CAMBRIDGE STUDIES IN PHILOSOPHY

Substance among other categories

This book revives a neglected but important topic in philosophy: the nature of substance. The belief that there are individual substances, for example, material objects and persons, is at the core of our commonsense view of the world, yet many metaphysicians deny the very coherence of the concept of substance. The authors develop a novel account of what an individual substance is in terms of independence from other beings. In the process many other important ontological categories are explored: Property, Event, Space, Time. The authors show why alternative theories of substance fail and go on to defend the intelligibility (though not the existence) of interacting spiritual and material substances.

"This is a well-informed and up-to-date contribution to an important topic in modern metaphysics, filling a significant gap in the recent literature." (E. J. Lowe, University of Durham)

CAMBRIDGE STUDIES IN PHILOSOPHY

General editor, ERNEST SOSA

Advisory editors JONATHAN DANCY, GILBERT HARMAN, FRANK JACKSON,
WILLIAM G. LYCAN, SIDNEY SHOEMAKER, JUDITH J. THOMSON

RECENT TITLES

Substance among other categories

Joshua Hoffman   *Gary S. Rosenkrantz*

UNIVERSITY OF NORTH CAROLINA AT GREENSBORO

CAMBRIDGE
UNIVERSITY PRESS

Published by the Press Syndicate of the University of Cambridge
The Pitt Building, Trumpington Street, Cambridge CB2 1RP
40 West 20th Street, New York, NY 10011-4211, USA
10 Stamford Road, Oakleigh, Melbourne 3166, Australia

© Cambridge University Press 1994

First published 1994

Printed in the United States of America

Library of Congress Cataloging-in-Publication Data
Hoffman, Joshua.
Substance among other categories / Joshua Hoffman, Gary S.
Rosenkrantz.
p.   cm. – (Cambridge studies in philosophy)
Includes bibliographical references and index.
ISBN 0-521-46101-4
1. Substance (Philosophy)   2. Soul.   I. Rosenkrantz, Gary S.
II. Title.   III. Series.
BD331.H57   1994
111′.1 – dc20   93-49101
                                         CIP

A catalog record for this book is available from the British Library.

ISBN 0-521-46101-4 hardback

For my wife, Ruth, and my parents, Jack and Bea
(J.H.)

For my wife, Sheree
(G.R.)

Contents

Acknowledgments

The seeds of this project began to take root some seventeen years ago when we became intensely interested in answering two fundamental philosophical questions. First, is it possible to analyze the ordinary concept of an individual substance in terms of ontological independence? Second, is it possible to state criteria of identity and individuation for such individual substances? We owe a debt of gratitude to Roderick Chisholm, whose metaphysics classes and seminars at Brown University in the mid-1970s are the source of our interest in these two questions. In addition, we would like to thank the following philosophers for their helpful comments or conversations: John Foster, John Heil, John King, Jonathan Lowe, C. B. Martin, Peter Simons, Barry Smith, Ernest Sosa, James Van Cleve, and Michael Zimmerman. And we are especially grateful to an anonymous referee for Cambridge University Press, whose many critical comments and suggestions for improvements were most helpful and guided us in making the final revisons of our work.

We have incorporated portions of the following coauthored or singly authored articles of ours: "The Independence Criterion of Substance," *Philosophy and Phenomenological Research* 51 (1991), pp. 835–853; "Are Souls Unintelligible?" *Philosophical Perspectives* 5 (1991), pp. 183–212; "Concrete/Abstract," in *Companion to Metaphysics,* edited by Jaegwon Kim and Ernest Sosa (Oxford: Basil Blackwell, forthcoming); "J. Rudner Boscovich," in *The Cambridge Dictionary of Philosophy,* edited by Robert Audi (Cambridge: Cambridge University Press, forthcoming); and "Mereology," in *The Cambridge Dictionary of Philosophy,* edited by Robert Audi (Cambridge: Cambridge University Press, forthcoming). We would like to express our gratitude to the editors of *Philosophy and Phenomenological Research, Philosophical Perspectives,* Basil Blackwell, and Cambridge University Press for kindly permitting us to include this material.

Introduction

This essay is an exploration of the ontological landscape of ordinary discourse and thought. Most philosophers would concede that there is an ordinary, commonsense, or "folk" conceptual scheme, and that this scheme has certain ontological presuppositions. Foremost among these is the idea that there are enduring things, or individual substances, continuants such as people, rocks, flowers, and houses. Other kinds of entities which common sense appears to recognize are events, places, times, properties, and collections, as well as surfaces, edges, shadows, and holes. Any ontologist must begin as a point of reference with a consideration of this folk or commonsense ontology, even if in the end he revises it in some way. At least since the time of Aristotle, philosophers have tried to organize and relate entities of the kinds which belong to the commonsense ontology, kinds which Aristotle called *categories*.

One of our primary aims is to analyze the ordinary or commonsense concept of an individual substance, and the other is to characterize the possible extension of this concept. These analytical enterprises do not involve any commitment to the existence of an individual substance so conceived. Our analysis of substance will be carried out in terms of a broad theory of ontological categories which covers both commonsense categories of the sort just referred to and categories of a more theoretical sort, which are scientific, mathematical, or philosophical in origin.

The main idea behind our analysis of substance is a venerable one: it is that a substance has a kind of *independence* which no other sort of entity enjoys. Many philosophers, including some of the greatest, such as Aristotle, Descartes, and Spinoza, have tried to characterize substance in terms of some sort of independence criterion, but the consensus is that none of them has provided an adequate account of the requisite notion of independence. Our novel analysis of substance in terms of independence incorporates the insight of Aristotle that the independence of substance is to be understood in terms of the relation of the category of Substance to the

1

other categories, and the insight of Descartes and Spinoza that a substance is in some way independent of any other substance.

Because our analysis of substance is partly in terms of the relation of the category of Substance to other ontological categories, we find it necessary to explore in some depth not only the nature of substances, but also the natures of entities belonging to these other categories. In particular, we investigate the natures of concrete entities such as times, places, events, tropes or concrete "properties," collections, privations, and limits and abstract entities such as properties, relations, propositions, and sets.

In Chapter 1, we begin by informally characterizing the ordinary or commonsense concept of substance and distinguishing it from other commonsense ontological categories. Next, we explain the difference between the analytical project which we undertake and the project of determining whether a substance actually exists. This is followed by a defense of our analytical project against objections of the sort put forward by anti-metaphysicians of various stripes, including radical empiricists and positivists. The next section develops a framework for a scheme of ontological categories to be employed in our analysis of substance. We provide an informal presentation of this framework and scheme as well as a more formal account. Our scheme of ontological categories embodies a hierarchy of levels of generality among such categories related as genera and species and singles out the particular level in the hierarchy at which reside Substance and other, peer categories, such as Time, Place, Event, and Property. Finally, we characterize the intuitive notion of a substance through a formal enumeration of the salient metaphysical features of a substance, and we also enumerate the salient features specific to various possible species of substance. These salient features serve as the data to which, *prima facie,* any analysis of the intuitive notion of substance must be adequate.

Chapter 2 surveys several historically prominent accounts of substance in order to reveal the shortcomings of these accounts and to glean from this survey whatever insights it may provide. We begin with two Aristotelean accounts. According to the first, a substance is that which can persist through change. The second Aristotelean account of substance is found in the *Categories,* and maintains that a substance is that which is neither "said of" a subject nor "in" a subject. The latter is often thought to be an account of substance in terms of independence, but we shall argue that it is not such an account. Next, we critically assess various substratum and inherence theories of substance, including theories which either identify a substance with a "bare particular" or claim that a bare particular is a constituent of a substance. Finally, we argue that Descartes's criterion of substance in terms of independence is inadequate.

Other philosophers have tried to identify a substance with a set or collection of nonsubstances. For our purposes, there are two senses in which one might *identify* an F with a G. In the first sense, the claim is that the concept of being an F is synonymous with the concept of being a G. This can be called a *meaning identification*. In a second sense, the claim is only that it is metaphysically necessary that something is an F if and only if it is a G, where something's being a G explicates what it is for something to be an F. Here there is no implication that the concepts of being an F and being a G are synonymous. This can be called a *philosophical analysis*. Those who identify a substance with a set or collection of nonsubstances are claiming either that being a substance is synonymous with being such a set or collection, or else that being a substance is analyzable in terms of being a set or collection of this sort. If either of these claims is correct, then logically necessary and sufficient conditions for substancehood can be stated in terms of sets or collections of nonsubstances. In Chapter 3, we criticize any attempt to identify a substance with a set or collection of nonsubstances, nonsubstances such as abstract properties, events, sense-data, or concrete "properties" (tropes). We argue that there are three main reasons why these identifications fail to provide logically necessary or sufficient conditions for being a substance: a categorial confusion of the abstract and the concrete, a lack of unity of qualities, and excessive essentialism.

In Chapter 4 we construct an analysis of the ordinary concept of a substance in terms of independence, and defend the adequacy of this criterion of substancehood by arguing that while a substance satisfies our criterion, no entity of any other peer category does so. We also offer a second, simplified analysis of the ordinary concept of a substance, one which is available on the assumption that a simple substance is possible. The adequacy of this second analysis is also defended, and the two analyses are compared in detail as to their relative advantages and disadvantages.

The subject of Chapter 5 is the possible extension of the category of Substance. One of the main issues discussed is the intelligibility of the concept of an immaterial substance or soul, and another is the intelligibility of the notion of causal interaction between souls and bodies. Many philosophers have argued that there are criteria of intelligibility which are satisfied by bodies but not by souls. In response to their attacks on the concept of a soul, we offer relative consistency arguments which show that given what these philosophers require for intelligibility, souls are no worse off than bodies. This sort of answer is also given in reply to some of the arguments against the possibility of causal interaction between souls and bodies. Other such arguments are answered in a number of different ways. The overall conclusion of this chapter is that the arguments in the literature critical of the intelligibility of souls and of interaction between souls and bodies are not persuasive.

Our book closes with two appendixes which further explore important metaphysical concepts which play a prominent role in our discussions. Appendix 1 offers an analysis of the distinction between concrete and abstract entities. This distinction is employed in the informal presentation of our hierarchy of categories in Chapter 1, and in any subsequent decision to classify a given entity as either concrete or abstract. The same *formal* framework for a scheme of ontological categories which is utilized in our account of substance is also used to analyze the concrete–abstract distinction.

In defending our account of substance, and in the accompanying exam-ination of other ontological categories at the same level of generality, we argue in favor of the Aristotelean view that sizeless point-positions and instants are not parts of spatial and temporal continua. Some philosophers have an opposing view and claim that the modern mathematical analysis of dense continua supports their position. In Appendix 2, we will argue that these philosophers are mistaken in thinking that the modern mathematical analysis of continuity lends credence to their claim that point-positions and instants are parts of spatial and temporal continua.

The overall conclusion of our study is that the ordinary concept of substance, understood as possibly instantiated by both bodies and souls, is both intelligible and subject to enlightening philosophical analysis in terms of metaphysical independence. Our account of substance, together with its supporting arguments, not only clarifies the nature of a substance, but also the natures of entities belonging to other peer ontological categories central to commonsensical or theoretical conceptual schemes, and the relationships between a substance and entities belonging to these other categories.

1

Substance and other categories

First philosophy, according to the traditional schedule, is analytic ontology, examining the traits necessary to whatever is, in this or any possible world. Its cardinal problem is that of substance and attribute.

D. C. Williams *Principles of Empirical Realism* 74 (1966)

[Categories are] . . . the different kinds of notions corresponding to the definite forms of existence . . . an enumeration of all things capable of being named, the most extensive classes into which things could be distributed.

"Category" *Oxford English Dictionary* (1971)

I. STATEMENT AND DEFENSE OF OUR PROJECT

Metaphysics has often been revisionary, and less often descriptive. Descriptive metaphysics is content to describe the actual structure of our thought about the world, revisionary metaphysics is concerned to produce a better structure.

P. F. Strawson *Individuals* 9 (1959)

One of the main projects in this book is to conduct a conceptual investigation of the notion of an individual substance as ordinarily understood, paradigm instances of which seem to be particular material objects and persons. In one of its ordinary senses, the term 'thing' means individual substance. For example, the term 'thing' is being used in this sense in the following sentences:

'Wisdom is not a thing, it is a quality of a thing'.
'Surfaces and holes are not things, they are limits and absences of them, respectively'.
'A chameleon's turning color is not a thing, it is a change in one'.

Accordingly, it is impossible for a thing or an object in this ordinary sense either to *occur* (as an event does) or to be *exemplified* (as some properties are). To suppose otherwise is to commit what Ryle called a category mistake. This is the source of the apparent absurdity of saying, for example, that Socrates occurs or is exemplified by something. Likewise, it is a category mistake to identify a thing or substance with an absence, such as a hole, or a limit, such as a surface. A hole is an absence, and a surface is a limit, *of* a thing, and, hence, each of these is *not* a thing or individual substance. Nor is it possible for a material substance to be identified with a place: for one, a material substance can move, but a place cannot. Furthermore, it is impossible for an enduring individual substance to be identified with an interval of time, since the latter has times as parts, but the former cannot.

The great philosophers of the past, of course, were intensely interested in the concept of individual substance. Aristotle, for example, believed that individual substances were the basic or primary existents, as did Descartes, Spinoza, Leibniz, Locke, and Berkeley. Kant went so far as to maintain that human beings cannot conceive of a reality in which substances are absent. All of these thinkers (and many others) spent much time and effort trying to elucidate the concept of an individual substance.

While there is a large body of recent work devoted to the production (or destruction) of philosophical analyses of concepts such as knowledge and causation, the concept of substance has been neglected in comparison. Yet, the presupposition that there are substantial material objects and selves seems to be at the core of our commonsense or folk ontology, with the result that much current philosophical research also has this presupposition. In addition, it is not clear that empirical science has dispensed with the existence of substances (science still makes reference to particles), despite certain tendencies in that direction in the area of theoretical physics. Moreover, even if empirical science has rejected the existence of substances, it is questionable whether it has done so justifiably.

In any case, it should be observed that there being an ordinary *concept* of individual substance does not entail that there is an *instance* of this ordinary concept. This observation is implicit in the following passage in which Hans Reichenbach rejects the existence of material substance on the empirical ground that its existence is ruled out by the wave–particle duality of quantum mechanics.

> It was a long way from Democritus' atoms to the duality of waves and corpuscles. The substance of the universe – in the physicist's sense . . . has turned out to be of a rather dubious nature, if compared with the solid particles in which both the philosopher and the scientist believed for some two thousand years. The conception of a corporeal substance, similar to the palpable substance shown by the bodies of our daily environment, has been recognized as an extrapolation from sensual experience. What appeared to the philosophy of rationalism as a requirement of reason – Kant called the

concept of substance synthetic a priori – has been revealed as being the product of a conditioning through environment. The experiences offered by atomic phenomena make it necessary to abandon the idea of a corporeal substance and require a revision of the form of the description by means of which we portray physical reality. With the corporeal substance goes the two-valued character of language, and even the fundamentals of logic are shown to be the product of an adaptation to the simple environment into which human beings were born.[1]

Toward the end of this passage, Reichenbach argues for the conditional, that if there are empirical observations which disconfirm the existence of corporeal substance, then there also are (or can be) empirical observations which disconfirm fundamental logical truths. However, in our view, the contention that there can be empirical observations which disconfirm fundamental logical truths is deeply problematic. We conclude that if the aforementioned conditional affirmed by Reichenbach is correct, then it is highly questionable whether the empirical observations which Reichenbach takes to disconfirm the existence of corporeal substance really do disconfirm the existence of corporeal substance.

In any case, since our project is to construct a philosophical analysis of the ordinary concept of an individual substance, and since there being such an analysis does not entail that there is an instance of this ordinary concept, the completion of our enterprise does not commit us to the actual existence of a substance, or, for that matter, to the existence of an entity of any particular ontological category. Instead, our project is an example of what D. C. Williams has called "analytic ontology."

> Concerned with what it means to be a thing or kind at all, [analytic ontology] is in some wise prior to and independent of the other great branch of metaphysics, speculative cosmology: what kinds of things are there, what stuff are they made of, how are they strung together?[2]

Williams's distinction between analytic ontology and speculative cosmology seems to be the same as Brian Carr's more recent distinction between *categorial description* and *categorial realism*.[3] According to Carr, there is a

> relatively minimal metaphysical activity which can make claims to a legitimate and central place in philosophy, perhaps even *the* central place, and

1 *The Rise of Scientific Philosophy* (Berkeley: University of California Press, 1951), pp. 189–190.
2 *The Principles of Empirical Realism* (Springfield, Ill.: Charles C Thomas, 1966), p. 74.
3 Brian Carr, *Metaphysics: An Introduction* (Atlantic Highlands, N.J.: Humanities Press International, 1987), chap. 1.

which has always been part of the wider activity of metaphysicians. Even if it is questionable whether the existence of God, the nature of the spatiotemporal universe, and the future of the human soul can be investigated and established by rational argument, the metaphysical activity which I want to identify and introduce falls under no such grave suspicions. And though it is a minimal activity within that wider contentious one, it is not itself unrewarding.

Metaphysics, in its minimal form, is the activity of categorical description. Its subject matter is the most fundamental aspects of the way we think and talk about reality, the most fundamental features of reality as it presents itself to us. We divide the world into horses and trains, people and mountains, battles and towns, and a whole complex structure of different kinds of things; our language is the repository of this enormously rich furnishing of the world. But we can discern within this richness some overall divisions, between things and their properties, for example, or between events and the times and places in which they happen, and it is with the overall pattern of our categorizing of elements of the world that metaphysics concerns itself with. The basic divisions which our thought and talk about reality entail are the quarry of categorical describers.[4]

On the other hand, a categorial realist is characterized by Carr as someone

who takes the categories, which he seeks to describe, as marking real kinds to be found in the things which collectively make up reality.[5]

In our view Williams and Carr are correct to distinguish theories about what kinds of entities exist from accounts of what characteristics a given kind of entity must have. While it is likely that the former have ultimately to be based at least in part upon empirical evidence, accounts of the latter sort are *a priori:* their ultimate goal is the construction of philosophical analyses of the various categories of being. Our conceptual investigation focuses on the ontological category signified by the ordinary notion of an individual substance. We aim to provide an adequate philosophical analysis of this notion or category. In doing so, and in distinguishing substances from entities of other ontological categories, we shall elucidate those other categories as well.

Prima facie, the ontological category of Individual Substance is no less legitimate than any other ontological category, for instance, Property, Space, Time, Event, Collection, and so forth. In other words, the burden of proof is on one who regards Substance as suspect.[6] There are several senses in which this can be understood: the onus of proof rests on one who

---

4 Ibid., pp. 1–2.

5 Ibid., p. 6.

6 Likewise, anyone asserting the impossibility of times, places, events, or properties, etc., assumes the burden of proof.

supposes either that the concept of substance is unintelligible, or that it is impossible for a substance to exist, or (even) that substances do not exist.[7] The foregoing considerations suggest both that our project of illuminating the nature of substance by employing the current methods of philosophical analysis is of philosophical significance, and that work on such a project is overdue.

Ordinary conceptions of ontological categories such as Substance, Time, Place, Event, Property, and Collection are either innate, as rationalistic philosophers such as Descartes and Kant maintain, or derived from (suggested by) certain relevant experiences, as empiricists hold. Indeed, the concept of individual substance seems to be at least as central to our conceptual scheme as any of these other concepts, and is probably more so.[8] Moreover, each concept gives rise to its own distinctive philosophical problems. True, there are problems about the nature of substance, and about the identity and individuation of substances, but there are other equally pressing problems about the nature, identity, and individuation of events, times, places, properties, et cetera. *Prima facie* there is no reason to think that these problems are intractable in the case of substance, or only in that case.

Nevertheless, there are philosophers who would contend that this project lacks philosophical interest. In this section, we answer these philosophers, and defend our claim that our project has philosophical significance. How would these philosophers support their contention about our project?

First, they might argue that the distinction between substance and nonsubstance is so scholastic (in a pejorative sense) that to seek an analysis of the notion of substance is philosophically pointless. In a somewhat similar vein, Pierre Bayle said of a related distinction between an *ens per se* and an *ens per accidens* that these expressions "are unintelligible phrases, a mere jargon of the Spanish logicians which have no meaning at all."[9] Are attitudes of this kind justified when directed upon the distinction between substance and nonsubstance? It seems not. Since the relevant notion of substancehood is a part of our ordinary conceptual scheme, the term

---

7 While we do not argue that substances exist, we believe that common sense supports such a view. Hence, the denial of their existence assumes the burden of proof. We will, however, dispute the claim that either the concept of substance is unintelligible or it is impossible for a substance to exist.

8 This point is suggested in remarks made by Bertrand Russell in *The Problems of Philosophy* (Oxford: Oxford University Press, 1943), chap. 9.

9 See note A in the article, "Gorlaeus, David," in Bayle's *General Dictionary, Historical and Critical*.

'substance' cannot simply be dismissed in this way as a piece of senseless philosophical jargon or an unintelligible relic of an outmoded scholastic philosophy.

To this it might be replied that the ordinary notion of substance is obscure or confused and impossible to clarify, and hence that there is no intelligible ordinary concept of substance. However, such an argument cannot support the contention that our project is philosophically pointless. This is because if we are successful in providing an adequate analysis of the ordinary concept of substance, then the fact that there *is* such an analysis answers the charge that this notion of substance is obscure or confused and unclarifiable.

Some comments are also in order about the point of view according to which it is impossible that there be substances.[10] From that perspective, material objects and persons are convenient myths or can be eliminated in favor of logical constructions upon instantaneous entities, for example, temporal stages or impressions. But even if such a view is correct, it does not follow that our project lacks philosophical significance. If what is impossible according to this view is the instantiation of an intelligible concept, namely, substance, then the discovery of an analysis of that concept would have philosophical significance. In particular, such an analysis would enhance our understanding of what it is that is impossible. Thus, this sort of skeptical view about substance seems to be in a position which parallels that of a certain kind of epistemological skeptic. For example, an extreme epistemological skeptic might assert that it is impossible for anyone to possess knowledge, but he would not find the concept of knowledge unintelligible. Such a skeptic ought to regard the project of analyzing the concept of knowledge as a philosophically worthwhile one.

Another way to justify a dismissive attitude toward our project is to appeal to the criteria of cognitive significance employed by radical empiricists and logical positivists.

One such argument is the following:

(1i) The term 'substance' is meaningful only if someone is directly aware of a substance.

(1ii) No one is directly aware of a substance.

(1iii) The term 'substance' is meaningless.

---

10 Here, and subsequently, when we employ modal terms such as 'impossible', 'necessary', and 'possible', we are using them in the sense of *metaphysical* impossibility, necessity, and possibility.

The only way that a defender of this argument can argue for premise (1i) is by appealing to some form of the radical empiricist theory of meaningfulness, for example, Hume's principle that there is no simple idea without a corresponding impression, and no other sort of idea which is not a complex of such simple ideas, or the verification principle. These are discredited theories. However, even if one grants such theories, one can still reject premise (1ii), by holding that a person can be directly aware (by introspection) of at least one substance, namely, himself.[11]

Another argument in the positivist tradition, advanced by Rudolph Carnap,[12] and based on the verifiability criterion of cognitive significance is as follows:

(2i) A sentence asserting the existence of a substance is meaningful or has cognitive significance only if it is empirically verifiable.

(2ii) No sentence asserting the existence of a substance is empirically verifiable.

(2iii) Any sentence asserting the existence of a substance is meaningless or lacks cognitive significance.

According to Carnap, although the sentence 'A table exists' is empirically verifiable, the sentence 'A substance exists' is not empirically verifiable. Rather, it is a "metaphysical" sentence devoid of cognitive significance. Of course, there is nothing in this view that applies exclusively to substance. The sentences 'An event exists', 'A property exists', 'A time exists', 'A place exists', and so forth should also be judged to be metaphysical and therefore nonsensical.[13]

We reply to this by noting that the sentence 'A table exists' implies the sentence 'A substance exists'. Hence, if the former has cognitive significance, then so must the latter. Thus, we deny premise (2ii) of the preceding argument. Of course, Carnap would deny that 'A table exists' implies 'A substance exists', but the burden is upon him to justify this denial. One way he might attempt to do so is by claiming that 'A table exists' can be translated into a sentence about sensations, whereas 'A substance exists'

11 Hume, of course, denies that there is this sort of awareness of the self. See *A Treatise of Human Nature*, ed. L. A. Selby-Bigge (Oxford: Oxford University Press, 1888), book 1, part 4, secs. 5 and 6.

12 Carnap, *Philosophy and Logical Syntax* (1935), chap. 1, reprinted in Morton White, *The Age of Analysis* (New York: Mentor Books, 1955), pp. 209–225.

13 As Francis Bacon has observed (anticipating Carnap): "We have no sound notions either in logic or physics; substance, quality, action, passion, and existence are not clear notions. . . . They are all fantastical and ill-defined. The notions of less abstract natures, as man, dove, and the immediate perceptions of sense, as heat, cold, white, black, do not deceive us materially. . . . All the rest which men have hitherto employed are errors, and improperly abstracted and deduced from things" (*Novum Organum*, 1:15–16).

cannot be so translated. This attempt fails for two reasons. First, such phenomenalist claims have never been substantiated by actually providing such translations, nor is there any prospect of actually providing translations of this kind. Second, it is not clear that if 'A table exists' *could* be translated into sensation sentences, then 'A substance exists' could not *also* be translated into sensation sentences which are implied by the former sensation sentences.

The fact that positivists regard physics as the very model of empirical significance provides a further reason for thinking that premise (2ii) is false. Physical laws cannot be formulated without the use of some concept or concepts such as substance, event, property, time, or place. Science itself must employ such "metaphysical" concepts, all of which Carnap regarded as equally meaningless. Hence, Carnap has no reason to assert that the sentence 'A substance exists' is not empirically verifiable.

Some philosophers are skeptical of substance because they cannot understand what more there is to a substance beyond the bundle of qualities associated with such a "substance." The claim is that if you take away these qualities, then there is nothing left to a substance.[14] Is a substance something in addition to the qualities that in itself has no qualities? Surely, such a qualityless entity is absurd. However, these doubts would appear to be ungrounded or based upon confusions, as such worries apply to any entity whatsoever, even qualities. That is, these worries, if consistently applied, imply metaphysical nihilism. For it is no easier to understand what more there is to an event (or a quality, a time, a place, etc.) beyond the bundle of qualities associated with such an entity. (When this skeptical argument is applied to qualities, it results in an infinite regress, that is, a first quality is no more than a bundle of other qualities associated with "it," those

---

14 For example, Hume: "As our idea of any body, a peach, for instance, is only that of a particular taste, color, figure, size, consistency, etc., so our idea of any mind is only that of particular perceptions without the notion of anything we call substance, either simple or compound" (*An Enquiry Concerning Human Understanding* [New York: Liberal Arts Press, 1955], p. 194). Berkeley provides another example: "And as several of these [ideas] are observed to accompany each other, they came to be marked by one name, and so to be reputed as one thing. Thus, for example, a certain colour, taste, smell, figure and consistence having been observed to go together, are accounted one distinct thing, signified by the name *apple;* other collections of ideas constitute a stone, a tree, a book" (*The Principles of Human Knowledge,* part 1, paragraph 1). It should be noted that Berkeley did not extend his view of the nature of *physical* objects to *souls,* which he, unlike Hume, regarded as utterly different from collections of ideas.

Leibniz was critical of views such as these: "it is rather the *concretum,* as wise, warm, shining, which arises in our mind, than the *abstractions* or qualities (for these and not the ideas are in the substantial object), as knowledge, heat, light, etc., which are much more difficult to comprehend" (*New Essays Concerning Human Understanding,* book 2, chap. 23)

qualities, in turn, are no more than bundles of qualities associated with "them," the latter qualities are no more than the bundles of qualities that "they" are associated with, and so forth.[15] Thus, there is no quality in the regress that exists; each one in the series gives way to collections of others. However, one would not expect this infinite regress to trouble a metaphysical nihilist.) Hence, this line of thought leads to the conclusion that no entity of any sort exists,[16] and cannot be directed specifically against the existence of substance.

An argument which combines elements from both positivism and the preceding argument is as follows:

(3i) The term 'substance' is meaningful only if someone has an experience of a substance in the absence of any awareness of its properties.

(3ii) No one has such an experience.[17]

(3iii) The term 'substance' is meaningless.

Premise (3i) *seems* plausible only because it is easily confused with the following:

(3i*) The term 'substance' is meaningful only if someone has an experience of a substance which is distinguishable from an awareness of the properties which it instantiates.

(3i*) *is* plausible. But the claim that no one has an experience of a substance which is distinguishable from an awareness of the properties it instantiates is implausible. For example, there is a clear distinction between intellectually grasping the properties, length and width, and having an

---

15 Surely, everything has a nature, and if there are properties, then for any property, P, the nature of P consists of a number of properties P possesses. Thus, for instance, even a simple quality has a multiplicity of qualities, e.g., simplicity, abstractness, propertyhood, monadicity, immutability. Hence, one should distinguish between a property's being simple, in the sense of not being analyzable into more basic properties, and a property's having but a single property, which is impossible. Since a property must have many properties, if a substance can be reduced to the many qualities it possesses, then why cannot a property as well?

16 Bruce Aune, in *Metaphysics: The Elements* (Minneapolis: University of Minnesota Press, 1985), p. 49, gives a similar reply to the skeptical argument that a thing is nothing more than the bundle of qualities associated with it.

17 The following passage indicates that Descartes accepts this premise: "But we do not come to know a substance immediately, through being aware of the substance itself; we come to know it only through its being the subject of certain acts"; see *The Philosophical Writings of Descartes,* trans. John Cottingham, Robert Stoothoff, and Dugald Murdoch (Cambridge: Cambridge University Press, 1984), 2:124. On the other hand, in *The Problems of Philosophy,* chap. 5, Bertrand Russell was inclined to reject the same premise. According to Russell, each of us is probably acquainted with himself, a substance, where acquaintance with a particular is logically independent of all knowledge of truths about that particular.

experience of the length and width of the table.[18] Thus, the premise one would need to derive (3iii) from (3i*) is implausible. Finally, if premise (3i) were true, then one could generalize it to construct arguments which proved that the terms 'property', 'time', 'place', 'event', et cetera are meaningless, since no one can experience a property, time, place, event, et cetera, in the absence of any awareness of *their* properties.

Our survey of challenges to the proposition that there is philosophical interest in the investigation of the concept of substance has found no persuasive deterrent to this investigation. We therefore proceed with our investigation.

II. ONTOLOGICAL CATEGORIES

> Logicians in almost every age have endeavoured to frame schemes of classification in which things should be arranged according to their real nature. To these the name of Categories has been given.
>
> Abp. Thomson *Outline of the Laws of Thought* § 97 (1849)

> For a century or so, psychologists pondering the brain's memory handling system have suspected that the brain had some system of putting information in categories, with a separate pigeon-hole for categories like dogs, plants, numbers, each in a separate network of cells.
>
> Philip J. Hilts *New York Times* (Sept. 15, 1992)

No comprehensive understanding of the world is possible without ontological presuppositions, commitments as to what kinds or categories of entities exist. Although the intuitive concept of a genuine ontological kind may be hard to analyze, it is necessary to use this notion both in the study of ontology in general, and in the framing of a particular ontology. Paradigm cases of such intuitive ontological categories include Property, Substance, Event, Time, Place, and Collection. Such categories are among the more general or fundamental kinds of beings. A system of classification which is composed of such categories and which is applicable to all possible kinds of beings helps clarify the nature of reality. Since our primary focus is on the category of Substance, our first task is to locate this category in such a system of classification.

We begin with the observation that a substance is a *concrete* entity or *concretum*. The distinction between *abstracta* and *concreta* seems indispensable in ontology: for example, the debate between realists and antirealists over the existence of universals presupposes this distinction. In this debate, the realist affirms the existence of abstract universals, whereas the antirealist

18 See n. 14.

14

maintains that only *concreta* or particulars exist. We assume (plausibly, we think) that this very general division between *concreta* and *abstracta* is exhaustive and exclusive: necessarily, every entity either belongs to the ontological category of the concrete or belongs to the ontological category of the abstract, and there could not be an entity belonging to both of these categories. To illustrate the concrete–abstract distinction, we will give examples of ontological categories which are species of *abstracta* and *concreta*, respectively, together with putative instances of these ontological categories. Species of *abstracta* include Property (e.g., redness, squareness), Relation (e.g., betweenness, identity), Proposition (e.g., *that horses are animals, that some animals are unicorns*), Set (e.g., the null set, the set of Plato and Aristotle), and Number (e.g., the number 8, the number 9). Species of *concreta* include Substance (e.g., material objects and spirits), Event (e.g., explosions and storms), Time (e.g., instants and durations), Place (e.g., points and extended regions of space), Limit (e.g., corners and surfaces), Privation (e.g., shadows and holes), Trope (e.g., the particular wisdom of Socrates, *that* particular redness), and Collection (e.g., the mereological sum of Mars and Saturn, the mereological sum of Mars, Saturn, and Neptune).[19] The intuitive distinction between *concreta* and *abstracta* is ser-

---

19 The term, 'mereological', derives from the Greek μέρος, meaning 'part'. Thus, mereology is the theory of parts, or more specifically, Lesniewski's formal theory of parts. See Stanislaw Lesniewski, *Collected Works* (Dordrecht: Kluwer, 1991).

Typically, a mereological theory employs terms such as the following: proper part, improper part, overlapping (having a part in common), disjoint (not overlapping), mereological product (the "intersection" of overlapping objects), mereological sum (a collection of parts), mereological difference, the universal sum, mereological complement, and atom (that which has no proper parts).

Formal mereologies are axiomatic systems. Lesniewski's Mereology and Nelson Goodman's formal mereology (which he calls the "Calculus of Individuals") are compatible with nominalism, i.e., no reference is made to sets, properties, or other abstract entities. Lesniewski hoped that his Mereology, with its many parallels to set theory, would provide an alternative to set theory as a foundation for mathematics. For Goodman's formal mereology see his *The Structure of Appearance,* 2nd ed. (Indianapolis, Ind.: Bobbs-Merrill, 1966).

Fundamental and controversial implications of Lesniewski's and Goodman's theories include their *extensionality* and *collectivism*. Extensional theories imply that for any individuals, x and y, $x = y$ just in case x and y have the same proper parts. One reason extensionality is controversial is that it rules out an object's acquiring or losing a part, and therefore is inconsistent with commonsense beliefs such as that a car has a new tire or that a table has lost a sliver of wood. A second reason for controversy is that extensionality is incompatible with the belief that a statue and the piece of bronze of which it is made have the same parts and yet are diverse objects.

Collectivism implies that any individuals, no matter how scattered, have a mereological sum or compose an object. Moreover, according to collectivism, assembling or disassembling parts doesn't effect the existence of things, i.e., nothing is created or

viceable even if we lack an analysis of it. However, we offer a novel analysis of the concrete–abstract distinction in Appendix 1.

As we have already indicated, ontological categories are of different levels of generality, and are related to one another as species and genus. Thus, these categories constitute a system of classification which reflects these logical relations. In what follows we shall, first, characterize this system, and second, analyze a level of generality (which we will call *level C*) within this system which is crucial to our later attempt to analyze the concept of substance.[20]

Step 1

(1D1) A category *being an F* and a category *being a G* are *equivalent* =df. $\Box$ $(\forall x)$ $(Fx \equiv Gx)$.[21]

---

destroyed by assembly or disassembly, respectively. Thus, collectivism is incompatible with commonsense beliefs such as that when a watch is disassembled, it is destroyed, or that when certain parts are assembled, a watch is created.

It should be noted that accepting that there *are* collections does not necessarily commit one to either extensionality or collectivism.

Because the aforementioned formal theories shun modality, they lack the resources to express the thesis that a whole has each of its parts *necessarily*. Whatever one might make of the more general thesis of mereological essentialism, which has recently been defended by Roderick Chisholm (*Person and Object* [La Salle, Ill.: Open Court, 1976], pp. 148–158), we find it evident that at least collections in the sense of mereological sums have their parts essentially.

20 According to the analysis of the concept of substance we shall develop in Chapter 4, a substance is an entity of a certain kind, i.e., of a certain ontological category. The basic idea of our analysis is that this category, Substance, is one whose instances meet certain independence conditions *qua* being instances of that category. This notion of an on-tological category needs to be explained, since every entity is of many different kinds or categories of varying degrees or levels of generality. Thus, if we are to develop our analysis we must specify the *degree* of generality of the ontological categories we have in mind. This is a kind of generality problem (of which there are many versions in philosophy). We will provide a solution to this problem by giving informal and formal accounts of the appropriate degree of generality of an ontological category or kind of entity.

21 In (1D1)–(1D4), the letters 'F' and 'G' are schematic, and are to be replaced with an appropriate predicate expression. The modalities employed here, and elsewhere in the book, are metaphysical ones. Although we make use of metaphysical modalities, which are, after all, part of the analytical metaphysician's stock and trade, we shall not attempt to provide an analysis of them. *De dicto* metaphysical modalities are illustrated by the follow-ing examples: necessarily, if something is red, then it is colored; it is impossible that there exists a spherical cube; and it is contingent that the last name of the president of the United States begins with a 'C', i.e., it is possibly the case that the last name of the president of the United States begins with a 'C', and possibly not the case that the last name of the president of the United States begins with a 'C'. Examples of *de re* metaphysi-cal modalities are as follows: the Atlantic Ocean is essentially (necessarily) extended and possibly nonliquid or frozen. Notice that the Atlantic Ocean is accidentally (con-

16

For example, being an event and being an occurrence are equivalent categories. Any two equivalent categories are at the same level of generality.

(1D2) A category *being an F* is *instantiated* =df. $(\exists x)\ (Fx)$.

(1D3) A category *being an F* is *instantiable* =df. $\Diamond\ (\exists x)\ (Fx)$.

(1D4) A category *being an F subsumes* a category *being a G* =df. (i) $\Box\ (\forall x)\ (Gx \rightarrow Fx)$, and (ii) $\Diamond\ (\exists x)\ (Fx\ \&\ {\sim}Gx)$.[22]

If *A* subsumes *B*, then *A* is at a higher level of generality than *B*. For instance, *being an abstract entity* subsumes *being a property*. Notice that in this technical or logician's sense of subsumption a noninstantiable category is subsumed by any instantiable category, and a category that must be universally instantiated subsumes any category that need not be universally instantiated.

Step 2

There is an intuitive notion of a hierarchy of levels of generality among ontological categories.[23] This hierarchy is depicted in Figure 1.1. At the highest level (*level A*) is the category of *being an entity* which everything instantiates and which is therefore a kind of limiting case. At a lower level (*level B*) are the categories of Concreteness and Abstractness. At a yet lower

<hr>

tingently) liquid if and only if the Atlantic Ocean is liquid and possibly nonliquid.

It is customary to understand attributions of modalities of these kinds in terms of possible worlds. Those propositions which are necessary are true in all possible worlds, those propositions which are impossible are false in all possible worlds, those propositions which are possible are true in some possible world, and those propositions which are contingent are true in some possible world and false in some possible world. On the other hand, an entity, *e*, which has a certain property, *P*, has *P* essentially just in case *e* has *P* in every possible world in which *e* exists; and an entity, *e*, which has a certain property, *P*, has *P* accidentally just provided that *e* lacks *P* in some possible world in which *e* exists. Finally, an entity, *e*, has necessary existence if and only if *e* exists in all possible worlds; and an entity, *e*, has contingent existence if and only if *e* exists in the actual world and *e* fails to exist in some possible world.

22 For the purposes of (1D1)–(1D4), a 'category' is just a property of any sort whatsover, as opposed to the subset of properties which 'category' denotes in all other contexts, namely, properties which are genuine ontological kinds, or which divide up the world in ontologically important ways. We depart from our usual use of the term 'category' in the case of (1D1)–(1D4) because we want them to define logical relations which apply to all properties, and not only to categories in the strict sense.

23 See Gary Rosenkrantz and Joshua Hoffman, "The Independence Criterion of Substance," *Philosophy and Phenomenological Research* 51 (1991), pp. 835–853.

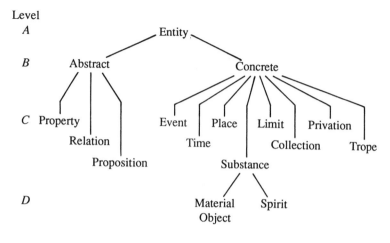

Figure 1.1

level (*level C*) are the categories which are the various types of *concreta* and *abstracta,* just provided that these categories are instantiable. Next, we list typical or core categories that are at level *C* on the foregoing proviso.

List *L:* Property, Relation, Proposition, Event, Time, Place, Limit, Collection, Privation, and Trope.[24]

Note that some categories which seem to be at level *C* are not on *L,* for example, Substance and Set. At a level of generality lower than *C* (call it *level D*) are those instantiable ontological categories which are the various types of the categories at level *C.* For instance, at level *D* we find types of Substance, for example, Material Object, or Spirit; types of Event, for instance, Material Event, or Spiritual Event; types of Limit, for example, Surface, or Line, or Instant; and types of Privation, for instance, Shadow, or Hole. More specific types are at lower levels of generality.

Presumably,

(A1) There are at least two (nonequivalent) instantiable categories of *concreta* at level *C* (at least one of which is on *L*), and there are at least two (nonequivalent) instantiable categories of *abstracta* at level *C* (at least one of which is on *L.*)

24 Cf. Aristotle, *Categories,* trans. J. L. Ackrill, in *Aristotle's Categories and De Interpretatione* (Oxford: Oxford University Press, 1963).

18

We employ ordinary or intuitive conceptions of the categories on L, and presuppose (plausibly, we think) that not every instance (actual or possible) of a category on L is identifiable with an instance of another level C ontological category. (The *irreducibility* of a category on L that this implies is consistent with the *eliminability* of an entity of such a category in favor of an entity of another ontological category.)[25] If the foregoing presupposition is mistaken, then the categories that make it so should be removed from L. The only limitation we place on this process of removal is that (A1) remains true, and that whatever categories satisfy (A1) be compatible with the foregoing presupposition.

In Step 3, we further clarify the intuitive notion of an ontological category at level C by providing an informative logically necessary and sufficient condition for this intuitive notion. This informative set of truth conditions for the intuitive notion of a level C category will qualify either as a philosophical analysis which enhances our understanding of that intuitive notion or as a criterion of application which provides a decision procedure for determining the extension of that intuitive notion. We do not think that it is incumbent upon us to provide such a set of truth conditions. In the light of our earlier account of the intuitive notion in question, we believe that this notion is sufficiently clear for our purposes without our providing a philosophical analysis or criterion of application for it. However, the discovery of a set of truth conditions of this kind answers anyone who claims that the intuitive notion of an ontological category *at level* C and our earlier account of it are unacceptably vague or unclear.

Step 3

(1D5) A category $C1$ is at level C =df. either (i) $C1$ is on L, and $C1$ is instantiable, or (ii) [(a) $C1$ is not on L, and $C1$ does not subsume an instantiable category on L, and no category on L subsumes $C1$, and (b) there is no category $C2$ which satisfies the conditions in (ii)(a) and which subsumes $C1$.][26]

While all categories are *properties*, some properties are not categories, for example, redness, squareness, bachelorhood, and (the disjunctive property

---

25 If an entity, e, is *eliminated*, in favor of $e^\star$, then e fails to exist. If an entity, e, is *reduced to* or *identified with* an entity, $e^\star$, then necessarily, e exists if and only if $e^\star$ exists.

26 $C1$'s being instantiable if it is not on L is guaranteed by the condition in (ii)(a) of (1D5) that no category on L subsumes $C1$, because (as noted earlier) a noninstantiable category is subsumed by an instantiable one, and because (A1) implies that some category on L is instantiable.

of) being a substance or a surface.[27] A property which is not an ontological category *ipso facto* fails to satisfy (1D5).

As noted earlier, the categories of being a substance and being a set are *not* on L but *are* at level C (if they are instantiable and irreducible). A category of this kind satisfies (1D5) by virtue of satisfying clause (ii) of (1D5). This clause has two parts, (a) and (b). Let us see why *being a substance* and *being a set* (if they are instantiable and irreducible) satisfy both of these parts. As Figures 1.2 and 1.3 illustrate, the category of Substance (Set) satisfies (ii)(a) of (1D5) because it is not on L and neither subsumes nor is subsumed by a category on L. In Aristotelean terms, the category of Substance (Set) is neither a genus nor a species of a category on L.[28] In

27 Do *Contingent Being* and *Necessary Being* count as ontological categories? If the contingent being–necessary being distinction is necessarily coextensive with the concrete–abstract distinction, then perhaps they do. On the other hand, it has often been maintained that there is a concrete being that has necessary existence, e.g., the theistic God. If so, then some substances, e.g., tables, are contingent beings and some are necessary beings. It has also been held that there are *sets* of ordinary concrete objects which are abstract and have contingent existence. If so, then some sets are contingent beings and some, e.g., the null set, are necessary beings. In that case, even though Substance and Set are ontological categories, neither Substance nor Set is subsumed by either Contingent Being or Necessary Being. However, a classificatory system of ontological categories is a hierarchial system of genera and species in which every ontological category is a genus or species. If the universal category, Entity, were to be divided into Contingent Being and Necessary Being, and neither Substance nor Set were subsumed by either Contingent Being or Necessary Being, then neither Substance nor Set would be an ontological category which is either a genus or a species in the classificatory system in question. This is contrary to our assumption that Substance and Set are such categories. Hence, a classificatory system of the sort required has not been provided, and the *modal categories* of Necessary Being and Contingent Being are not genuine ontological kinds or categories. Analogously, if Lion is a biological kind, a proper biological system of classification would not divide living things into two kingdoms Female and Nonfemale, since in that case Lion would not appear as a genus or species in the classificatory hierarchy: only Female Lion and Nonfemale Lion would so appear.

The problems discussed here would also arise for our categorial scheme if there could be both abstract and concrete substances, events, properties, relations, sets, times, places, tropes, and so forth. But we maintain that in each case there could *not* be both abstract and concrete entities of the sort in question. To suppose otherwise in any of these cases is to commit a category mistake. E.g., necessarily, if something is a substance, then it is concrete. In Chapter 3, we discuss the nature of the mistake we think is involved in the idea that abstract substances are possible. Also see Appendix 1, where we defend an analysis of the concrete–abstract distinction, an analysis which entails that there could not be both abstract and concrete substances, events, properties, times, places, tropes, and so on.

28 It might be objected that Substance is a species of *Collection*, viz., that, necessarily, a substance is a collection of other substances (its parts). In reply, we would argue that it is impossible for a material substance to be a collection of this kind, since it is essential to a material substance that its parts have some principle of unity, e.g., physical bonding,

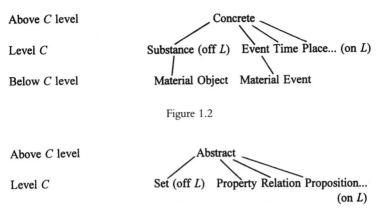

Figure 1.2

Figure 1.3

addition, the category of Substance (Set) appears to satisfy clause (ii)(b) of (1D5), since it seems that every category that subsumes Substance (Set) also subsumes an instantiable category on L. For instance, given (A1), *being concrete* is a category that subsumes Substance, and *being abstract* is a category that subsumes Set. Moreover, given (A1), *being concrete* subsumes some instantiable category on L, that is, *being a time,* or *being a place,* or *being an event,* et cetera, and *being abstract* subsumes some instantiable category on L, that is, *being a property,* or *being a relation,* or *being a proposition,* et cetera. It seems that parallel considerations apply to any category that subsumes Substance (Set).[29]

whereas it is not essential to a collection that its parts have any such principle of unity.

It seems that if two objects x and y physically bond with one another to form a complex material object at a time t, then at t there must be a definite distance d such that if x were farther than d from y at t, then x and y would not bond with one another. But, physicists tell us that x and y never actually touch because of repulsive forces between fundamental particles. However, notice that the assumption that $d > 0$ does not entail there is no distance d of the sort that appears to be required. E.g., there might well be a precise positive distance (or a definite spatial region) at which (or within which) the forces which bind x and y together and the repulsive forces which keep x and y apart come into a sort of balance or dynamic equilibrium, and it would be plausible to identify d with this distance (or with the maximum width of the region in question). We shall understand the attachment or bonding of two pieces of matter x and y, or the joining of a surface or edge of x to a surface or edge of y, in such a way that it is compatible with, but does not require, x's literally touching y.

29 Thus, our account of a level C category in terms of L and (1D5) generates a "list" of categories of being that is *open-ended*. In other words, (1D5) is logically compatible with

21

It should also be observed that a category, $C^\star$, *not* on L, which is at a *higher* level than C, both fails to satisfy (i) of (1D5), and fails to satisfy (ii)(a) of (1D5). This is because $C^\star$ subsumes some instantiable category on L. Thus, such a category, $C^\star$, does not meet (1D5). An example of the sort in question is the category of being concrete. Furthermore, a category, $C^\star$, at a level *lower* than C, that is subsumed by a level C category on L, fails to satisfy both (i) of (1D5) (inasmuch as $C^\star$ either will not be on L or else will not be instantiable) and (ii)(a) of (1D5) (because $C^\star$ is subsumed by some instantiable category on L). Hence, a category, $C^\star$, of this kind does not satisfy (1D5). An example of this sort might be the category of being a material event. In addition, a category, $C^\star$, at a level *lower* than C, that is subsumed by a level C category *not* on L, both fails to meet (i) of (1D5) (since $C^\star$ will not be on L) and fails to meet (ii)(b) of (1D5). Therefore, such a category, $C^\star$, does not satisfy (1D5). An example of this sort might be the category of being a material object.[30]

III. THE CATEGORY OF SUBSTANCE INTUITIVELY UNDERSTOOD

As nothing can be proved but by supposing something intuitively and evident without proof . . .

    S. Johnson *Preface to A Dictionary of the English Language* ¶ 43 (1755)

two things. First, that there are one or more level C categories which are *not* on L. Second, that one or more of the categories on L are *not* at level C (because they are not instantiable). Hence, (1D5) differs from Aristotle's list of the categories of being, which has a *fixed membership.* (See Aristotle's *Categories,* chap. 4.) Our general approach to the theory of categories is compatible with Brian Carr's account of the "metaphysical enterprise of categorial description" which "seeks to spell out the fundamental features of our thought and talk about reality, assuming *neither* the adequacy or otherwise of such categories to reality in itself *nor* the fixed or changing nature of that thought and talk" (*Metaphysics,* p. 9).

30 Since (1D5) presupposes (A1), which implies that there are at least two instantiable categories of *abstracta* at level C, a nominalist might object to (1D5), arguing that *no* category of *abstractum* is instantiable. As we have stated, we framed (1D5) in as ontologically neutral a fashion as possible. Nevertheless, an alternative to (1D5) *can* be framed which is compatible with nominalism. In that case, the category of being concrete would be necessarily coextensive with the category of being an entity, and categories of *concreta* such as Substance, Time, Place, etc., would be at the second level (level B). (A1) would be replaced with (A1$\star$): there are at least two (nonequivalent) instantiable categories of *concreta* at level B (at least one of which is on L). A formal account of a category being at level B would then parallel the account we provide of level C in (1D5), where the term, 'at level C', is replaced with the term, 'at level B'. Similarly, if an extreme Platonist were to object to (1D5) on the grounds that no category of *concretum* is instantiable, (1D5) could be revised in order to satisfy such a critic along lines parallel to the foregoing.

22

In this section, we shall characterize the intuitive notion of substance or thinghood by listing its most prominent metaphysical features: in each case, one of these features is either *necessarily predicated of all substances,* or necessarily predicated of *all of the members of a certain species of substance,* or *possibly predicated of some of the members of (a) certain species of substance.* Such a characterization provides the data for our later philosophical theory or analysis of substance.

(1) Every individual substance has features; each is characterizable in some way, for instance as being round or being sad.[31]

(2) Since any substance *has* certain features, these features are unified by it.

(3) No feature is a *part* of a substance.[32] Intuitively, the legs of a table *are* parts of the table, but the shape and size of the table are *not* parts of the table.

(4) Any individual substance is such that if it exists at a time, then it possibly exists at more than one time. Furthermore, (4a) possibly, some individual substance persists through changes in its intrinsic features.[33] For example, there could be a rubber ball that is spherical at t_1 and slightly ovoid when it bounces at t_2, or there could be a person who is depressed at t_1 and not depressed at t_2, and so forth. In addition, (4b) possibly, some individual thing persists through a change in its relational features, for example, a feature such as being five feet from a wall, or being seated in a chair.

(5) In some possible world, there is an individual substance, *x,* which has an intrinsic or relational feature at a time *t,* while *x* exists at *t* in some other possible world and lacks that feature. For instance, in some possible world, Jones is now depressed and seated in a chair, but in some other possible world he exists now and lacks these features. Thus, *being depressed now* and *being seated in a chair now* are *accidental* features of Jones, since Jones has these features, but Jones lacks them in a counterfactual situation or possible world in which he exists. On the other hand, *being extended* is an *essential* feature of a certain chair: the chair in question exists and there is no counterfactual situation or possible world in which it lacks extension.

(6) Possibly, there are substances which have contingent existence. Typically, (6a) such substances can be created and destroyed.

(7) Possibly, the length of time for which a substance exists is accidental. For instance, it is possible that there is a person who is killed in 1963, but could have lived until 1995.

---

31 This implies that a substance is not a propertyless substratum or "bare particular" as some philosophers seem to have thought. Recent defenders of the existence of substrata which are "bare particulars" include Edwin Allaire, "Bare Particulars," reprinted in *Universals and Particulars,* rev. ed., ed. M. Loux (Notre Dame, Ind.: University of Notre Dame, 1976), pp. 281–290, and Gustav Bergmann, *Realism* (Madison: University of Wisconsin Press, 1967). We will critically examine the substratum theory in Chapter 2, Section II.

32 If this intuitive datum is correct, then a theory which holds that a substance is a "bundle" or collection of features is mistaken. We shall discuss and criticize a variety of such theories of substance at length in Chapter 3.

33 This is one of Aristotle's definitions of individual or primary substance. See his *Categories,* chap. 5. We discuss this definition of substance critically in Chapter 2, Section I.

(8) Possibly, there are two individual substances which are indistinguishable with respect to their qualitative intrinsic features.

In addition to the intuitive characteristics of individual substances in general, there are intuitive characteristics specific to individual *material, nonmaterial physical,* and *spiritual* substances. We begin with the characteristics of material substances.

(1_m) Material objects are spatially three-dimensional. Thus, a cubical solid, which is a material object, has three spatial dimensions, while a face of a cubical solid has two spatial dimensions, and is therefore not a material object.

(2_m) Material substances have an inside and an outside. A spherical solid, which is a material substance, has both an inside and an outside, whereas the surface of the spherical solid (though three-dimensional) does not have an inside and an outside, and is therefore not a material substance.

(3_m) No two material objects exhaustively coincide in space.[34]

---

34 Some philosophers would distinguish between a statue, for example, and the piece of bronze which constitutes it, or, in other words, between a statue which can undergo mereological change and a spatially coincident physical object which has its parts essentially. If these philosophers are correct in recognizing physical objects of both of the aforementioned sorts, then there are two things of the same kind, viz., two physical objects, which are spatially coincident. We employ a "robust" notion of materiality whereby a *material* object is a piece of matter having its parts essentially. We remain neutral about whether there are *physical* (but nonmaterial) objects which can undergo mereological change. Hence, what principle (3_m) implies is that no two *pieces of matter* can exhaustively coincide in space. If there are such physical objects as statues which are distinct from physical objects which are pieces of matter, then objects of the former kind are what we call "nonmaterial physical objects" (see the subsequent discussion in the text).

However, we tend to think (though we do not require for the purpose of this book) that a physical substance can undergo mereological change only if it belongs to a natural kind that is instantiated by a natural functional system. Such a system has parts, e.g., a heart, and a stomach, that have natural functions, e.g., to pump blood, and to digest food, natural functions that are causally necessary for the continued existence of the system. A physical substance of this kind is a living thing, an instance of a natural kind such as Tree, Cat, or Human. In contrast, although an instance of a nonnatural or artifactual kind such as Statue, Car, or Engine is characterized by its function, its function is artificially or humanly imposed. Living things should also be contrasted with natural things such as mountains, rocks, and planets, whose criteria of existence and identity depend upon structural or compositional factors which are nonfunctional. We are inclined to argue that artifacts and natural things of this sort are ontologically suspect on the ground that their criteria of existence and perdurance are conventional. The conventionality of these criteria is evidenced by their inherent vagueness or indeterminacy, e.g., that a snowball must be *roundish,* that a pebble must be *small,* and that a table can survive having some material added to it, or subtracted from it, but not *too much* material. On the other hand, if the criteria of existence and perdurance for living things depend only upon the natural functions of their parts, then these criteria are nonconventional. Of course, to deny the existence of physical things such as statues and rocks is *not* to deny the existence of the complex material things which are widely thought to constitute them and which have their parts essentially. It seems that a complex material thing of the latter sort has strict

(4_m) A material substance in its entirety is not located in two places at once.

(5_m) The parts of a material object have a unity in virtue of their being bonded together. Thus, a material object can be created or destroyed by assembly or disassembly (except in the case of fundamental particles which are indivisible).

(6_m) A material substance occupies or is in space.

(7_m) A material substance only has a material substance or portion of matter as a part. The detachable parts of a material substance are material substances, while any nondetachable parts of a material substance are at least portions of matter (but may not be substances themselves).

(8_m) If a material substance is perceivable at all, then it has sensible features, is publicly observable, and is perceivable by more than one sensory modality.

(9_m) A material object possibly moves.

The intuitive characteristic specific to nonmaterial physical substances is the following.

(1_{nmp}) A nonmaterial physical substance either has fewer than three spatial dimensions or is such that two things of the kind of nonmaterial substance in question can exhaustively coincide in space. A Boscovichian point-particle is not spatially three-dimensional.[35] And some physicists theorize that there are fundamental particles exhibiting a phenomenon known as *transparency:* under certain conditions two fundamental particles of this sort can "pass through" one another, occupying for a moment the very same place.

Finally, the two intuitive characteristics specific to spiritual substances or Cartesian souls are as follows:

(1_s) A spiritual substance is not located in space.

mereological criteria of existence and perdurance which are precise and determinate, and it seems that these criteria are nonconventional.

35 Rudjer Josip Boskovic (1711–1787), or Roger Boscovich, is best known for *A Theory of Natural Philosophy Reduced to a Single Law of the Actions Existing in Nature.* For a recent edition see *A Theory of Natural Philosophy* (Cambridge, Mass.: M.I.T. Press, 1966). This work attempts to explain all physical phenomena in terms of the attractions and repulsions of point-particles (*puncta*) which are indistinguishable in their intrinsic qualitative properties. According to Boscovich's single law, *puncta* at a certain distance attract, until upon approaching one another they reach a point at which they repel, and eventually reach equilibrium. Thus, Boscovich defends a form of dynamism, or the theory that nature is to be understood in terms of force and not mass (where forces are functions of time and distance). By dispensing with extended substance, Boscovich avoided epistemological difficulties facing Locke's natural philosophy and anticipated developments in modern physics. Among those influenced by Boscovich were Kant (who defended a version of dynamism), Faraday, James Clerk Maxwell, and Lord Kelvin.

Boscovich's theory has proved to be empirically inadequate to account for phenomena such as light. A philosophical difficulty for Boscovich's *puncta,* which are physical substances, arises out of their zero-dimensionality. It is plausible that any power must have a basis in an object's intrinsic properties, and *puncta* appear to lack such support for their powers. However, it is extensional properties which *puncta* lack, and Boscovich could argue that the categorial property of being an unextended spatial substance provides the needed basis.

(2_s) A spiritual substance is capable of consciousness.

We have distinguished three species of the category of Substance: material, nonmaterial physical, and spiritual. It would be useful at this point to construct a figure correlating the eight intuitive characteristics of substance with the three species of substance just mentioned. This figure will indicate which of these characteristics necessarily or possibly apply to which species of substance. We start by defining the letters a–g as follows:

a = applies necessarily to all substances
b = applies necessarily to all material substances
c = applies necessarily to all nonmaterial physical substances
d = applies necessarily to all spiritual substances
e = applies possibly to some material substances
f = applies possibly to some nonmaterial physical substances
g = applies possibly to some spiritual substances.

First, we correlate a–g with the intuitive characteristics predicated of substances in (1)–(8), as follows:

(1) a; (2) a; (3) a; (4) a; (4a) e, f, g; (4b) e, f, g; (5) e, f, g; (6) e, f, g; (6a) e, f, g; (7) e, f, g; (8) e, f, g.

Second, we correlate a–g with the intuitive characteristics predicated of material substances in (1_m)–(9_m):

(1_m) b, f; (2_m) b, f; (3_m) b, f; (4_m) b; (5_m) b, f; (6_m) b, c; (7_m) b; (8_m) b; (9_m) b, c.

Third, we correlate a–g with the intuitive characteristic predicated of nonmaterial physical substances in (1_{nmp}):

(1_{nmp}) c.

Finally, we correlate a–g with the intuitive characteristics predicated of spiritual substances in (1_s)–(2_s):

(1_s) d; (2_s) d, e, f.

The preceding four sets of correlations in some cases stand in need of explanation. We shall provide such explanations, following the order of presentation of these three sets and of the items in them.

In correlating the feature predicated in (4a) with e–g, we allow for the possibility that some material, nonmaterial physical, and spiritual substances are necessarily unchanging with respect to their intrinsic features. For example, Democritus postulated immutable material atoms; Boscovich seems to have posited immutable point-particles; and God is traditionally thought of as being immutable.

We correlate the feature predicated in (4b) and (5) as we do in order to allow for the possibility of a "Spinozistic" material, nonmaterial physical, or spiritual substance:[36] that is, a substance of one of those sorts which is necessarily the only individual and which has all of its dated properties and relations essentially.

One reason that the features predicated in (6), (6a), and (7) are correlated as they are is to be consistent with the possibility of a necessary material, nonmaterial physical, or spiritual substance. A second reason is to allow for the possibility of an essentially eternal substance.

One reason for correlating the characteristic predicated in (8) as we do is the same reason as given in the case of (4b). Another is to allow for the possibility of a substance which is necessarily the only substance of its kind: for instance, God.

In the case of the feature predicated in (1_m), our correlation is compatible with the possibility of both three-dimensional nonmaterial physical substances and non-three-dimensional ones. An example of the former is one of three-dimensional "ghostly" objects which are *transparent* or which can interpenetrate or exhaustively coincide in space. An example of the latter is a zero-dimensional Boscovichian particle or a one-dimensional "superstring."

The case of the characteristic predicated in (2_m) is similar to that of the characteristic predicated in (1_m). Three-dimensional nonmaterial physical substances have an inside and an outside, but zero-dimensional ones do not.

As for the feature predicated in (3_m), we take account of the possibility of both Boscovichian particles which cannot coincide in space (because of repulsive forces) and ghostly objects which can.

Since Boscovichian particles lack parts, we take this into account in our correlation of the characteristic predicated in (5_m). On the other hand, a string, being extended (in one dimension) has parts. It might be argued it is *not* necessarily the case that all nonmaterial physical substances occupy space, contrary to our correlation of the feature predicated in (6_m) with c. Consider the possibility of a universe containing no extended occupant of space, but just a single zero-dimensional particle. Suppose that necessarily, if space exists, then space is relational. In that case, the aforementioned particle does not occupy space in the universe in question, for there would be no spatial relations between it and anything else. But the idea that a zero-dimensional particle can fail to occupy space is incoherent. To put

36 Spinoza's one substance is, of course, neither material, nor spiritual, nor nonmaterial physical. Instead, it has both thought and extension (as well as infinitely many other, unknown essential attributes).

this another way, it is impossible for there to be a point-particle which fails to occupy space (just as it is impossible for there to be a material object that fails to occupy space). We remind the reader that zero-dimensional means "spatial, but lacking extension"; hence, a soul is not zero-dimensional, but lacking spatial dimensionality altogether. Thus, we are forced to the conclusion that a world in which there is no extended occupant of space, but just a single zero-dimensional particle (a world which seems possible), must be a world in which space is absolute.

Nonmaterial physical substances cannot have material parts, else they would be material substances. Hence, the feature predicated in (7_m) is correlated with b and not with f.

Finally, since we know of no good reason to rule out the possibility of a capacity for consciousness which is had by some nonmaterial physical substance or by some material substance, nor any good reason to rule out the possibility that some material object or that some nonmaterial physical object is incapable of consciousness, we correlate the characteristic predicated in (2_s) with e and f.

2

Historically prominent accounts of substance

All modern philosophy hinges round the difficulty of describing the world in terms of subject and predicate, substance and quality, particular and universal.

A. N. Whitehead *Process and Reality* 64 ([1929] 1969)

Indeed, what has been sought after of old, and now, and always, and is always puzzled over, namely, What is being? is this: What is substance?

Aristotle *Metaphysics* Z 1028b

I. TWO ARISTOTELEAN THEORIES

The first substance is the individual which can neither exist in another nor be predicated of another.

W. Turner *History of Philosophy* 133 (1903)

. . . that which receives modifications and is not itself a mode . . .

"Substance" *Oxford English Dictionary* (1971)

As we have indicated, the concept of substance has played a prominent role in the history of philosophy. Any attempt to provide an analysis of substance should be informed by an awareness of the efforts of the great philosophers of the past to characterize the ordinary concept of substance, and of the strengths and weaknesses of those efforts. As will become evident, our own analysis of the ordinary concept of substance is rooted firmly in one of the traditional approaches to understanding this concept. In this chapter, we will survey and critically assess several historically important attempts to analyze the ordinary concept of individual substance.

The first historically important attempt to analyze the ordinary concept is due to Aristotle, and states that a substance is that which can persist through change. As he said,

> It seems most distinctive of substance that what is numerically one and the same is able to receive contraries. In no other case could one bring forward anything, numerically one, which is able to receive contraries.[1]

It is interesting to note that in terms of our list of eight necessary features of all substances, Aristotle's analysis of substance is framed in terms of (4a) and (4b), and, hence, in terms of (4). In effect, he is maintaining that the other features, if they are necessary features of substance, are implied by this one.

The first problem for this view, one which was noted by Aristotle himself, is that entities other than substances can undergo change. Aristotle gives the example of a belief which is at one time true and at another false.[2] Since a belief or a proposition is not a substance, but can undergo a change in truth-value, Aristotle's analysis appears not to provide a logically sufficient condition of being a substance. Aristotle's reply to this objection is to say that "in the case of substances it is by themselves changing that they are able to receive contraries . . . statements and beliefs, on the other hand, themselves remain completely unchangeable in every way."[3] Aristotle's reply presupposes a distinction between *intrinsic* and *relational* change, calling the former something's "changing by itself." His example suggests an argument that abstract entities can undergo change, and his reply is that such entities, unlike substances, can only undergo relational changes. If Aristotle is entitled to the distinction between intrinsic and relational change, then his reply to the example of changing abstract entities reveals that his actual analysis is in terms of intrinsic change, or in terms of (4a). In that case, Aristotle's reply to such a counterexample is cogent.

Nevertheless, it might be argued that the intrinsic–relational change distinction is unclear,[4] and that without an analysis of *it,* Aristotle cannot use it to reply effectively to the objection in question. Aristotle does not provide such an analysis. Does he need to? This is a matter of controversy, but let us explore the question of whether an analysis of this sort is possible.

Following Aristotle, let us say that for something to change is for it to

---

1 *Categories,* trans. J. Ackrill, in *The Complete Works of Aristotle,* 2 vols. (Princeton: Princeton University Press, 1984), 1:7. Unless otherwise indicated, all further references to Aristotle will be to this edition.
2 Ibid.
3 Ibid.
4 For a discussion of a sophisticated attempt to define the intrinsic–relational distinction, see David Lewis, "Extrinsic Properties," *Philosophical Studies* 44 (1983), pp. 197–200. Lewis concludes that this attempt does not succeed. Also see Ishtiyaque Haji, "The Unresolved Puzzle About Posthumous Predication," *Grazer Philosophische Studien* 38 (1990), pp. 187–193, and David-Hillel Ruben, "A Puzzle About Posthumous Predication," *Philosophical Review* 97 (1988), pp. 211–236.

instantiate contrary or contradictory properties at different times. Thus, it seems natural to say that if a thing undergoes an intrinsic change, then it instantiates contrary or contradictory *intrinsic properties* at different times, and if it undergoes relational change, then it instantiates contrary or contradictory *relational properties* at different times. Examples of intrinsic properties are redness, squareness, and being in pain, and examples of relational properties are being five feet from Smith, being thought of by Jones, and being between a rock and a hard place. So, if there is a lack of clarity in the distinction between intrinsic and relational change, then it appears that this is because the distinction between intrinsic and relational properties is obscure. Can this distinction be elucidated?

A first attempt to do so might be to say that P is an intrinsic property if and only if necessarily, for any x, if P is acquired or lost by x, then x is a substance. A relational property is then defined as a nonintrinsic property. This attempt is obviously circular in the context of trying to define substance. Furthermore, there seem to be relational properties that are essential to anything which instantiates them (hence, can be neither acquired nor lost), for example, being diverse from George Bush, or being such that $2 + 2 = 4$. If either of these examples is correct, then when one substitutes for P the property, being diverse from George Bush, or the property, being such that $2 + 2 = 4$, the antecedent of the definiens is necessarily false. Thus, the definiens is vacuously satisfied, and the definition falsely implies that the relational property, being diverse from George Bush, is an intrinsic property of Boris Yeltsin, or that the relational property, being such that $2 + 2 = 4$, is an intrinsic property of Boris Yeltsin. Hence, the foregoing definition of an intrinsic property does not provide a logically sufficient condition of being an intrinsic property. This counterexample cannot be avoided by permitting substitutions only of accidental properties, since Aristotle himself recognizes the existence of essential intrinsic properties.

A second attempt consists in defining an intrinsic property as (roughly) a property that is possibly exemplified when one and only one entity exists. A relational property is then defined as a property that is not intrinsic. The intuitive idea here is that it is possible for there to be one and only one thing, and for this thing to exemplify blueness (intrinsic property), while it is not possible for there to be one and only one thing, and for this thing to exemplify being five feet (apart) from Smith (relational property).

This second attempt, at least in the version stated, fails to distinguish correctly intrinsic from relational properties. No property is possibly exemplified when one and only one entity exists. Consider the foregoing example, where it is supposed that there is one and only one thing, and it is blue. Necessarily, if blueness is exemplified, then there exists not only a thing which is blue, but also blueness, being a color (which blueness must instantiate), parts of a blue thing, and, arguably, times, places, a surface of a blue thing, and so forth. Other possible versions along the lines of this second attempt to define an intrinsic property are not likely to avoid the kind of difficulties raised here.

Given the failure of various attempts to elucidate the intrinsic–relational distinction, it might be suggested that this distinction is both cogent and primitive. For the sake of the argument, let us grant this suggestion. Nevertheless, Aristotle's definition of substance as that which can undergo intrinsic change is subject to refutation by counterexample. First, consider the case of a snowstorm that has different intensities at different times. It is not unnatural to say of the snowstorm that it changes its intensity over time. Thus, this seems to be a case of a nonsubstance, that is, an event, which undergoes an intrinsic change. If so, then Aristotle's definition does not provide a sufficient condition for being a substance. However, this counterexample seems peculiar because it implies that changes can undergo change. Perhaps the peculiarity is brought out by the following considerations. It appears to be a distinctive feature of an event that if it occurs in its entirety at a time of length l, then it occurs in its entirety at a time of length l in every possible world in which it exists.[5] Moreover, it is a plausible principle that if any contingent entity, e, which is not necessarily eternal, begins to undergo an intrinsic change at a moment, m, then it is possible for e to have gone out of existence at m instead. These two propositions together imply that contingent events which are not necessarily eternal (such as our snowstorm) cannot undergo genuine intrinsic change. Hence, the example of the snowstorm which undergoes change is not a plausible counterexample to Aristotle's definition.

A second kind of counterexample may prove to be more convincing. Consider the surface of a rubber ball which undergoes a change in shape whenever the rubber ball does. This appears to be a case of a nonsubstance,

---

5 One way of defending this claim is by appealing to the following two premises: (a) necessarily, a temporally extended event has temporal parts, and (b) an event's temporal parts are essential to it. Admittedly, (b) is controversial. However, some philosophers would argue that if something has temporal parts, then it cannot undergo intrinsic change – it merely has parts which have different properties. These philosophers would infer from this argument together with (a) that events cannot undergo intrinsic change. Such an inference is drawn, e.g., by P. T. Geach in *Logic Matters* (Berkeley: University of California Press, 1972), pp. 302–318, and by D. H. Mellor in *Real Time* (Cambridge: Cambridge University Press, 1981), chaps. 7 and 8.

namely, a surface, undergoing an intrinsic change. Furthermore, we can think of no effective reply along the lines of the preceding discussion to this counterexample. Thus, it seems that the capacity to undergo intrinsic change is not a logically sufficient condition of being a substance. On the other hand, Aristotle would no doubt reply that surfaces do not really exist, not even in the attenuated sense in which entities in the ten categories other than Primary Substance exist, such as places, qualities, times, et cetera. Aristotle may or may not be right about the reality of surfaces. His list of categories is certainly arbitrary-seeming and redundant, and it is a matter of controversy whether entities such as surfaces exist.[6] A criterion of substance which did not presuppose a particular ontology, such as Aristotle's, would be preferable to one which does. So at the very least, Aristotle's definition of substance in terms of intrinsic change is *not ontologically neutral.*

There is another respect in which an Aristotelean definition of substance is not ontologically neutral. It rules out the possibility of Democritean atoms: necessarily indivisible particles which have volume and which are incapable of undergoing intrinsic change. Since Democritean atoms are material substances, if atoms of this kind are possible, then the capacity to undergo intrinsic change is not a logically necessary condition of being a substance. Aristotle rejected the existence of Democritean atoms, but to many it seems that such atoms are possible.

As the foregoing discussion demonstrates, Aristotle's attempt to analyze the ordinary concept of substance in terms of the possibility of undergoing change (or intrinsic change) is not successful.

Aristotle's definition of individual or "primary" substance appears in chapter 5 of his *Categories.* There he says that "a *substance* – that which is called a substance most strictly, primarily, and most of all – is that which is neither said of a subject nor in a subject, for example, the individual man or the individual horse."[7]

In chapter 4 of the same work, Aristotle provides a list of the ten categories of being (apart from Individual Substance). The list is as follows: (Secondary) Substance; Quantity; Quality or Qualification; Relative or Relation; Place; Time; Being-In-A-Position; Having; Doing; Being Af-

---

6 Two contemporary philosophers who affirm the existence of surfaces (and other entities of that sort) are Roderick Chisholm, "Boundaries," in *On Metaphysics* (Minneapolis: University of Minnesota Press, 1989), pp. 83–89, and Avrum Stroll, *Surfaces* (Minneapolis: University of Minnesota Press, 1988).
7 *Complete Works of Aristotle,* 1:4.

fected.[8] Earlier, Aristotle tries to explain what he means by something's being *said-of a subject* and by something's being *in a subject*.[9]

Standing in the way of an evaluation of Aristotle's explanations of the *said-of* and *in* relations is the fact that there is considerable scholarly controversy over their interpretation. To avoid having to choose among these interpretations, we shall present each of the major interpretations and argue that this second of Aristotle's accounts of substance is *not an independence criterion* no matter which interpretation is chosen.

The first major interpretation is that of John Ackrill (among others), who says that the text implies the following definitions of the *said-of* and *in* relations, respectively:[10]

(2D1) *A* is *said-of B* =df. *A* is a species or genus of *B*.
(2D2) *A* is *in*$_a$ *B* =df. (a) *A* is *in*$_b$ *B*, and (b) *A* is not a part of *B*, and (c) *A* is incapable of existing apart from *B*.

The 'in' which occurs in the definiens of (2D2) cannot on pain of circularity be the same 'in' that occurs in the definiendum. Ackrill offers the following plausible account of the former, which we label '*in*$_b$':

(2D2a) *A* is *in*$_b$ *B* =df. one could naturally say in ordinary language either that *A* is in *B*, or that *A* is of *B*, or that *A* belongs to *B*, or that *B* has *A*, (or that . . .).[11]

The 'in' which occurs in the definiens of (2D2a) is just the 'in' of ordinary language, as opposed to the technical terms defined by (2D2) and (2D2a).

According to Ackrill, Aristotle employs the notion defined in (2D1) to distinguish species and genera from individuals, and employs the notion defined in (2D2) to distinguish substances (primary or secondary) from nonsubstances. Thus, for Aristotle, only individual or primary substances are neither said-of nor in$_a$ a subject. In Aristotle's view, species and genera in the category of Substance (e.g., man, stone) are said-of a subject (e.g., Socrates is a man), but are not in$_a$ any subject (mankind can exist apart from Socrates). These are the so-called secondary substances, and are essences according to Aristotle. Individuals in categories other than Substance, individual characteristics, are in$_a$ a subject but are not said-of any subject (for instance, *this* courage is in Socrates). Finally, species and genera in categories other than Substance (accidental general characteristics) are

8 Ibid.
9 Ibid., p. 3.
10 These definitions are propounded persuasively by J. L. Ackrill in his translation with notes of Aristotle's *Categories and De Interpretatione* (Oxford: Oxford University Press, 1963), pp. 74–76. Ackrill's interpretation may be regarded as the standard reading of Aristotle.
11 Ibid., p. 74.

both said-of a subject (e.g., the knowledge of grammar is knowledge) and in$_a$ a subject (e.g., knowledge is in minds, minds have knowledge).

In what sense is Aristotle's criterion an *independence* criterion? Clearly, Aristotle *intends* to maintain that in some sense individual substances are the fundamental realities, and that every other kind of existent is dependent on these fundamental realities, but not vice versa. For example, he says in book 12, chapter 5, of the *Metaphysics,* that "some things can exist apart and some cannot, and it is the former that are substances."[12]

One clear explication of ontological independence is in terms of asymmetrical existential entailment. If the existence of x entails the existence of y, and not vice versa, then y is in this sense independent of x. Such a notion of ontological independence seems to be pertinent to Aristotle's analysis of primary substance: if that analysis *is* in terms of ontological independence, then this independence would seem to be of the metaphysical or logical sort just characterized.[13] Hence, Aristotle seems to be saying here and in the *Categories* that while entities in categories other than Individual Substance presuppose or entail the existence of an individual substance, the existence of an individual substance does not presuppose or entail the existence of any other sort of entity. In this sense, only individual substances can "exist apart." Such a situation would be one in which individual substances were logically independent of all other kinds of entities, but, for any other such kind of entity, not vice versa. Thus, this would be a situation in which individual substances were *asymmetrically independent* of all other kinds of entities, and one in which every other kind of entity would be *asymmetrically dependent* on individual substances.

There are three senses in which it could either be asserted that a primary substance is independent of other Aristotelean beings, or that properties are dependent on primary substances.

(i) Possibly [(F does not exist because F is not exemplified) & ($\exists x$)(x is a primary substance)].[14]

---

12 *Complete Works of Aristotle,* 2:1691. We recognize that most scholars find in the *Metaphysics* an account of individual substance incompatible with the one in the *Categories.* Nevertheless, there is no reason to think that Aristotle changed his view that individual substance is the fundamental reality or that it is independent of other entities.

13 It appears that the only alternatives to metaphysical or logical independence are mereological and causal independence. However, Aristotle's analysis of individual substance in the *Categories* is clearly not in terms of the mereological or causal independence of individual substances from entities of other categories.

14 'F' is a schematic letter which should be replaced by the name of a possible property, in the sense of an Aristotelean being which is not a primary substance.

(i) expresses the independence of the class of primary substances from any particular property.

(ii) Necessarily, if $\sim(\exists x)(x$ is a primary substance), then $\sim(\exists G)(G$ is a property).

(ii) expresses the dependence of the class of properties on the class of primary substances.

(iii) Necessarily, if F exists, then $(\exists x)(x$ is a primary substance which exemplifies F).[15]

(iii) expresses the idea that any particular property must be exemplified by some primary substance, and hence, that any particular property depends on some primary substance. To establish the *asymmetrical* independence of primary substances, it must be shown that the dependence relations which are the converses of those expressed in (i)–(iii) do *not* hold between primary substances and other beings.

Does Aristotle's criterion of primary substance (as that which is neither said-of a subject nor in$_a$ a subject) actually imply that individual substances are in any of the three senses just listed asymmetrically independent of other beings?

To begin answering this question, we shall ask whether the said-of relation is an asymmetrical dependence relation. It *is* an *asymmetrical* relation, for if A is said-of B, then B cannot be said-of A. According to the Aristotle of the *Categories,* Platonism is false, and every species or genus is a species or genus of primary substance. One consequence of this is that the dependence or independence relations expressed in (i)–(iii) hold between primary substances and secondary substances. (i) holds because, for example, it is possible that humanity is not exemplified and there is a (nonhuman) primary substance, for instance, a stone. (ii) holds because if there were no primary substances, there could be no secondary substances. And (iii) holds because, for example, if horseness exists, then there must be a primary substance which is a horse. Thus, the said-of relation is a relation which is such that if a secondary substance is said-of a primary substance, then the secondary substance is *dependent upon* the primary substance.

But does the holding of the said-of relation between primary substances and secondary substances imply that the former are *asymmetrically independent* of the latter?[16] To answer this question, we ask whether any of the

---

15 'F' is a schematic letter which should be replaced by the name of a possible property.
16 Note that from the fact that xRy is an asymmetric relation and the fact that xRy is a dependence relation, it does not follow that x is asymmetrically dependent on y. In general, from the fact that something has each of two properties, being-F and being-G, it

converse relations of (i)–(iii) hold between primary and secondary substances. The three converse relations are as follows:

(i★) Possibly, a does not exist & $(\exists G)(G$ is exemplified).[17]
(ii★) Necessarily, if $\sim(\exists G)(G$ is a property), then $\sim(\exists x)(x$ is a primary substance).
(iii★) Necessarily, if a is a primary substance, then $(\exists G)(a$ exemplifies $G)$.[18]

(i★) expresses the independence of the class of properties from any particular primary substance. (ii★) expresses the dependence of the class of primary substances on the class of properties. And (iii★) expresses the idea that any primary substance must exemplify some property, and hence that any primary substance depends on some property. Hence, either (i★) needs to be false and (i) true, or (ii★) false and (ii) true, or (iii★) false and (iii) true, of the relation between primary and secondary substances, if the said-of relation is to be an asymmetrical independence relation – with primary substances as the independent entities. We have already said that (i), (ii), and (iii) are true in the case of primary and secondary substances. But we now can observe that (i★), (ii★), and (iii★) are all *true* of the relation between primary and secondary substances.

In the case of (i★), it *is* possible for any particular primary substance not to exist, for example, Socrates, and for there to be a secondary substance, say, humanity, which is exemplified by someone, for instance, Boris Yeltsin. This shows that the class of secondary substances is independent of any particular primary substance *in the same sense* in which the class of primary substances is independent of any particular secondary substance.

does not follow that it has being-F G-ly. For example, because a property is abstract and interesting, it does not follow that that property is interestingly abstract (or abstractly interesting). Another (more specific) example is the relation, x is the undetachable right-hand Siamese twin of y. This relation is asymmetric, since if x is the right-hand Siamese twin of y, then y is not the right-hand Siamese twin of x (but the left-hand Siamese twin). Furthermore, this relation is a dependence relation, inasmuch as if x is the undetachable right-hand Siamese twin of y, then x cannot exist unless y exists. But it does not follow that x is asymmetrically dependent on y, because y is dependent in the same way on x. Two additional points. First, we do not deny the validity of the inference from the fact that something has each of two properties, being-F and being-G, that it has the conjunctive property, being-F-and-G. This is a trivially valid inference. Second, we do not deny that in *some* cases one can infer from the fact that something has the two properties, being-F and being-G that it has the property, being-F G-ly. For example, if a relation is spatial and dyadic, then it does follow that it is spatially dyadic. It may be that those who think that because a relation is asymmetric and a dependence relation that it is therefore an asymmetric dependence relation draw this inference under the influence of those cases where such an inference is warranted, or it may be that they are confusing this sort of inference with the different, trivial inference mentioned previously.

17 'a' is a schematic letter which should be replaced with the name of a primary substance.
18 'a' is a schematic letter which should be replaced with the name of a primary substance.

Turning to (ii*), we observe that necessarily, if there are no secondary substances, then there are no primary substances. This shows that the class of primary substances is dependent upon the class of secondary substances *in the same sense* in which the class of secondary substances is dependent upon the class of primary substances.

Finally, in the case of (iii*), we note that necessarily, if there is a primary substance, then there is a secondary substance which it exemplifies. This shows that any particular primary substance must exemplify some secondary substance, and hence, that any particular primary substance is dependent upon some secondary substance *in the same sense* in which any particular secondary substance is dependent upon some primary substance.

We conclude that the said-of relation on Ackrill's interpretation of Aristotle is *not* an asymmetrical independence relation holding between primary and secondary substances in which the primary substances are independent of the secondary substances.

Let us turn, next, to the in_a relation as defined by Ackrill's (2D2). Is this relation an asymmetrical relation? Yes, because if F-ness is in_a x, then x cannot be in_a F-ness. Moreover, conjunct (a) of the definiens of (2D2) expresses an asymmetrical relation, the one defined by (2D2a). However, this latter relation is *not* a dependence relation in any clear sense (i.e., of entailment). Furthermore, it is clear that conjunct (b) in (2D2) does not express a dependence relation, since A's not being a part of B in no way implies that A is dependent upon B. On the other hand, conjunct (c) in (2D2) expresses as strong a dependence relation as we could find in (a) of (2D2). Looking to conjunct (c) in (2D2), we find that this conjunct explicitly expresses a dependence relation. If A is in_a B, then A is incapable of existing apart from B. But recall that, according to Ackrill's interpretation, Aristotle holds that individuals in categories other than Substance, and species and genera in categories other than Substance, are the only existents that can be in_a a subject. Species and genera in categories other than Substance cannot be in_a individual substances because they can exist apart from any particular individual substance. Hence, it is only individuals in categories other than Substance (i.e., tropes)[19] that are in_a individual substances, for example, Socrates's courage is in_a Socrates.[20]

19 The term 'trope' as a name for such concrete "properties" is due to D. C. Williams, *The Principles of Empirical Realism* (Springfield, Ill.: Charles C Thomas, 1966). A trope such as Aristotle's wisdom would not, of course, itself be wise: it is Aristotle who is wise. Moreover, Aristotle's wisdom could only be possessed by Aristotle, though other wise individuals, e.g., Socrates, possess a particular wisdom of their own which could not be possessed by anyone else. Likewise, the particular squareness of a certain object could only be possessed by that object, and each square object possesses its own particular squareness

In order to evaluate the proposition that conjunct (c) in (2D2) expresses an asymmetrical dependence relation, where tropes are asymmetrically dependent upon primary substances, we shall first apply (i)–(iii) to tropes and primary substances. In doing so, we interpret (i)–(iii) as follows. First, substitutions for 'F' should be names of tropes. Second, quantified variables which formerly ranged over universals now range over tropes. Finally, 'exemplification' now expresses a relation of possession appropriate to a primary substance vis-à-vis a trope. Interpreted in this way, (i) expresses the independence of the class of primary substances from any particular trope. (ii) expresses the dependence of the class of tropes on the class of primary substances. Lastly, (iii) expresses the idea that any particular trope must be "exemplified" by some primary substance and, therefore, that any particular trope depends upon some primary substance. (i)–(iii) are true. (i) is true because, for example, possibly, Boris Yeltsin exists even though Socrates's courage does not. (ii) is true because, for example, it is not possible for Socrates's courage to exist unless Socrates exists. Lastly, (iii) is true because, for instance, if Socrates's courage exists, then it must be "exemplified" by Socrates.

But in clause (c) of (2D2) does the holding of the indicated relation between primary substances and tropes imply that the latter are *asymmetrically dependent* on the former? To answer this question, we ask whether any of the converse relations of (i)–(iii) hold between primary substances and tropes. The three converse relations are (i*)–(iii*) interpreted for the case of tropes and primary substances, as were (i)–(iii). So interpreted, (i*) expresses the independence of the class of tropes from any particular primary substance. (ii*) expresses the dependence of the class of primary substances on the class of tropes. And (iii*) expresses the idea that any primary substance must "exemplify" some trope, and hence that any primary substance depends on some trope. Hence, either (i*) needs to be false

which no other square object could possess. Furthermore, the particular squareness of a certain object shares the spatial location of that object. In addition, it appears that the particular squareness of a certain object *is* square, and hence possesses spatial parts. Many modern trope theorists do not postulate both tropes and universals, and many identify either everyday things, or substances, with collections of tropes. Examples of trope theorists include D. C. Williams and G. F. Stout, "Are the Characteristics of Particular Things Universal or Particular," symposium in *Proceedings of the Aristotelian Society*, suppl. vol. 3 (1923), pp. 114–122, and Keith Campbell, *Abstract Particulars* (Oxford: Basil Blackwell, 1990).

20 We shall have reason to question the coherence of this interpretation. Specifically, we shall have reason to question whether Aristotle could coherently allow for particular properties outside the category of Substance without allowing for them in the category of Substance.

and (i) true, or (ii*) false and (ii) true, or (iii*) false and (iii) true, of the relation between primary substances and tropes, if clause (c) of (2D2) is to express an asymmetrical dependence relation where tropes are the dependent entities. We have already said that (i), (ii), and (iii) are true in the case of primary substances and tropes. But we now can observe that (i*), (ii*), and (iii*) are all *true* of the relation between primary substances and tropes.

In the case of (i*), it *is* possible for any particular primary substance to not exist, for example, Socrates, and for there to be a trope, say, Boris Yeltsin's courage, which is exemplified by someone, for example, Boris Yeltsin. This shows that the class of tropes is independent of any particular primary substance *in the same sense* in which the class of primary substances is independent of any particular trope.

Turning to (ii*), we observe that necessarily, if there are no tropes, then there are no primary substances. This shows that the class of primary substances is dependent upon the class of tropes *in the same sense* in which the class of tropes is dependent upon the class of primary substances.

Finally, in the case of (iii*), we note that necessarily, if there is a primary substance, then there is a trope which it "exemplifies." This shows that any particular primary substance must "exemplify" some trope and, hence, that any particular primary substance is dependent upon some trope *in the same sense* in which any particular trope is dependent upon some primary substance. We conclude that the relation between tropes and primary substances expressed in clause (c) of (2D2), insofar as (i)–(iii) and (i*)–(iii*) can determine, is *not* an asymmetrical dependence relation in which tropes are dependent upon primary substances.

However, it would seem that in the case of an individual such as Socrates's courage, there is dependence of the desired asymmetrical sort: Socrates's courage cannot exist apart from Socrates, but Socrates can exist apart from it. In formal terms, the pair of converse dependence relations are as follows:

(iv) For any trope, G, $(\exists x)(x$ is a primary substance and G is necessarily such that it is possessed by $x)$.

(iv*) For any primary substance, x, $(\exists G)(G$ is a trope and x is necessarily such that it possesses $G)$.

On Ackrill's interpretation, (iv) is true while (iv*) is false. (iv) is true because on the present interpretation, a trope is a property of the form, the F-ness of a, and necessarily, if the F-ness of a is possessed by a primary substance, it is possessed by a. (iv*) is false because (according to Ackrill)

Aristotle's view is that all tropes are *accidents* (in categories other than Substance), and therefore, if *a* possesses the *F*-ness of *a*, then possibly, *a* does not possess the *F*-ness of *a*.

If Ackrill's interpretation were correct, then there *would* be a sense in which clause (c) of (2D2) expresses an asymmetrical dependence of tropes on primary substances. However, we do not believe that Ackrill's interpretation of Aristotle is coherent. More specifically, we shall argue on grounds of parity that if Aristotle accepts the existence of *accidental* tropes, he should accept the existence of *essential* tropes, for instance, Aristotle's humanity, Plato's substantiality, and so forth. These would be tropes or individual characteristics in the category of Substance, concrete isomorphs of secondary substances which are part of the nature of a primary substance, a possibility which Ackrill (and, if Ackrill is right, Aristotle) overlooked.

Given Aristotle's belief that there are secondary substances (general essences such as humanity), and accidental individual characteristics (e.g., Aristotle's wisdom), Aristotle *should* have held that Socrates's humanity exists, and that this individual characteristic is essential to Socrates. This is true for the following reasons. First, extremely plausible considerations of ontological parity imply that if Socrates's wisdom exists, then there also exists Socrates's humanity. Second, if humanity is essential to Socrates (as Aristotle supposes), then certainly Socrates's humanity is also essential to Socrates. We conclude: the view which Ackrill attributes to Aristotle, namely, that there are accidental tropes but no essential tropes, is incoherent, and therefore, if Aristotle holds that there are the former, then he should also hold that the latter exist.

Given this result, we shall now argue that clause (c) of (2D2) does *not* after all express an asymmetric dependence of tropes on primary substances. Let us reconsider (iv★) in the light of the existence of essential tropes. In that case, (iv★) is true: for example, if Aristotle exists, then there is a trope, Aristotle's humanity, which Aristotle must possess. Since (iv★) is true, primary substances depend upon tropes *in the same sense* in which (iv) expresses the dependence of tropes upon primary substances. Hence, clause (c) of (2D2) does not express an asymmetric dependence of tropes on primary substances. Since (c) is the only clause of (2D2) which expresses a dependence relation, the in$_a$ relation defined in (2D2) is not such an asymmetric dependence relation.

We have seen that on a coherent version of Ackrill's interpretation, neither those things that are said-of something nor those entities which are in$_a$ something are thereby asymmetrically dependent on that something. Hence, the disjunction, *A* is either said-of *B* or *A* is in$_a$ *B*, does not express

41

an asymmetric dependence of A upon B. A further consequence is that the negation of this disjunction, not-(A is said-of B) and not-(A is in$_a$ B), does not express an asymmetric independence of A from B. Thus, by characterizing an individual substance as that which is neither said-of nor in$_a$ a subject, Aristotle has not, after all, on this interpretation, provided an independence criterion of individual substance. He did not succeed in distinguishing individual substances from all other sorts of entities in terms of any of the indicated senses of independence.

Given Ackrill's interpretation, our argument that those entities which are in$_a$ something are not thereby asymmetrically dependent on that something is more controversial than our argument that those entities which are said-of something are not thereby asymmetrically dependent on that something. Nevertheless, as the following line of reasoning shows, even if it is conceded that A's being in$_a$ B expresses an asymmetric dependence of A upon B, Aristotle's characterization of an individual substance as that which is *neither* said-of nor in$_a$ a subject still fails to provide an independence criterion of individual substance on Ackrill's interpretation. First, an Aristotelean secondary substance cannot be in$_a$ anything. Second, as we have argued, the said-of relation between primary substances and secondary substances is *not* an asymmetrical dependence of secondary substances on primary substances. Consequently, on Ackrill's interpretation of Aristotle, even if A's being in$_a$ B expresses an asymmetric dependence of A upon B, Aristotle's account does *not* establish what it purports to establish: that primary substances are asymmetrically independent of *all* other beings. In particular, Aristotle's account fails to establish that primary substances are asymmetrically independent of secondary substances. Thus, Aristotle fails to give an independence criterion of primary or individual substance on Ackrill's interpretation.

Montgomery Furth defends an alternative interpretation of Aristotle.[21] According to Furth's interpretation, an individual characteristic which is *in* a subject is not a trope, but is rather a sort of universal: an accidental property of one or more individuals, a property which is a lowest species of one of the categories other than Substance.[22] To evaluate the proposition that on Furth's interpretation the *in* relation is an asymmetrical dependence relation, where accidental lowest species in categories other than Substance are asymmetrically dependent upon primary substances, we

---

21 In *Substance, Form, and, Psyche: An Aristotelian Metaphysics* (Cambridge: Cambridge University Press, 1988), chap. 1.
22 Ibid., pp. 15–21.

shall first apply (i)–(iii) to these lowest species and primary substances. In order to do so, we interpret (i)–(iii) as follows. First, substitutions for 'F' should be names of lowest species. Second, quantified variables range over primary substances. Interpreted in this way, (i) expresses the independence of the class of primary substances from any particular lowest species. (ii) expresses the dependence of the class of lowest species on the class of primary substances. Finally, (iii) expresses the idea that any particular lowest species must be exemplified by some primary substance, and, therefore, that any particular lowest species depends upon some primary substance. (i)–(iii) are true. (i) is true because, for example, possibly, Boris Yeltsin exists even though a certain specific variety of courage does not exist because it is not exemplified. (ii) is true because, for example, it is not possible for a specific variety of courage to exist unless there is a primary substance which exemplifies that variety of courage. Lastly, (iii) is true because, for instance, if a certain specific variety of courage exists, then it must be exemplified by some primary substance.

But does the holding of the indicated relation between primary substances and lowest species imply that the latter are *asymmetrically dependent* on the former? To answer this question, we ask whether any of the converse relations of (i)–(iii) hold between primary substances and lowest species. The three converse relations are (i⋆)–(iii⋆), interpreted for the case of lowest species and primary substances, as were (i)–(iii). So interpreted, (i⋆) expresses the independence of the class of lowest species from any particular primary substance. (ii⋆) expresses the dependence of the class of primary substances on the class of lowest species. And (iii⋆) expresses the idea that any primary substance must exemplify some lowest species, and hence that any primary substance depends on some lowest species. Hence, either (i⋆) needs to be false and (i) true, or (ii⋆) false and (ii) true, or (iii⋆) false and (iii) true, of the relation between primary substances and lowest species, if lowest species being *in* primary substances is an asymmetrical dependence relation where lowest species are the dependent entities. We have already said that (i), (ii), and (iii) are true in the case of primary substances and lowest species. But we now can observe that (i⋆), (ii⋆), and (iii⋆) are all *true* of the relation between primary substances and lowest species.

In the case of (i⋆), it *is* possible for any particular primary substance to not exist, for example, Socrates, and for there to be a lowest species, say, a certain specific variety of courage, which is exemplified by some other primary substance, for instance, Boris Yeltsin. This shows that the class of lowest species is independent of any particular primary substance *in the same sense* in which the class of primary substances is independent of any particular lowest species.

Turning to (ii★), we observe that necessarily, if there are no lowest species, then there are no primary substances. This shows that the class of primary substances is dependent upon the class of lowest species *in the same sense* in which the class of lowest species is dependent upon the class of primary substances.

Finally, in the case of (iii★), we note that necessarily, if there is a primary substance, then there is a lowest species which it exemplifies. This shows that any particular primary substance must exemplify some lowest species and, hence, that any particular primary substance is dependent upon some lowest species *in the same sense* in which any particular lowest species is dependent upon some primary substance.

We conclude that on Furth's interpretation a lowest species being *in* a primary substance, insofar as (i)–(iii) and (i★)–(iii★) can determine, is *not* an asymmetrical dependence relation in which lowest species are dependent upon primary substances.

Furth's understanding of Aristotle's said-of relation is substantially the same as that of Ackrill. Since we have already shown that on Ackrill's reading this relation is not an asymmetrical dependence relation, it follows that on Furth's interpretation of Aristotle, this relation is also not an asymmetrical dependence relation. Thus, for reasons which are parallel to those we gave in the case of Ackrill's interpretation, on Furth's reading of Aristotle, the definition of primary substance as that which is neither said-of nor *in* a subject is not a definition of primary substance in terms of an asymmetric independence relation.[23]

---

23 Frank Lewis, in *Substance and Predication in Aristotle* (Cambridge: Cambridge University Press, 1991), chap. 2, offers another view of the *Categories*. Lewis addresses the "asymmetry of Aristotle's dependency claims. Dependency cannot consist solely in the fact that, for example, a given nonsubstance, pallor (say), can exist *only if* some individual substance or other exists, for this condition on the existence of pallor is matched by an exactly parallel condition on the existence of individual substances: Socrates, for example, can exist only if some nonsubstance or other exists and is in him. On this showing, there will be no grounds for the priority of either kind of entity over the other, given the standard and most nearly relevant definitions of priority." So far, Lewis is in accord with the main thrust of our critique of Aristotle, as brought out by our use of (i)–(iii) and (i★)–(iii★). But Lewis appears to defend Aristotle's position that in virtue of being neither said-of nor *in* a subject, primary substance is asymmetrically independent of other entities. According to Lewis, Aristotle can get "the asymmetry he needs: an individual nonsubstance can exist only if, *and only because,* some individual substance or other exists, but it is not the case that any given individual substance can exist only because some nonsubstance or other does so. In particular, the existence of things other than individual substances is grounded

While Aristotle's analysis of individual substance is not an independence criterion of individual substance, the question remains of whether this analysis is correct. To this question we now turn.

First of all, consider the property of being both round and square (or the property of being a horned horse). Since it is impossible (false) that the class of things that are both round and square (horned horses) have a member, this class cannot (does not) subsume any other class. Nor is it possible (true) that the property of being round and square (being a horned horse) is exemplified. Hence, this property cannot be (is not) said of anything. Furthermore, in the relevant Aristotelean sense, the property of being round and square (being a horned horse) is not "in" anything. On Ackrill's reading, this is because one could *not* naturally say in ordinary language (where A = being round and square or being a horned horse) either that A is in x, or that A is of x, or that A belongs to x, or that x has A, (or that . . .), for any x. On Furth's reading, this is because there could not be (is not) a lowest species of being round and square (being a horned horse), since a lowest species must be exemplified. Consequently, it appears that on either reading, Aristotle's analysis implies that the property of being round and square and the property of being a horned horse are neither *in* nor said-of anything, and therefore are primary substances. Since this is absurd, it seems that Aristotle's analysis does not provide a sufficient condition of being a primary substance.

Doubtless, since Aristotle would say that every property is exemplified, he would answer this objection by asserting that there is no such property as being round and square or being a horned horse. Because Aristotle must make this reply to avoid this objection, his analysis presupposes a certain ontology of properties. This ontology is controversial. It would be preferable to have an analysis of individual substance that is neutral with respect to such controversies.

Moreover, on Ackrill's interpretation, Aristotle's analysis is subject to a more serious objection. Consider an individual substance such as a stone, s.

in that of individual substances by the two core relations of (metaphysical) predication; *since these relations are asymmetric, the grounding is also asymmetric, as required* [our emphasis]" (p. 69, n. 41). Lewis appears to be saying that because the said-of and *in* relations are asymmetric relations, and because they are dependence relations, they are therefore asymmetric dependence relations. This, of course, does not follow, as we have been careful to emphasize (see n. 16). On the other hand, if Lewis only means to attribute this inference to Aristotle, then it is Aristotle alone who fallaciously draws this conclusion. We do think that Aristotle draws this conclusion, and as we shall argue, we diagnose the mistake as due to a conflation of ontology with syntax.

Obviously, *s* cannot be said of anything. On the other hand, *s* cannot exist apart from space, is not a part of space, and one *could* say in ordinary language that *s* is in space. Therefore, it appears that *s* *is* in$_a$ something, namely, space. If so, then on Aristotle's definition *s* is *not* an individual substance, and his definition (as understood by Ackrill) does not provide a necessary condition of being an individual substance.[24]

It might be replied on behalf of Aristotle that in the ordinary sense of 'in' employed in (2D2a), *s* is not in space. We see no rationale for this assertion. For such a reply to carry any weight, it would have to be supported by an analysis of the relevant ordinary sense of 'in' which ruled out our case but let in all of the desired ones. An analysis of this kind is noticeably absent in Aristotle, and it is difficult to see how one could be forthcoming. Hence, our second counterexample to Ackrill's reading of Aristotle's definition reveals a serious defect: that of employing inessential linguistic criteria where straightforwardly ontological ones are needed.

Many commentators have observed that in formulating his analysis of primary substance in the *Categories,* Aristotle was guided by a certain grammatical or linguistic belief: that only terms for primary substances can exclusively function as grammatical subjects in categorical sentences. He seems to have assumed that this belief indicates a deeper metaphysical one, namely, the independence of individual substance. We think that Aristotle was correct in supposing that individual substance must enjoy ontological independence,[25] though his attempt to characterize it in terms of the said-of and *in* relations, as we have argued, fails, perhaps because he hewed too closely to his linguistic model.

II. SUBSTRATUM AND INHERENCE THEORIES

> That which manifests its qualities, – in other words, that in which the appearing causes inhere, that to which they belong, is called their *subject,* or *substance,* or *substratum.*
>
> Sir William Hamilton *Lectures on Metaphysics* viii I. 137 ([1836–1837] 1859)

---

24 This criticism of Aristotle seems to have been anticipated by Alfred North Whitehead in *Process and Reality* (Toronto: Collier-Macmillan, 1969), p. 75. According to Whitehead, "the actual entity, in virtue of being *what* it is, is also *where* it is [and this is] inconsistent with Aristotle's phrase, 'neither asserted of a subject, nor present in a subject.'"

25 We defend this claim in Chapter 4. The sort of independence of individual substance argued for in Chapter 4 is more complex than Aristotle's, though it makes use of some of his ideas.

All the philosophers . . . when they divide a substance from an accident, mean by a substance that which can subsist in it self without a subject of inherence.

Jeremy Taylor *The Real Presence* 211 (1654)

According to some interpretations, philosophers such as Descartes and Locke held that a substance is a substratum in which properties subsist or inhere.[26] According to this doctrine, a substance is a propertyless or bare particular which gives unity to the properties which inhere in it. For example, Locke wrote that,

> not imagining how these simple ideas can subsist by themselves, we accustom ourselves to suppose some *substratum* wherein they do subsist and from which they do result, which therefore we call *substance*.[27]

And Descartes stated that

> *Substance.* This term applies to every thing in which whatever we perceive immediately resides, as in a subject, or to every thing by means of which whatever we perceive exists. . . . The only idea we have of a substance itself, in the strict sense, is that it is the thing in which whatever we perceive . . . exists, either formally or eminently.[28]

He also said that

> We do not have immediate knowledge of substances, as I have noted elsewhere. We know them only by perceiving certain forms or attributes which must inhere in something if they are to exist; and we call the thing in which they inhere a 'substance'.[29]

That either Descartes or Locke actually subscribed to the substratum theory is a matter of scholarly controversy. In the case of Descartes, some have taken the quotations cited here to be expressing not a commitment to a substratum, but to be merely expressing the point that one cannot apprehend or conceive of a substance except in terms of its properties or

26 Concerning Descartes, see Louis Loeb, *From Descartes to Hume: Continental Metaphysics and the Development of Modern Philosophy* (Ithaca, N.Y.: Cornell University Press, 1981), chap. 2. For Locke, see D. J. O'Connor, *John Locke* (New York: Dover, 1967), and R. Woolhouse, *Locke's Philosophy of Science and Knowledge* (New York: Barnes and Noble, 1971).

27 *An Essay Concerning Human Understanding,* 2 vols., rev. ed., ed. John Yolton (New York: Dutton, 1965), vol. 1, chap. 23, p. 245.

28 *The Philosophical Writings of Descartes,* trans. John Cottingham, Robert Stoothoff, and Dugald Murdoch (Cambridge: Cambridge University Press, 1984), 2:114.

29 Ibid., p. 156.

attributes.[30] In the case of Locke, some have interpreted the quoted passage (and others like it) to be part of an *attack* on rather than a defense of the substratum theory.[31]

The idea of a substratum arises perhaps in the following way. All of the properties associated with a substance are ordinarily thought to be possessed by, to be exemplified by, or to inhere in a single object which provides their *unity*. This unity requires an explanation in terms other than that of the properties themselves. That which accounts for this unity is an underlying support or substratum in which the properties subsist or inhere. Hence, this theory of substance defines a substance as that entity which lacks properties but in which properties subsist or inhere, thereby uniting them.

A second role attributed to the substratum is that of *concretizer*. Given that properties are abstract, but that ordinary things such as a ball, a flower, and Socrates are concrete, the substratum is the explanation of why it is that a ball, a flower, and Socrates are concrete. A ball, on this theory, is a complex of abstract properties and a concrete substance or substratum which somehow is responsible for the concreteness of the complex.

Third, some substratum theorists favor the substratum for its role as *individuator*. Given the possibility of two qualitatively indistinguishable spheres, the fact that one sphere is composed in part of substratum 1 while the other is composed of substratum 2 is supposed to account for the diversity of the two spheres.[32]

A fourth argument for the substratum theory is that the substratum is needed to explain the *persistence* of a substance through intrinsic qualitative change. The idea is that the substance persists because its substratum is unchanged.

A first objection to a theory which identifies a substance with a substratum, or which takes a substance to be a complex of a substratum and properties, is that the idea of a substratum is incoherent and self-

---

30 This reading of Descartes is suggested, at least, by M. Wilson, *Descartes* (London: Routledge and Kegan Paul, 1978).

31 See, e.g., Jonathan Bennett, *Locke, Berkeley, Hume: Central Themes* (Oxford: Oxford University Press, 1971); M. R. Ayers, "The Ideas of Power and Substance in Locke's Philosophy," in *Locke on Human Understanding: Selected Essays,* ed. I. Tipton (Oxford: Oxford University Press, 1977), pp. 77–104; and Martha Bolton, "Substances, Substrata, and Names of Substances in Locke's *Essay,*" *Philosophical Review* 85 (1976), pp. 488–513.

32 E.g., Gustav Bergmann, *Realism* (Madison: University of Wisconsin Press, 1967).

contradictory.[33] A substratum exemplifies no properties.[34] It is incoherent because it is a necessary truth that any entity exemplifies properties. Nor can anyone grasp or apprehend or conceive of anything which fails to exemplify any property. It is self-contradictory because the substratum theorist himself must attribute various properties to the substratum: for example, the property of being such that properties can subsist or inhere in it, the property of being concrete, the property of being a substance, and (absurdly) the property of lacking all properties! Finally, another serious difficulty for the theory is that it asserts both that properties subsist or inhere in the substratum *and* that the substratum fails to exemplify any property. Yet the following seems to be a necessary truth: if a property P inheres in x, then x exemplifies P. Thus, if by subsisting or inhering in a substratum, the substratum theorist means just that a property is *exemplified* by the substratum, then he contradicts himself in also asserting that the substratum is "bare." On the other hand, if by subsisting or inhering in a substratum, the substratum theorist does not mean that a property is exemplified by the substratum, then it is not clear what if anything is meant by subsisting or inhering in a substratum. In common parlance, a substance or thing literally *has* certain properties, that is, exemplifies them (in technical terminology). But according to the substratum theorist, it does not follow from a property's inhering or subsisting in a thing that the thing literally has that property. Hence, the substratum theorist owes us an explanation of just what he has in mind here, an explanation which is not forthcoming and without which one has no clue to the nature of the relation in question.

Second, the theory that an individual substance is a substratum (call this *ST1*), and the theory that an individual substance is a complex of a sub-

33 If Locke and Descartes are substratum theorists, then they seem to hold the version according to which a substratum is a substance. Bergmann, on the other hand, seems to hold the view that both a substratum and properties are constituents of a given substance, e.g., a flower, person, or rock. The latter view has the advantage of endorsing the commonsense belief that ordinary objects such as flowers, people, and rocks *are* substances.

34 According to some more recent versions of the substratum theory, e.g., Bergmann's, a substratum exemplifies properties, but has no nature, i.e., exemplifies no property essentially. Call this view *ST3*. According to ST3, a substratum *possibly* exemplifies no properties, since, if it has the property of having properties, then it has this property accidentally. Thus, ST3 is also incompatible with the necessary truth that an entity exemplifies some properties, and so does not escape our criticism that the substratum theory is incoherent. We have concentrated on the historically more prominent substratum theories, according to which a substratum is propertyless.

stratum and properties (call this *ST2*), conflict with several of the data for a philosophical theory of substance.

We begin with ST1. ST1 conflicts with the following data enumerated in Chapter 1, Section III: (1) no individual substance can be featureless; (4a) possibly, some individual substance persists through a change in its intrinsic features; (4b) possibly, some individual substance persists through a change in its relational features; and (5) possibly, some individual substance has an accidental intrinsic or relational feature and has an essential intrinsic feature. Clearly, ST1 conflicts with all of the foregoing features of ordinary substance because a substratum literally has no features at all (although, as we have seen, it is said to bear some unexplained relation to various features). Since ST1 conflicts with *so much* of the data for an account of what an individual substance is, ordinarily conceived, and since its very coherence is questionable, we conclude that this theory of substance is highly implausible.[35]

ST2 holds that a substance is a complex of a substratum and properties. This conflicts with the following data enumerated in Chapter 1, Section III. (3) no substance has a feature as a part. Since ST2 maintains that a substance is a (concrete) collection of a substratum and certain properties, it follows that a substance has those properties as parts. (4a) Possibly, a substance persists through a change in its intrinsic features. According to ST2, a substance is a *complex* or *collection* of a substratum and properties. It appears that the parts of such a collection are essential to it. Furthermore, it seems also that these parts are either an item (a substratum) which has no intrinsic features, or else are items (properties) which have all of their intrinsic properties essentially. Finally, the relations between the substratum and the properties of the substance are fixed by the fact that they are related in a *sui generis* metaphysical way (rather than in some empirical way, e.g., spatially), while the properties are related only in a purely logical way to one another. Thus, it appears that a complex or collection of a substratum and properties has all its intrinsic features essentially. Note that although, according to ST2, a substance has certain intrinsic and relational features, it has the wrong ones. According to ST2, a ball does not have the property of being round, does not have the property of being made of rubber, does not have the property of being pink, and does not have the property of being a ball! Rather, a ball is a complex or collection which

---

35 For some related criticisms of the claim that substrata are substances, see Brian Carr, *Metaphysics: An Introduction* (Atlantic Highlands, N.J.: Humanities Press International, 1987), chap. 2.

includes a substratum in which roundness, being rubber, being pink, and being a ball subsist or inhere. The ball itself has the property of being a complex, the property of having a substratum and certain properties as parts, and so forth.[36]

In addition, we find the four arguments which motivate the substratum theory to be unsound. The first is the argument that the substratum is needed to unify the properties of an ordinary thing. A much better candidate for this role is the ordinary object itself. Thus, we would hold that *the ball* unifies the properties of the ball, that the flower unifies the properties had by the flower, and so forth.

A second argument holds that a substratum is what makes an ordinary object concrete. One reply to this is that it is by no means clear that a complex of abstract properties and a concrete substratum is itself concrete. For example, a *set* of abstract properties and a concrete substratum is *abstract,* not concrete, and a *collection* of objects in the sense of their mereological sum, which *is* a concrete entity, cannot have an abstract entity as a part. A second reply is that there is no need to postulate any entity other than an ordinary thing like a ball in order to explain why the ball is concrete: a ball is concrete because it is a substance, and because it is a material object, and because it is in space and time, and so forth.

The third motivating argument postulates substrata in order to explain the diversity of ordinary objects (as is made clear by the possibility of there being two qualitatively indistinguishable ordinary objects). But if ordinary objects require substrata as individuators, why don't substrata themselves require some entity in order to individuate them? Properties can't individuate them, for they have none. Whatever else might serve to individuate substrata (i.e., something other than further substrata, e.g., location) would serve to individuate ordinary objects without having to invoke substrata. Thus, consistency seems to imply either that substrata require further substrata as individuators (an absurdity), or else that substrata are not required in order to individuate ordinary objects.

The fourth argument motivates the introduction of substrata by arguing that substrata explain how ordinary objects can persist through intrinsic qualitative change. A substratum is an unchanging core which is a constit-

---

36 As Michael Loux has observed, a theory like ST2 "drives us to . . . the view that the ordinary way of thinking about the ball is wrong. The ball does not literally possess the properties associated with it; something else does"; see *Substance and Attribute* (Dordrecht: Reidel, 1978), pp. 109–110. This something else is of course the substratum. And, as we have pointed out, it is not in any ordinary sense that the substratum literally "possesses" these properties.

uent of an ordinary object. As we showed earlier, ST2 implies that an ordinary object (a substance) cannot undergo intrinsic qualitative change. ST1 differs from ST2 only in designating the substratum as the substance. Hence, ST1 also implies that an ordinary object cannot undergo intrinsic qualitative change. Thus, this fourth argument does not provide any motivation for either ST1 or ST2. Moreover, a more commonsense view of substance can explain the persistence of an ordinary object through intrinsic qualitative change. The explanation is that an ordinary object has an essence or nature which it cannot lose. The ordinary object persists through intrinsic qualitative change because it retains its essence or nature. Jones may undergo a change of mood, but Jones persists because he retains his humanity, and so forth.

For all of the reasons we have provided in the foregoing discussion, substratum theories do not give adequate accounts of substance. We turn next to what we call the *inherence* theory of substance.

The inherence theory of substance can be distinguished from the substratum theory in that the former defines a substance as that in which properties inhere, without implying, as does a substratum theory, that the subject of inherence could exist without any properties. The fact that the inherence theory does not imply a substratum is not always realized. An example of the inherence theory seems to be provided by Descartes in the following quotation:

> *Substance.* This term applies to every thing in which whatever we perceive immediately resides, as in a subject, or to every thing by means of which whatever we perceive exists.[37]

The gist of this definition of substance is that a substance is that in which properties "reside" (inhere). But the definition suffers from being too general, that is, it does not provide a logically sufficient condition of being a substance. Since the definition implies that if there are substances, then there are properties, and since every entity must possess properties, the definition also implies that if there are substances, then there are properties in which properties inhere. For example, the property of being round has the property of being a property, et cetera. Hence, the inherence theory implies that if a substance exists, then a property is a substance. This is because what the inherence theory provides a definition of is not a substance, but a subject of predication, which every entity is. It is entityhood and not substancehood which is defined in this way.

37 *Philosophical Writings of Descartes,* 2:114.

III. INDEPENDENCE THEORIES OF SUBSTANCE

> For of the other categories none can exist independently, but only substance.
>
> Aristotle Metaphysics Z 1028a

Another kind of theory of substance, examples of which are found in Aristotle and Descartes, is in terms of substance as that which is uniquely independent of all other entities. Thus, Aristotle:

> Some things can exist apart and some cannot, and it is the former that are substances.[38]

And Descartes:

> The answer is that the notion of *substance* is just this – that it can exist all by itself, that is without the aid of any other substance.[39]

Descartes's definition seems to suffer from the fatal flaw of conceptual circularity, since it explicates the notion of substance in terms of the notion of substance. However, Descartes also provided the following definition:

> By *substance*, we can understand nothing other than a thing which exists in such a way as to depend on no other thing for its existence.[40]

This definition is noncircular if 'thing' means entity. According to Descartes, God is the only entity that satisfies this definition of substance. But, Descartes also says:

> But as for corporeal substance and mind (or created thinking substance), these can be understood to fall under this common concept: things that need only the concurrence of God in order to exist.[41]

From these citations and the surrounding text, it seems that Descartes has something like the following overall account of individual substance in mind.

(2D3) x is a basic substance =df. it is possible that x exists without any other entity existing.

In Descartes's view, God is the only basic substance.

---

38 *Complete Works of Aristotle*, 2:1691.
39 *Philosophical Writings of Descartes*, 2:159.
40 Ibid., p. 210. A similar contemporary definition is offered by David Armstrong: "a particular is a substance, logically capable of independent existence. It could exist although nothing else existed." *Nominalism and Realism* (Cambridge: Cambridge University Press, 1978), 1:115.
41 *Philosophical Writings of Descartes*, 2:159.

(2D4) x is a nonbasic substance =df. it is possible that x exists without any other entity existing, except God.

(2D5) x is a substance =df. x is either a basic substance or a nonbasic substance.[42]

It would appear that there are a number of difficulties with this Cartesian account of substance. In the first place, since (2D4) and (2D5) presuppose the existence of God, Descartes's theory of substance suffers from an extreme form of lack of ontological neutrality. Clearly, it would be better for a theory of substance not to be committed to the existence of God than for it to be so committed.

Second, since Descartes holds that God has certain essential properties, for example, omnipotence, omniscience, and omnibenevolence, it seems that God could not exist unless some other entities exist, that is, his essential properties. If so, then (2D3) mistakenly implies that God is not a basic substance. In that case, (2D3) does not provide a necessary condition for being a basic substance. It follows that (2D5) is incorrect.[43] Descartes might answer this difficulty by appealing to the doctrine of divine simplicity. According to this doctrine, all of God's properties are identical with one another and with God. However, this doctrine is of questionable coherence.[44]

In any event, there are also apparent counterexamples to Descartes's (2D4). For example, consider a typical nonbasic substance, say, a table (call this table a). It is plausible that if a exists, then a is necessarily such that some other substances exist as well, that is, parts of a.[45] Furthermore, it

42 Another advocate of an independence criterion of substance is Spinoza. He wrote as follows. "By substance, I understand that which is in itself and is conceived through itself; in other words, that, the conception of which does not need the conception of another thing from which it must be formed" (*Ethics,* part I, definition 3). For Spinoza, God is the only substance. Unlike Descartes, Spinoza does not countenance created or nonbasic substances. Thus, unlike Aristotle, Descartes, and ourselves, Spinoza's theory rules out the possibility of a plurality of individual substances.

43 If nominalism were true, then Descartes's definition would not be subject to this objection. But his definition would still be subject to other difficulties, including some developed here.

44 For a defense of the coherence of the doctrine of divine simplicity, see "Epistemology Supernaturalized" by William Mann, and for a critical commentary on this essay and a rejoinder, see "Necessity, Contingency, and Mann" by Gary Rosenkrantz, and "Reply to Rosenkrantz" by William Mann, in that order, all of which appear in *Faith and Philosophy* 2, no. 4 (1985), pp. 436–456, 457–463, and 464–467, respectively.

45 This criticism of Descartes's definition of substance is directed at Descartes's definition considered as compatible with the commonsense belief that there is a plurality of material objects. Descartes appears to have rejected this belief in favor of the view that there exists one and only one material substance, i.e., the entire material world conceived of as a single indivisible object. While the aforementioned criticism of Descartes's definition of substance does not apply to this conception of material substance (because such a substance has no parts which are themselves substances), it can be reformulated to apply to

seems that a cannot exist without there being certain nonsubstances, for instance, certain places, properties, and surfaces.[46] Consequently, it is not possible for a to exist without any other entity existing except God. Thus, (2D4), Descartes's definition of nonbasic substance, mistakenly implies that a is not a nonbasic substance, and (2D4) does not provide a necessary condition of nonbasic substance. Hence, (2D5) is inadequate.

There is an important alternative reading of Descartes's theory of substance, one framed in terms of *causal* independence instead of purely logical or metaphysical independence.[47] On this reading of Descartes, his theory of substance can be stated in terms of the following definitions:

(2D3★) x is a basic substance =df. it is possible that x exists without being caused to exist by any other entity.

(2D4★) x is a nonbasic substance =df. it is possible that x exists without being caused to exist by any other entity except God.

(2D5★) x is a substance =df. x is either a basic substance or a nonbasic substance.

This theory of substance is also subject to several serious criticisms. First, like its predecessor, it presupposes theism. Second, the theory is framed in terms of causal independence, but only some categories of beings can be caused to exist. Those entities which cannot be caused to exist but which are not substances will satisfy (2D3★). For example, if there are properties or sets which are uncaused necessary beings, then they will satisfy (2D3★). In this case, (2D3★) implies that such properties and sets are basic substances, while they evidently are not. Hence, (2D3★) does not provide a sufficient condition for being a basic substance.

Descartes might reply to the second objection by arguing that properties, sets, and so forth, in fact, are all causally dependent on God. There are two versions of such a reply. According to the first, properties are *directly* casually dependent upon God, and on the second, properties are *indirectly* causally dependent upon God. A property, P, is directly causally dependent upon God if and only if God causes the existence of P, but does not do so by causing the existence of something other than P which causes the existence of P. A property, P, is indirectly causally dependent upon God just

this conception of material individual substance. The reformulated criticism is that on this conception of individual material substance, a material substance cannot exist without there being parts of that substance (i.e., nonsubstantial parts).

46 This point appears to have been made by Alfred North Whitehead in *Process and Reality*, p. 75. As he observes: "The actual entity, in virtue of being *what* it is, is also *where* it is. . . . This is the direct denial of the Cartesian doctrine '. . . an existent thing which requires nothing but itself in order to exist.'"

47 Loeb, *From Descartes to Hume,* chap. 2.

provided that God causes the existence of P, but does so by causing the existence of something other than P which causes the existence of P.

If properties are directly causally dependent on God, then they seem to satisfy (2D4⋆), and such properties turn out to be nonbasic substances. Thus, if Descartes's reply is that properties are directly causally dependent on God, then (2D4⋆) implies that properties and sets are nonbasic substances, while they obviously are not. Thus, if this is Descartes's answer, then (2D4⋆) does not provide a sufficient condition for being a nonbasic substance.

Alternatively, since Descartes seems to accept the Aristotelean view that every first-order property[48] must inhere in an individual,[49] he might reply instead that all properties must be caused to exist by God insofar as the individuals in which they inhere must be caused by God. And if such properties are causally dependent upon those individuals, then they must be *indirectly* causally dependent upon God: God causes (directly or indirectly) all individuals other than himself, and in virtue of the fact that a first-order property cannot exist unless there is an individual in which it inheres, properties are causally dependent for their existence upon individuals. Hence, God causes a property to exist *by* causing an individual to exist which in turn causes the property to exist. If Descartes could defend this claim about properties, then he could dispute the idea that properties satisfy (2D4⋆).

However, the following line of reasoning shows that properties do not have this sort of causal dependence upon the individuals in which they inhere. First, efficient causation is an *asymmetrical* dependence relation: if x causes y to exist, then y does not cause x to exist. Second, although on Aristotelean Realism a first-order property must inhere in an individual, our critique of Aristotle's account of primary substance in the *Categories* implies that Aristotelean properties are *not* thereby *asymmetrically* dependent upon individuals. Such properties do not causally depend upon individuals in virtue of their necessarily inhering in them, any more than do the individuals causally depend on their properties in virtue of their necessarily having properties. We conclude that if properties are causally dependent on God, then Descartes has provided no reason to deny that they

---

48 A *first-order* property is a property which could only be had by a concrete individual.
49 Descartes appears to accept this Aristotelean view in the following passages taken from *The Philosophical Writings of Descartes*. "It follows that, wherever we find some attributes or qualities, there is necessarily some thing or substance to be found for them to belong to . . ." (1:196). "We know them [substances] only by perceiving certain forms or attributes which must inhere in something if they are to exist" (2:156).

satisfy (2D4★), and hence no reason why such properties do not turn out to be nonbasic substances. Nor is there any other obvious argument for the conclusion that properties are indirectly causally dependent upon God. If properties are causally dependent on God, then, it seems, (2D4★) once more implies that properties and sets are nonbasic substances, though they evidently are not. Thus, once again (2D4★) does not provide a sufficient condition for being a nonbasic substance.

Finally, some philosophers have argued that the nondivine actual causal origins of certain substances are essential to those substances. For example, Kripke and others have argued that any human being is a material substance which is essentially caused to exist by a certain sperm–egg pair.[50] If this is correct, then a human being cannot exist without being caused to exist by something other than God, and that human being would fail to satisfy (2D4★). If so, (2D4★) would not provide a logically necessary condition for being a nonbasic substance. Descartes, of course, did not think that human beings were individual material substances. Nevertheless, he may have been wrong about this, and given the aforementioned Kripkean view, it would be enough to refute (2D4★) if it were even *possible* for there to be a human being who is a material substance and essentially came from a certain sperm–egg pair. In any case, even if Descartes is right to rule out the possibility of material human beings, his theory of substance is not neutral with respect to this issue, as other theories are.

None of the preceding important historical attempts to analyze the ordinary notion of substance is successful. And in Chapter 3, we shall argue that another such attempt does not succeed, namely, the theory that a substance is identifiable with a bundle or collection of features. Nevertheless, in Chapter 4 we shall argue that the independence criterion of Descartes and others, and Aristotle's scheme of categories, contain elements and insights which can be employed in constructing an adequate independence criterion of substance.

50 Saul Kripke, "Naming and Necessity," in *Semantics of Natural Language,* ed. D. Davidson and G. Harman (Dordrecht: Reidel, 1972), pp. 253–355.

3

Collectionist theories of substance

Bundle: A collection of things bound or otherwise fastened together; a bunch; a package, parcel.

"Bundle" *Oxford English Dictionary* (1971)

The former recited particulars, howsoever improperly . . . bundled up together.

F. Greville *The Life of the Renowned Sir Philip Sidney* 235 (1628)

I. WHAT IS A COLLECTIONIST THEORY OF SUBSTANCE?

The idea of a substance is nothing but a collection of simple ideas that are united by the imagination and have a particular name assigned them by which we are able to recall, either to ourselves or to others, that collection.

D. Hume *A Treatise of Human Nature* I. iv. 6 (1739–1740)

A distinction needs to be drawn between two sorts of *collectionist* theories about substance.[1] The *eliminative* collectionist theory holds that there are no substances. Instead, there are collections of entities of another sort, which collections are not to be identified with substances. This view usually maintains that what are taken to be substances are really collections of nonsubstances. A proponent of this view seems to be the Hume of the *Treatise*.[2] Hume is the sort of eliminationist who thinks that there is no

---

1 One variety of collectionist theory is what has traditionally been called a "bundle theory." The latter term is usually associated with a theory which is concerned with collections of (abstract) properties or (concrete) tropes.
2 Hume's radical empiricist argument against substance was outlined in Chapter 1, Section I. Nevertheless, even Hume sometimes speaks as though substances exist and can be identified with collections of sense-impressions, as witness the quotation cited at the head of this section (*Treatise,* book 1, part 4, sec. 6). Indeed, such an authority of ordinary English usage as *Webster's Third New International Dictionary* (1976) cites this quotation in its article on "Substance," maintaining that in Humean Philosophy 'substance' means "a collection of qualities regarded as constituting a unity."

intelligible concept of substance, but it is possible to be an eliminationist and also hold that the concept of substance is a coherent one.

A second kind of collectionist theory *identifies* substances with collections of nonsubstances. Such a theory attempts to provide a philosophical analysis[3] of the concept of an individual substance as ordinarily understood in terms of a collection of this kind. Consequently, it maintains that necessarily, x is a substance if and only if x is a collection of nonsubstances of an appropriate sort. The basic idea of this theory is that the substantiality of a substance is just the collecting of those nonsubstances in a certain way. Since we are interested in attempts to analyze the ordinary concept of substance, it is this second sort of collectionist theory which concerns us. We are not sure that any collectionist theorist has both clearly distinguished the eliminative and noneliminative versions of the theory, and subscribed to the latter version. This is not of great concern to us, for someone *could* do so. What matters is whether such a theory is correct.

Our strategy is to frame various versions of the collectionist theory which identifies substances with collections of nonsubstances, and then to test such theories by determining whether they are compatible with the intuitive characteristics of substance discussed in Chapter 1.

Theoretical parsimony is often the motivation for the attempt to identify substances with some other sort of entities. Since substances cannot be identified with properties, events, tropes, or similar items,[4] apparently the only alternative for those who seek to reduce substance to or identify substance with an entity of another kind or ontological category is to reduce a substance to or identify a substance with a *collection* of properties, events, tropes, or similar entities.

What possible reductions or identifications need to be considered? They would appear to be these: that a substance can be identified with a collection or set of either abstract entities, that is, properties, or of concrete entities, that is, tropes, ideas, sense-data, events, or the like.[5] We shall call all such accounts of substance *collectionist* theories of substance.

---

3 In the sense of a logically necessary and sufficient set of conditions which are also explanatory. See our Introduction for a discussion of the distinction between a philosophical analysis and a meaning identification.

4 See Chapter 1, Section I.

5 The collectionist sees the collection as functioning as a kind of substitute for a substratum, a substitute in which the items collected allegedly inhere, in the sense that they are qualities of the substance which is identified with the collection. Since events cannot inhere in anything (they are too substance-like for this), it is not plausible to regard a substance as a collection of events. Thus, we will not single out event-collectionism for any special consideration. Nevertheless, a number of our criticisms of collectionism will apply to the

II. SETS OR COLLECTIONS OF ABSTRACT
ENTITIES

> It is a complete mistake to ask how a concrete particular fact can be built up
> out of universals. The answer is, "In no way."
> A. N. Whitehead *Process and Reality* 24 ([1929] 1969)

We first consider what might be called naive collectionist theories. These theories identify substances with sets or collections of properties.[6]

A collectionist theory which identifies a substance with *a collection of properties* faces a serious criticism. As we indicated earlier in our discussion of categories of being, a collection is properly understood as being necessarily a collection of concrete entities, which are the parts of the collection. A collection is therefore a mereological sum of those parts. Thus, the idea of a collection of *abstract* entities such as properties is incoherent: a *concretum* such as a collection cannot have abstract parts. Formally put, this criticism is based on the following argument:

(1i) Necessarily, every entity is either abstract or concrete but not both.

(1ii) Necessarily, if a collection exists, then it is concrete.[7]

(1iii) Necessarily, if there is a concrete entity, then it does not have an abstract entity as a part.[8]

(1iv) Necessarily, if a property exists, then it is an abstract entity.

(1v) Necessarily, if there is a collection of properties, then there is a concrete entity which has an abstract entity as a part.

_____

(1vi) Necessarily, there is not a collection of properties.

claim that substances can be identified with collections of events as much as to other forms of collectionism.

6 We remind the reader that as we employ the term, a 'property' is an abstract entity. We use the term 'trope' to designate a concrete feature.

7 In saying this, we believe that we are drawing out an implication of the intuitive notion of a collection. However, it might be argued that there is another possible category, call it Collection★, which is a category of abstract entities. A collection★ can only have abstract entities as parts. We have no objection in principle to such a level *C* category provided that the nature of entities of this sort could be coherently defined.

8 Of the three kinds of parts that readily come to mind, viz., spatial, temporal, and logical parts, it is clear that properties are not parts of concrete entities in any of these three senses. On the widely held assumption that properties are not in space, they cannot be spatial parts of anything. Moreover, it is necessarily the case that for any *x, if x* is a spatial part of a concrete entity, then *x* is a concrete entity, and not an abstract entity (such as a property). Because properties can only be logical parts, e.g., conjuncts, disjuncts, and negands, of abstract entities, they cannot be logical parts of concrete entities. We take it to be obvious that properties cannot be temporal parts of anything. We can think of no further sense of parthood which would support the idea that a concrete entity could have an abstract entity as a part. We conclude that premise (1iii) is highly plausible.

Thus, the theory that a substance is a collection of properties implies that a substance is impossible. This is not the intent of this theory: according to its proponents, it is supposed to allow for the possibility of substances.

A second naive collectionist theory identifies substances with *sets* of properties rather than collections of properties. In the case of a collection of properties, the properties in question are parts of that collection, while in the case of a set of properties, the properties in question are not parts but *elements* of that set, where the being-an-element relation is defined by the axioms of set theory.[9]

A telling first criticism of the view that a substance is a set of abstract universals is readily available. How can a concrete thing, a substance, be an abstract thing like a set? In other words, it is absurd to suppose that a concrete thing is an abstract entity.[10] This seems to be a category mistake.[11]

A second criticism of the theory in question is much discussed in the literature.[12] This criticism arises from the fact that while it is possible for there to be two qualitatively indistinguishable substances, it is not possible for there to be two qualitatively indistinguishable sets of qualitative properties. Since a set is individuated by its elements, then, for example, if set *a* has only elements *x, y,* and *z,* and set *b* has only elements *x, y,* and *z,* then set *a* = set *b.* Thus, if set *c* is a set which has certain properties as elements, and set *d* has the same elements, then set *c* = set *d.* Hence, there cannot be *two* sets whose membership consists of the same qualitative properties, and if substances are sets of qualitative properties, then there cannot be two

---

9 We defend this distinction between parts and elements in Appendix 1.

10 H. N. Castañeda seems to imply that a concrete thing is an abstract entity in "Individuation and Non-Identity: A New Look," *American Philosophical Quarterly* 12 (1975), pp. 131–140. Likewise for Bertrand Russell in *Human Knowledge: Its Scope and Limits* (New York: Simon and Schuster, 1948), p. 83.

11 Keith Campbell in *Abstract Particulars* (Oxford: Basil Blackwell, 1990), describes tropes as "abstract particulars." In our terminology, this description is unintelligible, amounting to the description of a trope as both abstract and concrete. But Campbell explains that what he means by 'abstract' in this context is something like "has normally to be abstracted from its surroundings." If he had said that tropes are *abstracted* particulars, then his usage would have been compatible with our terminology. By a 'particular' we mean a *concretum,* not a nonuniversal, i.e., we do not mean by a *concretum* something which is incapable of multiple exemplification, although all *concreta* satisfy that description. The problem is that some *abstracta* also are incapable of multiple exemplification, e.g., sets. Hence, in our terminology, a set is a nonuniversal *abstractum.*

12 E.g., see Michael Loux, *Substance and Attribute* (Dordrecht: Reidel, 1978), chap. 6; James Van Cleve, "Three Versions of the Bundle Theory," *Philosophical Studies* 47 (1985), pp. 95–107; and William Carter, *The Elements of Metaphysics* (New York: McGraw Hill, 1990), chap. 4.

qualitatively indistinguishable substances. This seems to be an unintuitive consequence of the identification of substances with sets of qualitative properties. While this criticism has some plausibility, we are not sure that it is decisive in itself. A defender of the theory in question could reply that sets of properties which are identical with substances have *nonqualitative* properties as members, for instance, the property of being at place *p* at time *t,* or the property of being identical with Socrates. This reply raises a host of other issues and problems concerning the nature, legitimacy, and admissibility of these properties and the concrete entities to which they pertain. We shall not discuss these issues and problems any further, since we think that our first criticism of the identification of sets of properties with substances is decisive.

III. COLLECTIONS OF CONCRETE ENTITIES

> The thought of any object is not that of a mere bundle of qualities.
> E. Neale *The Analogy of Thought and Nature Revealed* 40 (1863)

In order to avoid the problems raised in the preceding paragraphs, a collectionist might turn to the theory that a substance is a collection of *concrete* entities, for example, tropes. A collection of concrete entities avoids the incoherence of the idea of a collection of abstract entities. Moreover, a collection of concrete entities, unlike a set of concrete entities, is concrete, as it should be if it is to be identified with a substance. Finally, since there can be two qualitatively indistinguishable tropes, on the view that substances are collections of tropes, there is no special difficulty in allowing for the possibility of two qualitatively indistinguishable substances as there was for the theory that substances are sets of properties. In the case of two qualitatively indistinguishable substances, the corresponding collections of tropes would be qualitatively indistinguishable, and yet have as parts different tropes. Hence, the theory that a substance is a collection of tropes has several advantages over the theory that a substance is a set (or collection) of properties.

In what follows, we shall develop three criticisms of this sort of collectionist theory. The first criticism will apply to the theory that substances are collections of tropes, and parallel criticisms will apply to the theory that substances are collections of properties, sense-data, ideas, events, or the like. The second and third criticisms will apply to the theory that substances are collections of tropes, and parallel criticisms will apply to the theory that substances are collections (or sets)[13] of properties, and to theories which identify substances with collections (or sets) of other *concreta*, such as sense-data, ideas, or events.[14]

A first objection to this sort of collectionist theory is based on our list of the data for a philosophical theory of the intuitive notion of a substance, the notion which the collectionist in question is trying to analyze or explicate in terms of collections.[15] According to datum (3), from Chapter 1, Section III, no feature of a substance is a part of that substance. For example, the right half of a material object, *o*, is a part of *o*, but the color of *o* is not a part of *o*. But, according to the collectionist, *o* is a collection of tropes, one of which is the color of *o*, and since the items which a collection collects are parts of the collection, the color of *o* is, according to the collectionist, a part of *o*.[16] Thus, the collectionist theory conflicts with datum (3). The implication that the color of *o* is a part of *o* also conflicts with another datum for a theory of substance: datum (7_m), which says that the parts of a material substance are either material substances or portions of matter. That collectionism has implications which conflict with data (3) and (7_m) is an indication of a category mistake in the identification of

---

13 I.e., these criticisms will apply to sets as well as collections. On the other hand, the first kind of criticism applies to collections but not to sets.

14 Although we intend the latter two kinds of criticisms to apply to both collections and sets, henceforth we will refer only to collections and their parts with the understanding that parallel remarks apply to sets and their elements. Likewise, although we will refer only to tropes as parts of collections (and implicitly as elements of sets), we do so with the understanding that parallel observations apply to properties, sense-data, ideas (in the sense of Locke, Descartes, Berkeley, and Hume), and events.

15 See Chapter 1, Section III, for our discussion of these data.

16 In a recent article, "Substance Without Substratum," *Philosophy and Phenomenological Research* 52 (1992), pp. 705–711, Arda Denkel disputes the claim that "the bundle theory entails that the elements of the bundle (particular properties) are *parts* of the bundle" (p. 706). He gives the following argument for denying this claim. First, he argues that (a) "the different parts of a whole may either overlap or be discrete." Second, Denkel understands (a) to imply that (b) "the parts of a whole either overlap in space and in the sense of sharing parts, or else are both spatially and part-wise discrete." Thus, (a) is intended to rule out the case where there are parts of a whole which overlap spatially but not part-wise. He goes on to point out that the tropes which comprise a bundle overlap spatially but share no parts, e.g., the particular roundness and the particular redness of an apple are in the same place but have no part in common. However, (b) is false: a *collection* of the redness of the apple and the roundness of the apple has as parts those two tropes (this is a direct consequence of the axioms of collection theory, and not subject to dispute). Yet the two tropes are spatially coincident without sharing a part.

(b) seems to be true when restricted to wholes which are material substances and to parts of such wholes which are portions of matter. But Denkel's principle (b) is wholly unrestricted, and needs to be, for his purposes. We conclude that Denkel has not provided any good reason for thinking that the tropes in a bundle are not parts of the bundle.

substances with collections. A collection can have *any* kind of concrete entity as a part, but a material substance can only have a material substance or portion of matter as a part.[17]

In the foregoing argument, we appealed to certain data concerning the intuitive concept of an individual substance. As we have pointed out, an analysis of substance should, *prima facie,* be compatible with such data. Since such data are only *prima facie* regulative of any analysis of substance, there are circumstances in which some of the data (but not all of them) can be overturned. More specifically, a *prima facie* datum can be overturned only if there is good reason to think that it is incompatible with either another *prima facie* datum or a conjunction of other such data. It is, of course, illegitimate to defend the view that the shape of a physical object is a part of that physical object simply by rejecting the intuitive datum that a feature of a thing is not a part of that thing. That is, this defense is illegitimate *because* it does not involve a demonstration that the datum in question is incompatible with other data for being a substance. After all, the point of a philosophical analysis of substance is to explicate the *intuitive* concept of substance. Nor does it appear likely that any defense of the proposition that a substance has properties as parts *could* be made. For it does not seem likely that it could be shown that the datum that, necessarily, a substance does not have properties as parts is incompatible with other data for being a substance. In any case, the burden of proof is on one who would reject this datum.[18]

Two other main difficulties, of which we will give a preliminary sketch, confront the collectionist in question.

First, there is the *unity of qualities* problem.[19] Consider the collection of the greenness of an apple, the taste of a pickle, the sound of a ball bouncing, the shape of an orange, the smell of an onion, and so forth. Alternatively, consider a collection of diverse psychological qualities of different persons. For instance, consider the collection of S_1's belief that the sky is blue, S_2's feeling of depression, S_3's sensation of blue, S_4's fear of snakes, S_5's feeling of pain, and so on, where each one of the persons S_1, S_2, S_3, S_4, S_5, et cetera, is diverse from all of the others. Collections of this kind are *not*

---

17 Of course, necessarily, for any x, if x is a soul or immaterial substance, then x does not have parts. On the other hand, necessarily, for any x, and for any y, if x is a nonmaterial physical substance, and y is part of x, then y is either a nonmaterial physical substance or a portion of nonmaterial physical stuff.

18 Of course, such strictures apply to an attempt to reject any of the data for being a substance which we have presented and to which we often appeal in this book.

19 This problem arises because of the need for a collectionist theory to be compatible with datum (2) on our list of data for a philosophical theory of substance.

substances, but it is not clear that a collection theorist can provide an adequate account of this fact. The items collected in these two examples may be interpreted in terms of either tropes, properties, ideas, sense-data, or events. On any of these interpretations, however, there is a perfectly good collection of items, but certainly such a collection is not an individual substance. Notice that since such an account should distinguish a nonsubstantial collection from a substance in any *possible* case, it appears that it ought to do this *both* in the case of material objects and immaterial (Cartesian) souls.[20]

Second, there is the problem of *excessive essentialism*. It seems that there could be individual substances that have accidental qualities and endure through changes in some of their intrinsic qualities. However, since it is extremely plausible that a collection has its parts essentially,[21] it is hard to see how a collectionist can satisfactorily account for the full range of such accidental qualities and changes.

The challenge for the collectionist is to provide a satisfactory account of the distinction between those collections which are substances and those which are not. This requires a unifying relation holding only among the parts of those collections that are substances. One part of this challenge is to specify a relation which overcomes the unity of qualities problem, and the second part of the challenge is to specify a relation which overcomes the problem of excessive essentialism. We shall next discuss attempts to specify a relation among the parts of a collection which solves the unity of qualities problem for a collectionist account.

What might such an attempt look like? It must not presuppose the existence of any noncollectionist substances, whether material or spiritual, else it fails of its purpose. There are five possibilities: (Pi) The parts of the collection are unified by their all being in the same place at the same time.[22] (Pii) The parts of the collection are unified by their each standing

---

20 In Chapter 5, we shall defend the claim that immaterial souls are possible or intelligible.

21 Just as plausibly, sets have their elements essentially. For a defense of the proposition that sets have their elements essentially, see James Van Cleve, "Why a Set Contains Its Members Essentially," *Nous* 19 (1986), pp. 585–602.

22 In order to prevent a possible confusion over what it is for tropes which belong to an object to be in the same place at the same time or be *spatially coincident,* consider the case of a rectangular object, x, whose right half is red and whose left half is black. Obviously, the particular redness of x's right half, which is located where x's right half is located, and the particular blackness of x's left half, which is located where x's left half is located, are *not* spatially coincident. But does either of these tropes belong to x? Since x is neither red nor black, but checkered, i.e., half red and half black, neither of these tropes belongs to x. Rather, the tropes in question belong to x's right half and x's left half, respectively. On the

in some causal connection to the others. Perhaps it is supposed that this causal connection is analogous to the causal connection in a human body between the heart, the lungs, the kidneys, the brain, the liver, the blood, et cetera. If any of these organs ceases to function then this would cause all of the other organs to cease to function. (Piii) There is a logically or metaphysically necessary connection among the parts of the collection. (Piv) The parts of the collection are unified by some combination of the foregoing criteria. (Pv) There is some other unifying relation among the parts of the collection.

There are a number of problems confronting (Pi). First, (Pi) presupposes the existence of physical space, and so is incompatible with theories which deny the existence of physical space, such as idealism and phenomenalism, theories that are attractive to some of those who would support collectionism. Moreover, (Pi) is incompatible with Cartesian dualism or substance dualism. (Pi) explains the unity of a substance in terms of the spatial coincidence of its properties. Since an immaterial soul is not in space, the unity of its properties cannot be so explained. Thus, (Pi) implies the impossibility of souls and, consequently, of Cartesian dualism. Since souls seem possible,[23] (Pi) appears not to provide a logically necessary condition for a collection of tropes being a substance.

Second, it is possible that there is an item such as a lightning flash or the like which is an event and not a substance. But an entity of this kind can possess spatiotemporally coincident tropes of shape, size, charge, and so forth. Hence, spatiotemporal coincidence of tropes is not a logically sufficient condition for those tropes belonging to a substantial collection. It might be replied that if the collectionist advocating (Pi) restricts himself to the goal of providing a collectionist account of material substance (and, as

other hand, there is a trope of having a particular red-and-black pattern of color (a particular checkeredness) which *does* belong to x. *This* trope of x is located where x is located, and therefore is spatially coincident with all of x's other particular properties, e.g., x's particular shape, size, mass. Thus, when we say that two entities are spatially coincident at t, we mean that they both fully occupy the same place, p, at t, and that there is no other place that is not a subplace of p which is occupied by either entity at t. Notice that in the case of x, x's right half partially occupies the place that x fully occupies, and that x's left half partially occupies the same place – the place that x fully occupies. Therefore, there is *some* sense in which the two halves of x and their respective color tropes of red and black occupy the same place. But, as we have tried to make clear, they are not as a consequence spatially coincident.

23 As we have already indicated, in Chapter 5 we shall argue that the concept of an immaterial soul is an intelligible one. Given this argument, it is not open to the bundle theorist to just dismiss the possibility of souls in defense of his theory.

we have already implied, he must do so in an attempt to avoid the first problem for (Pi)), then he can specify the requisite criterion of a substantial collection in terms of spatiotemporal coincidence of tropes by requiring that such a collection include a trope of having a certain quantity of matter or having a certain inertial mass (having a certain impenetrability). But, it is problematic that an appeal to either of these tropes can be of any help. First, since necessarily, for any x, x is a material substance if and only if x is a quantity of material stuff whose parts are suitably bound together, and a collectionist substance is merely a collection of tropes, it follows that the trope of having a certain quantity of matter cannot be included in the collection unless a certain quantity of material stuff whose parts are suitably bound together is exhibited as a collection of tropes. And the problem of exhibiting the latter seems no more tractable than the problem of exhibiting a material substance as such a collection. Second, a particular impenetrability is the trope of a certain material substance's being such that no other material substance can occupy the same place at the same time. Since this trope pertains to other possible material substances, it would be conceptually circular to include this trope as a part in a collection with which a substance is to be identified. Similarly, it would be circular to include some trope of being a particular substance in such a collection. (And more generally, it would be viciously circular to employ the intuitive notion of substance in the *analysans* of a putative analysis of this intuitive notion.) This criticism cannot be answered by defining a particular impenetrability as a trope such that no other *tropes* can occupy the same place at the same time, since possibly, other tropes *are* spatiotemporally coincident with a given collection of spatiotemporally coincident tropes. For example, if a certain shape, size, and color are spatiotemporally coincident (and no other tropes are coincident with them), then, possibly, a certain taste and temperature are spatiotemporally coincident with that shape, size, and color. Nor can the criticism that a collection of tropes is penetrable be answered by defining a particular impenetrability as a particular extension such that no other particular extension can occupy the same place at the same time. Suppose that a particular chair c has a particular extension e_1 in place p at time t. Suppose that c is green at t. Then (possibly) c's being green, an event, has a particular extension e_2 which also exists in place p at time t. e_1 and e_2 are tropes of different individuals and, hence, cannot be the same trope. Thus, it is not (necessarily) true that the extension of a material substance excludes the extension of all other entities: rather, it necessarily excludes the extensions of other material substances.

It might be thought that the collectionist can answer the second problem for (Pi) by requiring that a trope of *being a particular nonevent* (or, synonymously, a trope of *being a particular nonoccurrent*) be included within a collection of tropes which are spatially coincident. Notice that such a putative analysis of substance makes use of the concept of a nonevent in its *analysans*. Even if this putative analysis provides a logically necessary and sufficient condition for a collection's being a substance, the following considerations imply that this revision of (Pi) is viciously circular.

It would seem that if substance is analyzable in terms of a collection of spatially coincident tropes, then event can be so analyzed as well. In particular, it appears that if substance can be analyzed in terms of a collection of tropes which are spatially coincident, one of which is a *being a particular nonevent,* then event can be analyzed in terms of a collection of tropes which are spatially coincident, one of which is a *being a particular nonsubstance.* Observe that a putative analysis of this kind makes use of the concept of a nonsubstance in its *analysans*. However, to employ the negative concept ~F is to make use of the concept F; for example, to employ the concept of a nonevent is to make use of the concept of an event, and to employ the concept of a nonsubstance is to make use of the concept of a substance. Since substance can be analyzed in terms of the concept of a nonevent, and since event can be analyzed in terms of the concept of a nonsubstance, it follows that substance can be analyzed in terms of the concept of an event, and event can be analyzed in terms of the concept of a substance. However, there is a vicious circularity involved in the attempt to analyze substance in terms of the concept of an event, and analyze event in terms of the concept of a substance. Thus, it is impossible that substance is analyzable in terms of the concept of an event, and event is analyzable in terms of the concept of a substance. Since substance being analyzable as a collection of tropes which are spatially coincident and which include a *being a particular nonevent* seems to imply this impossibility, we conclude that substance is not analyzable as such a collection of tropes.

Alternatively, the collectionist might try to answer the second problem for (Pi) either by (Ra) requiring that a trope of *a particular lacking of any temporal part* be included within a collection of tropes which are spatially coincident, or by (Rb) requiring that a trope of *having a particular capacity to undergo intrinsic qualitative change* be included within a collection of tropes which are spatially coincident. Because necessarily, any event *has* a temporal part, if (Pi) is modified as indicated in (Ra), then an event cannot satisfy this modified version. And on the assumption that it is *impossible* for an event to undergo intrinsic qualitative change, if (Pi) is revised as specified in (Rb), then an event cannot satisfy this revised version.[24] But if the collectionist attempts to distinguish those collections of spatially coincident tropes which are substances from those collections of spatially coincident tropes which are events by modifying (Pi) as indicated in either (Ra) or (Rb), then he is faced with the following problem. It is doubtful whether either *lacking any temporal part* or *being capable of undergoing intrinsic qualitative change* is a logically necessary condition of being a substance. First, it is arguable that it is possible for there to be a four-dimensional space-time continuum containing material substances, and that such material substances would have temporal parts.[25] Second, it seems possible that there are Democritean atoms, such atoms being indivisible material substances which are incapable of undergoing intrinsic qualitative change. Thus, if (Pi) is modified along the lines of either (Ra) or (Rb), then it is problematic whether the resulting modified version of (Pi) provides a logically necessary condition for being a substance.

Is there another way of modifying (Pi) which requires the inclusion of some special trope within a collection of spatially coincident tropes and which holds out more promise to the collectionist than the ones which we have considered? We cannot think of one. Thus, we doubt that the collectionist can provide an adequate solution to the second problem which we have raised for (Pi).

A third problem for (Pi) arises from this seeming possibility: there could be two completely penetrable, spatially extended substances, that is, non-material physical substances, having the same shape and size that can interpenetrate, so that the two can occupy the same place at the same time.[26] Two such objects can separate and occupy different places at the same time as well. At the time when the two substances are in the same

24 The assumption that it is impossible for an event to undergo intrinsic qualitative change is controversial. However, we have given an argument which supports this assumption in Chapter 2, Section I.

25 Powerful arguments which support the claim that there could be a four-dimensional space-time continuum containing material substances which have temporal parts can be found in Mark Heller's *The Ontology of Physical Objects: Four Dimensional Hunks of Matter* (Cambridge: Cambridge University Press, 1990). On the other hand, P. T. Geach in *Logic Matters* (Berkeley: University of California Press, 1972), pp. 302–318, and D. H. Mellor in *Real Time* (Cambridge: Cambridge University Press, 1981), chaps. 7 and 8, have argued powerfully that substances do not have temporal parts. Both of them argue that substances can change and entities which have temporal parts cannot. However, their arguments establish at most that *actual* substances lack temporal parts, and not that it is impossible for there to be an immutable substance which has temporal parts and which exists in a four-dimensional space-time continuum. For the purposes of our argument here the mere possibility of such a substance is sufficient.

26 An example of this is provided in Chapter 1, Section III.

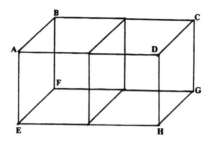

Figure 3.1

place, there is no one substance in that place which has all of the tropes that each of the two objects has, as (Pi) requires. Hence, spatiotemporal coincidence is not a logically sufficient condition for substantial unity in a collection of tropes.

A final difficulty for (Pi) is illustrated in Figure 3.1. Suppose that two cubes are touching (in the ordinary sense) but not joined (they do not adhere to one another). In this way, it would seem, because ABCDEFGH is visually and tactually continuous, that a particular trope of a noncubical rectangular solid ABCDEFGH is formed. This cannot be denied on the ground that there is no substance that possesses the trope of ABCDEFGH, since if substances are *collections* of tropes, then some trope can exist without belonging to a substance. And ABCDEFGH is spatiotemporally coincident with other tropes of size, color, and so on. Yet, it is very plausible that in such circumstances there is no noncubical rectangular solid, since the mere touching of two cubes is not enough to create a third noncubical rectangular substance of which they are parts. More seems to be required, namely, some kind of adherence or fusion of these parts. It follows that spatiotemporal coincidence among tropes is not a logically sufficient condition for a collection of those tropes being a substance.

However, it appears that there may be a reply to this final objection on behalf of the collectionist. What distinguishes a substance from the collection which coincides with the trope of ABCDEFGH is that a substance cannot be pulled apart as easily as can the two cubes in question. A substance has a kind of *causal unity* which ABCDEFGH lacks. If tropes can be relata of the causal relation, and if one can speak of the parts of particular extensions being causally related, then perhaps the collectionist can distinguish a substantial collection from a nonsubstantial collection by

70

means of requiring the parts of the particular extensions of substantial collections to be causally related to their neighboring parts in such a way as to bind them together. If the collectionist takes this way out, then, of course, he no longer is satisfied with (Pi) as an account of substance, for he has supplemented (Pi) with a further condition of substantial unity, namely, the causal condition described earlier. Hence, this way out for the collectionist is an instance of (Pv). Note that this instance of (Pv) does not escape either the criticisms lodged earlier against collectionism in general or the other criticisms lodged against (Pi).

(Pii) attempts to characterize the concept of a substance in terms of a relation of causal dependence holding between the parts of a collection of tropes. This approach holds out the hope of avoiding some of the difficulties which beset (Pi). For example, (Pi) could not allow for immaterial substances or for penetrable nonmaterial physical substances, but it isn't as obvious that (Pii) could not do so.

What would the causal relation among the parts or elements of a collection be? There are two proposals for causal criteria that need to be considered. The first is given by the following definition:

(3D1) $a, b, c, \ldots$ are the tropes which are parts of a substantial collection $\Leftrightarrow$ in *every* nomically possible situation, if any one of them goes out of existence, then its going out of existence causes all of the other tropes which are parts of the collection to go out of existence.

The second proposed criterion can be stated as follows:

(3D2) $a, b, c, \ldots$ are the tropes which are parts of a substantial collection $\Leftrightarrow$ in *some* nomically possible situation, if one of them goes out of existence, then its going out of existence causes all of the other tropes which are parts of the collection to go out of existence.

The attempt to characterize the unity of a substantial collection of tropes in terms of their causal relations stated by (3D1) is subject to the following decisive objection. Every substance possesses some particular quality essentially, for example, its particular quality of being a substance. Hence, (3D1) rules out the possibility of a substance's undergoing a change in an intrinsic quality, since on (3D1), if any particular intrinsic quality of a substance, x, goes out of existence, then all of the intrinsic qualities of x go out of existence, including those essential to x, implying that x ceases to exist. Thus, (3D1) is incompatible with one of the intuitive data for a theory of the intuitive notion of substance, namely, datum (4a): possibly, a substance undergoes a change in one of its intrinsic features (without the substance going out of existence), that is, it loses one of its intrinsic features

71

without losing all of them. For instance, an object's particular color is not physically necessary for its particular shape, and vice versa; an object's particular shape is not physically necessary for its particular volume; and an object's particular volume is not physically necessary for its particular shape. In addition, a cubical piece of rubber having a volume of eight cubic inches can either be stretched into a noncubical rectangular solid (eight by one by one inches) having a volume of eight cubic inches, or be compressed into a cube of a smaller volume, respectively.[27] Thus, a substance can change one of its particular intrinsic features without changing all of them, contrary to what (3D1) implies. We call this problem the *problem of excessive nomic essentialism,* for (3D1) states so strong a unifying condition for the parts of a collection of tropes that the tropes cannot be causally "pried apart" at all.

Clearly, (3D1) must be modified if the causal collectionist is to avoid the problems just stated. A revision of (3D1) might be offered to avoid these counterexamples. As a first step, consider the following:

(3D1*)   *a, b, c,* . . . are the tropes of an *atomic* substantial collection ⇔ in *every* nomically possible situation, if any one of them goes out of existence, then its going out of existence causes all of the other tropes to go out of existence.

(3D1*) defines the notion of an atomic substantial collection of tropes. Such collections are supposed to be identical with atomic substances, that is, substances which are unbreakable or indivisible. A second definition, which we shall not formally state, would say that a substantial collection is one which is either atomic or composed of atomic substances. In the latter case, the parts of the particular extensions of the atomic substantial collections would be required to be causally related to their neighboring parts in such a way as to bind them together. The idea behind (3D1*) is to avoid the counterexamples to (3D1) by defining the idea of substantial collections which, because they cannot undergo intrinsic change at all, satisfy the condition that if one of their tropes goes out existence, then all of them do. The assumption is that the only way that a trope which belongs to an atomic substance can go out of existence is for the substance in question to

---

27   Similar kinds of counterexamples will apply in the case of souls, that is, in the case of an attempt to analyze the unity of a soul's features in terms of causal relations of the sorts indicated holding between psychological tropes. Such an analysis assumes some sort of nomic necessity which applies to spiritual entities. One such counterexample is the possibility of a soul which at first has feelings of anxiety and jealousy, but then ceases having feelings of anxiety without thereby ceasing to have feelings of jealousy.

be destroyed, and in that case, all of the tropes belonging to that substance go out of existence as well.

Unfortunately, counterexamples to (3D1*) are also readily forthcoming. To begin, there seem to be several kinds of possible atomic substances which can undergo intrinsic qualitative change, and which therefore can change some of their particular intrinsic qualities while retaining others.

First, souls are possible, a soul is an atomic substance, and a soul can undergo intrinsic qualitative change. For example, a soul which is thinking about mathematics can cease thinking about mathematics and think about baseball instead. This counterexample, if correct, implies that (3D1*) does not provide a logically necessary condition for being an atomic substance.

Second, it even seems possible that there be material atoms which undergo intrinsic qualitative change, where such an atom is a necessarily indivisible particle which has volume. For example, it seems possible that there is an atom of this kind which *stretches*. Even if one assumes mereological essentialism for atoms, it seems possible that there is an atom which uniformly stretches without changing the relative arrangements (relevant to mereological essentialism) of any of its parts. Such an atomic object would have the same volume after stretching as it did before stretching, but not the same shape. It would lengthen in some direction and shorten in another.[28] If it is thought impossible for an atom to stretch, we reply that unbreakability does not imply unstretchability, since an object could be indefinitely stretchable if it were made of continuous matter. Some portion of it would get thinner and thinner, and this could go on indefinitely, but no matter how thin a portion became, it could not break. After all, if an atom is unbreakable, then so must any portion of it be, no matter how small. Another possibility is that an atom could stretch up to a certain point, and then be unstretchable. Democritus and those in the atomist tradition seemed to have denied that atoms can undergo intrinsic qualitative change. However, the reason for this is that they assumed, like other pre-Socratic naturalists, that if there can be change, then there must be an immutable subject of change, that is, a substance, and atoms were their choice for this role. As we have implied, this principle of change is not self-evidently true. It seems to us that there could be basic laws which govern fundamental intrinsic changes that have no underlying mechanism.

A second example of an atom which undergoes intrinsic qualitative change is the possibility that there is a necessarily indivisible voluminous

---

28 This is because the atom has a certain amount of matter, which is fixed. There are no spaces between the parts of the atom. Hence, its volume must remain constant.

particle which undergoes a change in color (e.g., from red to blue), where color is a primary quality of such atomic particles. Even though it seems not to be the case that there are atoms which have color as a primary quality, it seems possible that there are atoms of this kind. Empirical evidence would in that case support the conclusion that there are fundamental laws of nature which govern the having of colors on the part of atoms. It might, for example, be empirically confirmed that, as a matter of fundamental law, atoms of the same color repel, whereas atoms of different colors attract. These two examples of material atoms which can undergo intrinsic qualitative change, if correct, imply that (3D1*) does not provide a logically necessary condition for being an atomic substance.[29]

Third, matter, for all we know, is infinitely divisible. Hence, it seems possible for there to be material substances which are not composed of atoms. This possibility is incompatible with the companion to (3D1*), which attempts to define the concept of a substance in terms of (3D1*). More specifically, if there could be material substances which are not atomic and are not composed of atoms, then the companion to (3D1*) does not provide a logically necessary condition for being a substance.

(3D2) avoids the objections to (3D1), since (3D2) requires only that in *some* circumstances the going out of existence of some particular feature of a substance causes all of the other particular features of that substance to go out of existence. This is compatible with the possibility, in other circumstances, of the persistence of a substance through change. Thus, the defender of (3D2) would assert that any case in which a substance is annihilated is a case in which the going out of existence of one particular feature, for example, an essential trope of a material object such as its being extended, causes the going out of existence of all of its other particular features. It seems that (3D2) provides a logically necessary condition of a collection's being a substance. But the trouble arises when we ask whether (3D2) provides a logically *sufficient* condition of a collection's being a

---

29 Earlier we claimed that, possibly, there is a Democritean atom, i.e., a necessarily indivisible particle which has volume and which could *not* undergo a change in any of its intrinsic qualitative properties. Notice that this claim is compatible with our present argument that, possibly, there is a non-Democritean atom of a certain sort, i.e., a necessarily indivisible particle which has volume and which *could* undergo a change in some of its intrinsic qualitative properties, e.g., a change in its shape or color. A Democritean atom and a non-Democritean atom of this kind would differ in a crucial way with respect to their natures or essential properties, since the former would be necessarily unchangeable and the latter would not. Thus, it is perfectly coherent to suppose both that a Democritean atom is possible and that a non-Democritean atom of the aforementioned sort is possible.

substance. Consider the following example. A pair of crystal glasses are next to one another. Then there is a collection, c, whose parts are the particular features of the two glasses. In some nomically possible situation, a ball causes the first glass to crash into the neighboring one, thereby destroying both of them. The going out of existence of the particular being-at-rest of the first glass causes the going out of existence of all the features of both glasses, that is, all the other features collected by c. Thus c qualifies as a substance on (3D2), but c is not a substance.[30] Hence (3D2) does not provide a logically sufficient condition for being a substance.

It is hard to think of any alternative nomic, causal, or counterfactual proposals for defining the notion of a substantial collection of tropes that are not vulnerable to objections of the kinds that we have presented.

According to strategy (Piii), one can define a substantial collection in terms of metaphysically necessary connections holding among the tropes belonging to the collection. Thus,

> (3D3) $a, b, c, \ldots$ are the tropes which are parts of a substantial collection $\Leftrightarrow$ in any possible situation, if any one of them exists, then its existing metaphysically necessitates the existence of all the others.

(3D3) is subject to all of the same counterexamples as is (3D1). Therefore, we need not discuss (3D3) any further. Note that there are analogs to (3D1★) and its companion.

> (3D3★) $a, b, c, \ldots$ are tropes which are parts of an *atomic* substantial collection $\Leftrightarrow$ in every possible situation, if any one of them exists, then its existence metaphysically necessitates the existence of all the others.

(3D3★)'s companion, which we shall not formally state, would say that a substantial collection is one which is either atomic or composed of atomic substances. In the latter case, the parts of the particular extensions of the atomic substantial collections would be required to be causally related to their neighboring parts in such a way as to bind them together. Since (3D3★)'s companion is subject to all of the same counterexamples as (3D1★)'s companion, it is not necessary to consider (3D3★)'s companion any further.

Strategy (Piv) attempts to analyze the concept of a substantial collection of tropes by combining earlier approaches. One such attempt combines spatial coincidence with causal interdependence.

---

30 Note that the domino-like dependence of one material object on another could also obtain in the case of two souls, such that the going out of existence of one would cause the other to go out of existence, given an appropriate notion of spiritual nomic connections. Such a possibility generates a counterexample to any attempt to analyze the unity of features of a soul in terms of causal dependence between psychological tropes along the lines of (3D2).

(3D4)   *a, b, c, . . .* are tropes which are parts of a substantial collection ⇔ (i) *a, b, c,*
   . . . are spatially coincident, and (ii) *a, b, c, . . .* are such that in *every* nomically
   possible situation, if *any* one of them goes out of existence, then its going
   out of existence causes all of the other tropes which are parts of the collection to go out of existence.

Far from being an improvement over (3D1) or the spatial coincidence
criterion, (3D4) is subject to some of the defects of both. It is refuted by
the possibility of souls, since souls, being nonspatial, are substances which
do not satisfy (i) of (3D4), and by the possibility of intrinsic qualitative
change in substances, because (ii) of (3D4) incorrectly rules out this possibility as we have argued. The attempt to define an *atomic* substance in terms
of spatial coincidence and causal interdependence also founders because of
counterexamples of this kind. The possibility of nonspatial atomic substances (souls) is incompatible with the requirement that the tropes which
are parts of an atomic substance be spatially coincident, while the possibility of intrinsic qualitative change in an atomic substance (a soul or a
material atom) is incompatible with the requirement that the tropes which
are parts of an atomic substance be causally interdependent in the way
needed. But perhaps another combination would do better.

(3D5)   *a, b, c, . . .* are tropes which are parts of a substantial collection ⇔ (i) *a, b, c,*
   . . . are spatially coincident, and (ii) *a, b, c, . . .* are such that in *some* nomically
   possible situation, if *some* one of them goes out of existence, then its going
   ·out of existence causes all of the other tropes which are parts of the collection to go out of existence.

Like (3D4), the possibility of souls argues against (3D5), for a soul is a
substance which fails to satisfy (i) of (3D5). Thus, (3D5) does not provide a
logically necessary condition for being a substance. Moreover, there could
be an *event* all of whose particular features are spatially coincident and
satisfy (ii) of (3D5). For example, possibly, a piece of metal's being cubical is
an event (call it *e*). Consider the collection, *c*, of tropes which belong to *e*.
We assume that events reduce to collections of tropes if substances do. So
there is some nomically possible situation in which if one of *e*'s tropes goes
out of existence, for instance, its particular cubicalness, then its going out
of existence causes *e* to go out of existence, and hence, causes all of the
other tropes which are parts of *c* to go out of existence.[31] Hence, because *c*
is a nonsubstantial collection but satisfies (3D5), (3D5) does not provide a
logically sufficient condition for being a substance.

31 Note that since *e* is the event of a certain piece of metal's having a certain shape, *e* itself has
   that same shape, viz., being cubical. Thus, the particular cubicalness of the piece of metal
   is exactly similar to the particular cubicalness of *e*, and is spatially coincident with it,
   though presumably not identical with it.

An important and ingenious recent instance of strategy (Piv) is the collectionist theory of Peter Simons.[32] Simons combines spatial coincidence with a complex of logical relations in order to analyze the concept of a substantial collection. He distinguishes between the core or essential tropes belonging to such a substance and the peripheral or accidental tropes of such a substance. Simons's account of the core of a substantial collection can be expressed as follows:

(3D6) $a, b, c, \ldots$ are tropes which belong to a core collection, $C, \Leftrightarrow$ (i) $a, b, c, \ldots$ are spatially coincident, and (ii) $a, b, c, \ldots$ are such that in every possible situation, if any one of them exists, then its existence metaphysically necessitates the existence of all the others.

Next, Simons's analysis of the periphery of a substantial collection can be stated in the following manner:

(3D7) $a, b, c, \ldots$ are tropes which belong to the periphery of a core collection, $C,$ $\Leftrightarrow$ (i) $a, b, c, \ldots$ are spatially coincident with the tropes belonging to $C,$ and (ii) each of $a, b, c, \ldots$ is such that in every possible situation, if any one of them exists, then its existence metaphysically necessitates the existence of the tropes belonging to $C,$ and (iii) (x) (if x is one of $a, b, c, \ldots,$ then x is such that in some possible situation, the tropes belonging to C exist without x existing).

Finally,

(3D8) x is a *substantial collection* $\Leftrightarrow$ x is a collection which consists of a core of tropes and a periphery of tropes which belongs to that core.[33]

Simons's theory may be illustrated with an example of a commonsense material object, a particular quantity of frozen water in the form of a cube. According to Simons, if there was such an object, then its core would include tropes of extension and waterhood, while the periphery would include tropes of cubicalness, coldness, and solidity. Each of the latter entails[34] each of former, but not vice versa, and all of the former entail one another. Thus, the particular extension of the water entails the particular waterhood of the water, and vice versa. The particular solidity of the frozen water entails its particular extension, but not vice versa: the water can melt and change from being solid to being liquid.

32 "Particulars in Particular Clothing: Three Trope Theories of Substance," read at the University of North Carolina at Greensboro, Annual Symposium in Philosophy, *The Real Things: Studies in Ontology,* 1992, forthcoming in *Philosophy and Phenomenological Research.*
33 Simons is noncommittal about exactly what tropes are to be found in the core of a material object. He regards this as an empirical question to be resolved by science.
34 By saying that a trope T1 'entails' a trope T2 we mean that the existence of T1 metaphysically necessitates the existence of T2.

A first problem for this account reveals that despite its complexity, the account is not yet complex enough. The problem is that (3D8) does not allow for the possibility of a substance all of whose properties are essential. For example, there seems to be a possible world in which the only substance is a Democritean atom. Such a substance (if one assumes that space and time are relational) would consist of just a core collection without a periphery, whereas (3D8) requires that any substance consist of both a core and a periphery. In order to surmount this objection, Simons would need somehow to distinguish between those cores which by themselves amounted to substances from those cores which in order to be substances stand in need of peripheries.

A second objection to Simons's theory of substantial collectionhood is that because (3D6) requires the parts of the core of a substance to be spatially coincident, (3D6) rules out the possibility of nonspatial substances, that is, souls. An adequate response to this objection would consist in breaking up each of (3D6) and (3D7) into two disjuncts, one for spatial substances, and one for souls. The disjuncts of (3D6) and (3D7) for spatial substances would require spatial coincidence plus the indicated entailments, while the disjuncts for souls would require the entailments and the condition that any trope belonging to a soul not be spatially located.

A third objection to Simons's theory can be developed out of the following propositions. (2i) According to Simons's theory, the tropes belonging to a particular material substantial collection, c, are parts of that collection, and these tropes must be spatially coincident with one another. Furthermore, these tropes must be located where the substance with which c is identified is located. In other words, if a material substance has tropes, and these tropes are located, these tropes must be located where the substance is. Thus c itself is spatially coincident with each of the tropes which belong to it. Hence, (2ii) all of the tropes belonging to a substantial collection which is a material substance are extended and have spatial parts.[35] For example, a sphere, S, has a right half, H, and S has a particular sphericity, s, while H has a particular hemisphericity, h. (2iii) Evidently, the tropes belonging to a substantial collection are features of the substance which is identified with that collection. (2iv) Necessarily, parthood is a transitive relation: if x is part of y and y is part of z, then x must be part of z. (2iv) implies that, (2v) necessarily, a part of a part of a collection is a part of

---

35 In other words, because a trope of a material object is spatially coincident with that material object, and because a material object is spatially extended, a trope of a material object is spatially extended.

that collection. Now, consider our sphere, S. S is according to Simons a collection of tropes. s, the particular sphericity of S, is a part of the substantial collection which is S. By (2ii), s has spatial parts, one of which is h. Since s is a part of S, and h is a part of s, by (2v), h is a part of S. But if h is a part of S and s is a part of S, then by (2i) and (2iii), this implies a contradiction: that S is a hemispherical sphere!

A fourth, related objection to Simons's theory derives a contradiction from (2i), (2ii), (2iv), and (2v), without making use of (2iii). Consider once again our sphere, S. S is according to Simons a collection of tropes, all of which are spatially coincident [from (2i)]. s, the particular sphericity of S, is a part of the substantial collection which is S. By (2ii), s has spatial parts, one of which is h. Since s is a part of S, and h is a part of s, by (2v), h is a part of S. Then h is spatially coincident with S and with s. But h is a proper spatial part of s. That h is spatially coincident with s and also a proper spatial part of s implies a contradiction.

Hence, (3D8) and all of its descendants which we suggested were needed to meet earlier objections imply contradictions, and do not provide a logically necessary condition for something's being a substance. Our diagnosis of what has gone awry in Simons's account is that the axioms of collection theory do not cohere with the logical conditions which he places on the inclusion of tropes in a substantial collection.

The foregoing argument shows that if material substances are possible, then Simons's account of substance harbors an inconsistency. The following argument implies that if God exists along with contingent souls, then Simons's theory implies yet another contradiction.

God by definition is a necessary being. If God exists and a contingent soul, s, exists, then the existence of any one of the tropes belonging to s metaphysically necessitates the existence of the core tropes belonging to God, but not vice versa. Furthermore, because s is a soul, the tropes belonging to s are not spatially located. Hence, given our expansion of Simons's theory to let it apply to souls as well as material substances, the tropes belonging to s meet all of the conditions for being in the periphery of God's core tropes. Thus, on Simons's theory, God has accidentally all of the tropes belonging to any contingent soul, for instance, tropes of non-omnipotence and nonomniscience. This is, of course, impossible. In God's *core* are to be found tropes of omnipotence and omniscience, among other tropes. From the preceding it follows that God would be, for example, both essentially omnipotent and accidentally nonomnipotent, and essentially omniscient and accidentally nonomniscient.

Hence, given the possible existence of God and contingent souls, (3D8) and all of its descendants imply contradictions, and do not provide a logically sufficient condition for something's being a substance. In this case, our diagnosis of what has gone awry in Simons's account is that the same kind of connections, namely, ones seemingly both necessary and synthetic, which he postulates as holding between tropes of the same substantial collection, also could hold between the core of a necessary substance and the tropes of certain contingent substances.

A final objection to Simons's pursuit of strategy (Piv) shows that this theory fails to provide a logically sufficient condition either for being a material substance or for being a soul. This objection is similar to the second objection which we raised to strategy (Pi), or the spatiotemporal coincidence theory of the unity of substantial collections. The tropes of a concrete material event, e, will, as we said earlier, be spatially coincident. But we may now observe further that such an event will have a core of tropes which are essential to the existence of e. The same is true, of course, of a spiritual event, $e^\star$, whose core tropes are not spatially coincident. It seems to be the case, as well, that both e and $e^\star$ will have a periphery of accidental tropes containing at the least certain relational tropes. An argument which parallels the one given in the case of a collectionist theory, which pursues strategy (Pi), shows that Simons's theory cannot distinguish substantial collections from event-collections. Therefore, for yet another reason, Simons's theory fails to provide a logically sufficient condition for being a substance.

A final approach to solving the problem of unity for the collectionist theory falls under (Pv), that the unity of a substantial collection is provided by some hitherto as yet unremarked relation. What might this nonspatial, noncausal, nonlogical relation be? One sort of answer is given by the contemporary metaphysicians, Bertrand Russell and Hector Neri-Castañeda.[36] According to each of them, there is a *primitive* relation which does the job, a relation which Russell calls "compresence" and a relation which Castañeda calls "consubstantiation." Each of these undefined relations is supposed to account for the synchronic unity of the parts or elements of substantial collections or sets.[37] Adopting this relation as prim-

36 Russell, *Human Knowledge: Its Scope and Limits,* chaps. 7–8; H. N. Castañeda, "Thinking and the Structure of the World," *Critica* 6, no. 18 (1972), pp. 43–81, and "Perception, Belief, and the Structure of Physical Objects and Consciousness," *Synthese* 35 (1977), pp. 285–351.

37 Castañeda's substantial collections or sets contain not tropes but what he calls "ontological guises." Guises themselves are said by Castañeda to be concrete entities constructed out of abstract properties (for Castañeda, substances are "bundles of bundles"). Sim-

itive is unsatisfactory, since it would seem that without an account of this relation we have no notion of what this relation is. For instance (Castañeda):

> We take physical objects to be very special systems of guises intimately related to one another by just one very special relation that cannot receive a better name than *consubstantiation*.[38]

Of course, it won't do to say that, for example, red and round are consubstantiated just when an object is red and round, inasmuch as this presupposes the ordinary concept of individual substance, and an account of this ordinary concept cannot appeal to this ordinary concept. Nor will it do to say the following (Russell):

> Two events are 'compresent' when they are related in the way in which two simultaneous parts of one experience are related. At any given moment, I am seeing certain things, hearing others, touching others, remembering others, and expecting yet others. All these percepts, recollections, and expectations are happening to me now; I shall say that they are mutually 'compresent'.[39]

A reduction of substances to collections cannot rely on a unifying relation which has no intuitive content other than a relation of mutual inherence in a substance. In the quotation from Russell, there is an explicit appeal to the self as that to which various mental items are related. It would appear, therefore, that what Russell said in another context applies to his own and Castañeda-type attempts to provide a unifying relation for substantial collections: they have all the advantages of theft over honest toil!

We turn now to the problem for collectionism of excessive essentialism. Even if the problem of the unity of qualities can be solved, the collectionist faces this second problem. To begin with, according to datum (4a)[40] characterizing the intuitive notion of substance, it is possible for some

---

ilarly, Russell's collections or "complexes" contain universals. Nevertheless, their basic strategy for unifying guises or universals into substances can be adapted by a trope collectionist.

38 In "Perception, Belief, and the Structure of Physical Objects and Consciousness," Castañeda offers a set of axioms for the consubstantiation relation (the "Law of Communion," the "Law of Conditional Reflexivity," etc.). However, these axioms do not explicitly *define* consubstantiation, since that notion occurs within them. Nor do we accept the idea that they provide a so-called implicit definition of consubstantiation, since more than one relation could satisfy the axioms. In our view, without an intended interpretation, axioms are mere uninterpreted schemata. For a defense of this view, see Gary Rosenkrantz, "The Nature of Geometry," *American Philosophical Quarterly* 18 (1981), pp. 101–110.

39 *Human Knowledge: Its Scope and Limits*, p. 329.

40 See Chapter 1, Section III.

individual substance to undergo a change in its intrinsic qualitative properties while remaining numerically one and the same. For instance, suppose that Socrates at time t_1 is drunk and is identical with a collection of tropes, c, one of whose parts is that trope which is a particular drunkenness, and all of whose parts exist at t_1. Socrates can change from being drunk at t_1 to being sober at a later time, t_2. But it would seem that if Socrates were identical with c, then he could not undergo such a change. This is because it is extremely plausible that the parts of a collection are essential to it. Since c contains Socrates's particular drunkenness as a part at t_1, and does not contain his particular sobriety at t_1, c cannot exist at time t_2 while containing the latter property nor exist at time t_2 while failing to contain the former property. Yet, at t_2, Socrates does have a particular sobriety. Hence, Socrates is not identical with c.

It might be thought that a bundle theorist who identifies a substance with a set of abstract properties is better off with respect to the problem of excessive essentialism vis-à-vis change. On the view we have in mind, a changing object is to be identified with a special kind of set of abstract entities. For each time that the object exists, and for each of the properties belonging to that object at that time, there is a corresponding temporally indexed or dated property which is an element of the set in question. A particular substance is identified with such a set, and the properties of the substance at a given time are determined by those properties in the set which are indexed to the time in question. Thus, the set with which Socrates is identified contains being drunk at t_1 and being sober at t_2. It might seem at first that this view can accommodate Socrates's changing from being drunk to being sober, inasmuch as this view seems to imply that Socrates is drunk at t_1 and sober at t_2. However, because the elements of a set are essential to it, such a view implies that *any* temporally indexed feature had by an object is an essential feature of that object. For example, if Socrates is drunk at time t, then the property of being drunk at t is essential to Socrates. But, surely, this property is not essential to Socrates. In other words, as datum (5), from Chapter 1, Section III, characterizing the intuitive notion of substance implies, possibly, Socrates exists at t and is not drunk at t. It follows that an individual substance cannot be reduced to or identified with a set of properties of the sort indicated.[41]

---

41 For cogent criticisms of a variant of the view we have just rejected, see James Van Cleve, "Three Versions of the Bundle Theory." According to this variant, a substance is identical with a set of world-indexed dated properties, with the world-indexing having the aim of

Another attempt to avoid the problem of excessive essentialism identifies a changing object, *o*, with a temporal sequence, *s*, of collections of tropes such that for any time, *t*, at which *o* exists, *s* has as a part the collection of *o*'s tropes at *t*. Strictly speaking, this is not a collectionist theory of substance, for it does not identify a substance with a collection, but rather with a *temporal sequence*.[42] Nevertheless, such a sequentialist theory of substance is a natural extension of collectionism, and so is appropriately dealt with here.[43]

avoiding just the problem about change we raised in the text. We remind the reader that we reject all views which identify substances with sets of abstract properties on the grounds that such sets, unlike substances, are abstract.

42 It might be thought that a temporal sequence is merely a collection *over* time – a four-dimensional collection – and hence that the category of being a temporal sequence is a subspecies of the category of being a collection. However, the following line of reasoning shows that this idea is mistaken. First of all, it is presumably *possible* that three-dimensional space and one-dimensional time exist, and it is therefore *not necessary* that if there is a temporal sequence, then four-dimensional space-time exists. However, necessarily, if there exists a collection (in time, as opposed to in space-time), then that collection could not continue to exist *after* one of its parts ceased to exist, but possibly, there is a temporal sequence (in time, not in space-time) which continues to exist after one of its parts ceases to exist (if there is a part in the sequence which succeeds the part that has ceased to exist). It follows that it is possible for there to be a temporal sequence (one which is in time, as opposed to in space-time) which is not identical with a collection. Hence, the category of being a temporal sequence is *not* a subspecies of (is not subsumed by) the category of being a collection.

43 An example of sequentialism is provided by Russell: "A piece of matter, which we took to be a single persistent entity, is really a *string of entities,* like the apparently persistent objects in a cinema. And there is no reason why we should not say the same of a mind: the *persistent ego* seems as fictitious as the *permanent atom*. Both are only strings of events having certain interesting relations to each other." See Bertrand Russell, "Philosophy of the Twentieth Century," in *Twentieth Century Philosophy*, ed. Dagobert D. Runes (New York: Philosophical Library, 1943), p. 247. Russell's is a sequentialism of events rather than of collections of tropes. Russell offers a fuller development of this theory in *Human Knowledge: Its Scope and Limits*. In that work, Russell makes clear that according to him, events are themselves collections of "compresent" qualities (p. 83). Thus, his developed view is that a substance is a sequence of collections of such qualities: "A complex of compresence which does not recur takes the place traditionally occupied by 'particulars'; a single such complex, or a string of such complexes causally connected in a certain way, is the kind of object to which it is conventionally appropriate to give a proper name" (p. 307). Hence, if his theory is a reductionist and not an eliminationist one with respect to substances and events, then Russell identifies a substance with an event or string of events. The view that a substance is an event is one we criticized earlier as a category mistake, while the view that it is a string of events is subject to criticisms parallel to those we make later of other forms of sequentialism. As for Russell's identification of events with collections of qualities, we have already criticized the idea that a *concretum* can be identified with a collection of *abstracta*. It was for that reason that we found versions of collectionism which identify substances with collections of tropes to be superior to the sort of theory Russell embraces.

83

Our first two criticisms of sequentialism are based on the intuition that the parts of a temporal sequence are essential to it: if a temporal sequence, s_1, in a possible world $W1$, and a temporal sequence, s_2, in a possible world $W2$, have different parts in $W1$ and $W2$, respectively, then s_1 does not count as the same sequence as s_2. This intuition supports two different criticisms of sequentialism. The first is that sequentialism does not allow for genuine intrinsic qualitative change in a substance.

If Socrates is such a sequence, then he doesn't really *change* from being drunk to being sober (although this might appear to be the case). The argument for this conclusion is as follows. Recall our principle that if a contingent entity which is not necessarily eternal undergoes change, then it could have gone out of existence instead of changing.[44] Socrates is a contingent entity who is not necessarily eternal and who undergoes change, for example, from being drunk to being sober. Thus, when Socrates is drunk, he could subsequently have gone out of existence instead of having become sober. Suppose Socrates was drunk at t_1 and became sober at t_2. Then he could have gone out of existence at t_2 instead of having become sober. But if Socrates is a sequence of collections of tropes, then those collections are essential parts of the sequence. And since the collections essentially include those tropes which are their parts, it follows that each such trope is an essential part of the sequence (or at least essentially belongs to the sequence). From these propositions, we can infer that if Socrates is a sequence of collections, then it is essential to Socrates that his particular drunkenness (the drunkenness we stipulated as having belonged to him at t_1) be followed by his particular sobriety (the sobriety we stipulated as having belonged to him at t_2). This, however, is incompatible with our earlier principle, which implies that Socrates could have gone out of existence after being drunk instead of having become sober. Thus, it follows from the principle in question that if Socrates is a sequence of collections of tropes, then he did not, despite appearances, actually undergo any change from t_1 to t_2. Instead, one might say that Socrates is a static, temporally expansive entity which displays qualitative variegation over his temporal expanse from t_1 to t_2.

It might be objected that if Socrates is identifiable with a sequence, S, of the sort indicated, then to *say* that Socrates changes from being drunk at t_1 to being sober at t_2 is *not* to say that (and does not imply that) S changes, but to say that S is such that it includes drunkenness at t_1 and sobriety at t_2, and to *say* that Socrates could have gone out of existence at t_2 is *not* to say

44 See Chapter 2, Section I.

that (and does not imply that) S could have gone out of existence at t_2, but to say that there could be a sequence *other* than S which is just like S up to t_2 and which is such that there is no post-t_2 sequence of the appropriate sort.

However, this objection is incompatible with the principle of the indiscernibility of identicals. According to that principle, for any x and y, if $x = y$, then x has every property y has and y has every property x has. Given the indiscernibility of identicals, if Socrates $= S$ and Socrates has the property of being such that he undergoes intrinsic qualitative change, then this implies that S has the property of being such that he undergoes intrinsic qualitative change, and if Socrates $= S$ and Socrates has the property of being such that he could have gone out of existence at t_2, then this implies that S has the property of being such that it could have gone out of existence at t_2. But the objection under discussion denies both of these implications. Hence, this objection is incompatible with the principle of the indiscernibility of identicals. Since we regard the principle of the indiscernibility of identicals as a necessary truth known *a priori*, we find the objection in question to be unacceptable.

A second criticism of sequentialism is an implication of some of the premises for the first criticism: that the collections which are parts of a temporal sequence are essential to that sequence, and that the tropes which are the parts of each collection are essential to that collection. The implication is that if Socrates is a sequence of the sort indicated, then his qualitative life history is essential to him. All of the features of Socrates at the first moment of his existence are essential to him, as are all of the features he has at each subsequent stage of his existence. Thus, the implication is that Socrates could not have been any different qualitatively from the way he actually was – a consequence at odds with the intuitive data for the ordinary concept of substance.

In order to avoid the two criticisms of sequentialism just discussed, the sequentialist might reject our assumption that the parts of a sequence are essential to it. We find the assumption in question extremely plausible, and would insist on its correctness. Nevertheless, it is worth examining the proposal which such a sequentialist might put forward based on the rejection of our essentialist assumption, and we shall find that the proposal suffers from a related form of excessive essentialism.

The proposal is that a temporal sequence of particulars is individuated by its first stage and, given that first stage, could have any number of different later stages. For example, if a, b, c, d, and e are the first five stages of sequence S, respectively, S could have had different stages e, f, g, and h, as its second through fifth stages instead of b, c, d, and e, respectively. Alternatively, S could have gone out of existence after its first stage (or after its second, etc.) instead of having persisted beyond it. We concede that if a sequence of particulars with identity conditions of this kind was possible, then it would avoid the two criticisms of sequentialism voiced earlier. On the other hand, a third criticism applies to this sort of sequentialism. On the view in question, the initial stage of a sequence is essential to it. The initial stage is a collection of tropes whose parts are essential to it. Thus, by identifying a substance with such a sequence, this view implies that for any feature, f, which a substance initially has, the property of initially having f is essential to that substance. For example, if a chair comes into existence five feet from the workbench, this view implies that in every possible world in which the chair exists, it is initially five feet from the workbench. Or, if the chair was a certain shade of green when first coming into existence, this view implies that the chair is initially that certain shade of green in every possible world in which it exists. These implications are at odds with the intuitive data for the ordinary concept of a substance: surely, the chair could have been assembled a little closer or further from the workbench, and just as surely, the chair could have been assembled out of parts whose particular shade of green had faded slightly.[45]

45 Recently, Harold Noonan, "Constitution Is Identity," *Mind* 102 (1993), pp. 133–146, has given an argument which implies that for any entities x and y, and some predicate G, such that the sentences 'x is possibly G' and 'y is not possibly G' are both true, x may nevertheless be identical with y provided that there are strong philosophical reasons for identifying x and y, and a Lewisian counterpart theory of modality is correct. On Lewis's theory, the property attributed by a given modal predicate is relative to, and varies with, the *sort* of individual which is the subject of the predication. E.g., Noonan argues that a statue, Goliath, is identical with Lumpl (the matter constituting Goliath) despite the fact that Goliath is not possibly such that it is compressed into a ball and survives, and Lumpl is possibly such that it is compressed into a ball and survives. Noonan maintains that this is compatible with Leibniz's Law, on the ground that the predicate 'possibly such that it is compressed into a ball and survives' signifies a different property when ascribed to Goliath than it does when ascribed to Lumpl. He argues that in the former case it ascribes the property of bearing the statue–counterpart relation to something which is compressed into a ball and survives (a property which Goliath lacks), and in the latter case it ascribes the property of bearing the matter–counterpart relation to something which is compressed into a ball and survives (a property which Lumpl has).

It might be claimed that the sort of argument given by Noonan can be used to defuse the problems of excessive essentialism we have raised for collectionism and sequentialism. We have three replies to this claim. First, we are unwilling to concede that a Lewisian, or any other reductive account of modality, is plausible. We reject all such accounts in favor of the standard possible worlds account involving transworld identity. For an argument in support of the standard account, see Gary Rosenkrantz, *Haecceity: An Ontological Essay*

Sequentialism of any kind also suffers from a diachronic analogue to the synchronic unity of qualities problem. How does the sequentialist insure that a later stage of a sequence is a stage of the same substance as an earlier stage? What is to prevent the unwanted infiltration into the sequence of stages from other (e.g., exactly similar) substances? Suppose two substances, x and y, coexist throughout their histories, are exactly similar at every stage, and undergo changes. x is identified with a sequence of collections of tropes, a, b, c, d, and y is identified with a sequence of distinct collections of tropes, e, f, g, h. Sequentialism seems to falsely imply that there is also a substantial sequence consisting of the stages a, f, c, h. A possible solution to the unity problem just posed which properly rules out the existence of such a substance requires that the stages of any substantial sequence be united by a relation of spatiotemporal continuity. We shall argue in Chapter 5 that spatiotemporal continuity is neither logically necessary nor logically sufficient for the persistence of a material substance (or any of its parts). Furthermore, for obvious reasons spatiotemporal continuity cannot be logically necessary or sufficient for the stages of a substantial sequence to be united if that sequence is to be identified with an immaterial soul. Thus, we do not regard this route to a solution to the problem of unity as a promising one. Nor do we think that a causal criterion of unity over time offers much hope of resolving the difficulty. As shown in our earlier discussion of causal criteria, such criteria for unity at a time are unable to provide a logically sufficient condition for that sort of unity. We believe that parallel problems will emerge for unity over time (because of possible relations of causal dependence holding between the stages of different substances). Further justification for this belief, including an example which illustrates this problem for causal criteria, may be found in Chapter 5. Finally, there is the Castañeda-like view that a primitive

(Dordrecht: Kluwer, 1993). Second, in the light of the unity of qualities problem for collectionism, there cannot be said to be strong philosophical reasons for identifying substances and sequences of collections of nonsubstances. Finally, it is not clear how Noonan's strategy is supposed to clear collectionism or sequentialism of the charge of excessive essentialism. This is because our arguments do not depend on our saying, for some predicate, G, that a substance is possibly G, and a sequence or collection is not. E.g., the argument we give for saying that our last variety of excessive essentialism applies to sequentialism instead depends on our claim that for some feature, being F, a substance is such that possibly *it* was not originally F, and a sequence is such that it does not possibly lack a first *member* which was F. Parallel comments apply to our other arguments for saying that some variety of excessive essentialism applies to some form of collectionism or sequentialism.

relation of "transubstantiation" unifies the stages of a substantial sequence. According to Castañeda:

> In such a view, the clustering of consubstantiated clusters along a spacetime vector must be viewed as another contingent genuine relation: the transubstantiation of consubstantiation clusters.[46]

We regard such a view as unsatisfactory: for parallel reasons, both it and the claim that an unanalyzable relation of consubstantiation is what unifies the features of a substance at a time lack content.

In conclusion, theories which identify substances either with sets or collections of properties, tropes, ideas, sense-data, events, or the like, or with sequences of such collections, face at least two intractable problems: that of the unity of qualities and excessive essentialism.[47] Having refuted these theories, in the next chapter, we will defend our own nonreductionist theory of substance: substance as that which possesses a unique kind of independence. Our theory will imply that a substance cannot be identified with a set or collection of properties, tropes, and so forth.

---

46 "Thinking and the Structure of the World," pp. 67–68.
47 This includes both theories which attempt to provide a philosophical analysis of substance in terms of sets, collections, or sequences of the sorts described, and theories which claim that the concept of a substance and the concept of such a set, collection, or sequence are identical in meaning. An account of the distinction between a philosophical analysis and a meaning identification may be found in the Introduction to this book.

4

The independence criterion of substance

A Being of itself and independent from any other.
> Bp. Pearson *Exposition of the Creed* I. 31 ([1659] 1682)

A substance is a being which can subsist by itself, without dependence upon any other created being.
> I. Watts *Logick: Or the Right Use of Reason in the Enquiry After Truth* I. ii. § 2 (1725)

I. PROBLEMS FOR THE INDEPENDENCE CRITERION

The chain of dependence which runs throughout creation.
> J. Tyndall *The Glaciers of the Alps* I. xxvii. 199 (1860)

The substance is not enough, unless it be clothed with its circumstances.
> Gracian's (B.) *Courtiers Oracle, or the Art of Prudence* ii (1685 trans.)

According to a traditional view, an individual substance is that which could exist all by itself or which in some sense is "independent." In this chapter, we construct a new version of an analysis of the ordinary notion of substance in terms of independence, and argue for its adequacy.

Our project is to construct an adequate philosophical analysis of this ordinary notion of thinghood. In setting forth our analysis we shall rely on our earlier arguments that a thing in this ordinary sense, that is, an individual substance, is not reducible to or identifiable with an entity of another kind or ontological category, for example, a set or collection of either properties, ideas, sense-data, or events. (This does not rule out the possibility that substances can be *eliminated* in favor of entities of another kind or ontological category.)

Since there is considerable disagreement among philosophers about what categories of entities could be instantiated, and since such disagreement is difficult to resolve, there is an advantage, epistemically speaking, in providing an analysis of substance which is ontologically neutral. Accord-

89

ingly, we aim to provide an analysis of substance which is ontologically neutral in the sense that it is compatible with the existence of entities belonging to any intelligible categories, given some plausible view about the natures, existence conditions, and interrelationships of entities belonging to those categories. The epistemic advantage of this procedure is that we can put forward and defend an analysis of substance without having to argue (questionably) that entities belonging to certain categories could not exist. As we shall see, such an ontically neutral analysis of substance provides an adequate criterion by which objects of discourse that would be nonsubstantial entities if they were to exist – for instance, events, after-images, properties, times, places, surfaces, and shadows – can be distinguished from genuine substances.

However, it seems that entities of indefinitely many ontological categories could be advocated, and there is sometimes disagreement among philosophers over whether an entity of a given category is intelligible. In the light of this, it does not seem reasonable to expect a single essay to provide both an analysis of substance and a complete argument that this analysis is ontologically neutral in the specified sense. Accordingly, in this essay we will only attempt to show that our analysis of substance is at least neutral with respect to a wide range of apparently intelligible ontologies encountered in philosophical literature.

Some of the particular ways in which our analysis of substance is neutral, and which help to enable this analysis to achieve the requisite ontological neutrality, are as follows. With respect to space and time, we are neutral both about whether they are absolute or relational, and about whether they are infinite or finite in extent. With respect to Property and other categories of *abstracta,* we are neutral about whether all instances of them have necessary existence or at least some instances have contingent existence. Moreover, we are neutral between property realism and nominalism. That is, our analysis of substance does not presuppose the existence of *abstracta.* Although we refer to various ontological categories, which are perhaps naturally construed as *abstracta,* if the nominalist program we have in mind were to be successful, it would have the resources to paraphrase all such references in nominalistic terms, including any references of these sorts which involve attributions of a metaphysical modality, *de dicto* or *de re.*[1] We do not rule out the possibility of such a nominalist program being

---

1 It should be noted that although we have occasionally made use of *de re* metaphysical modalities, our account of the concept of substance will be wholly couched in terms of *de dicto* metaphysical modalities.

successful. With respect to Event, we are neutral about whether the occurrence of an event entails the existence of a substance, or a time, or a property. With respect to Substance, we are neutral about the materialism–dualism–idealism controversy, and about whether there is a single necessary immaterial substance and whether there are necessary material substances. We are also neutral about whether material substances are infinitely divisible (i.e., about whether there are material atoms). Moreover, we take no position on the question of whether physical objects are material, three-dimensional objects or objects of some other dimensionality, for instance, point-particles, superstrings, or four-dimensional space-time objects.

As we have seen, several pivotal figures in the history of philosophy have defended an independence criterion of individual substance, including Aristotle and Descartes. Recall Aristotle's formulation of this idea:

> Some things can exist apart and some cannot, and it is the former that are substances.[2]

And we cite once again two of Descartes's statements of such a criterion. The first goes as follows:

> The answer is that the notion of *substance* is just this – that it can exist all by itself, that is without the aid of any other substance.[3]

As noted earlier, this definition appears to be viciously circular, since it defines the notion of substance in terms of the notion of substance.[4] However, Descartes's second definition of substance is the following:

> By *substance*, we can understand nothing other than a thing which exists in such a way as to depend on no other thing for its existence.[5]

As we have observed, this second definition is noncircular if 'thing' means entity. As indicated in our earlier discussion of Descartes, however, there is a general problem facing this and related attempts to analyze the notion of substance in terms of the possibility of a substance existing all by itself or in terms of some other form of independence. This general problem is that it

---

2 *The Complete Works of Aristotle,* trans. J. Ackrill, 2 vols. (Princeton: Princeton University Press, 1984), 2:1691.

3 *The Philosophical Writings of Descartes,* trans. John Cottingham, Robert Stoothoff, and Dugald Murdoch (Cambridge: Cambridge University Press, 1984), 2:159.

4 However, this definition might be read as putting forward the condition that a substance is an entity of an ontological category that could have one and only one instance. Notice that a definition of substance in terms of such an independence condition is clearly *not* conceptually circular. As we shall see, our definition of substance will incorporate a condition of this kind.

5 *Philosophical Writings of Descartes,* 2:210.

would seem that if there is a substance, then there must be other entities too. There are a number of different sorts of examples of this problem, each of which presents a different aspect of the problem.

First, suppose that there is a substance, for instance, a stone (call this stone b). It is arguable that b is necessarily such that there exist many other entities as well. These other entities include some substances, for example, entities which are parts of b, and some nonsubstances, for instance, b's surface, properties of b (observe that if a property, P, is either an essential characteristic of b or a necessary being, then b's existence entails P's existence *specifically*), locations in space and time which b occupies, occurrences involving b (such as b's having a certain shape at a particular time), and propositions about b. Moreover, theists would add God (a substance) to this list.

Second, consider the class, ϕ, of all kinds of torus-shaped material objects, examples of such objects being certain bagels and doughnuts. Arguably, in ϕ there is a kind of substance such that: any substance of this kind is necessarily such that there is a nonsubstance, that is, a hole.

Third, it has been argued that any human being is necessarily such that he originated from certain other temporally prior substances, namely, a certain sperm and egg.[6]

Finally, husbands are substances, as are both widowers and husbands-to-be. However, necessarily, if a husband (widower, husband-to-be) exists, then this entails that another substance exists (did exist, will exist), that is, a wife.

Each one of these four examples suggests that independence is not a logically *necessary* condition of substancehood. However, a Humean might argue that independence is not a logically *sufficient* condition of substancehood. To see this, assume for the sake of argument a neo-Humean ontology in which the only existents are instantaneous concrete events (inspired by Hume's *impressions*), none of which is necessarily connected in any manner to another. Clearly, such an event is not a substance, but on Humean assumptions it is possible for one such entity to exist all by itself.[7]

---

6 See Chapter 2, Section III, n. 50.
7 Hume gives an extreme version of an argument of this kind in his *Treatise of Human Nature*, ed. L. A. Selby-Bigge, (Oxford: Oxford University Press, 1888), book 1, part 4, sec. 5, p. 233. He asserts there that "if . . . anyone should [say] that the definition of a substance is *something which may exist by itself;* and that this definition ought to satisfy us . . . I shou'd observe, that this definition agrees to every thing, that can possibly be conceiv'd." Of course, this assertion is incorrect, as shown by the counterexamples to the logical necessity of a naive independence criterion of substance, provided in the main text.

Note that the assumption that there could be just one instantaneous event implies that

II. A PROPOSED FIRST SOLUTION

> The instances are independent of one another.
> W. Paley *Horae Paulinae* I. ¶ 13 (1790)

In what follows, we develop an analysis of substance in terms of a notion of independence. This analysis will be both ontologically neutral and compatible with objections of the aforementioned kinds. According to our analysis, a substance is an entity of a certain sort or of a certain ontic category. The fundamental idea of our analysis is that this category of Substance is one whose exemplifications meet certain independence conditions *qua* being exemplifications of that category. This conception of an ontological category should be explicated, since every entity falls under many different kinds or categories of varying degrees or levels of generality or specificity. Hence, in the development of our analysis we ought to specify the degree of generality of the ontological categories in question. A solution to a generality problem of this kind consists in giving informal and formal accounts of the appropriate degree of generality of an ontological category or kind of entity. The explication of an intuitive notion of a hierarchy of levels of generality among ontological categories in Chapter 1, Section II, above, is such an account. Our analysis of substance will make use of a concept formally explicated in that account, the concept of a level C category. This level includes categories such as Property, Relation, Proposition, Event, Time, Place, Trope, Collection, Limit, Privation, and, of course, Substance itself.

As we noted in the preceding section, the instantiation of properties such as being a husband and being a torus have certain troublesome exis-

---

time is absolute, not relational. (It would seem that there cannot be just one temporally *extended* event, for it appears that such an event would of necessity have parts which are themselves events.) Events are essentially temporal, so that the assumption in question is incompatible with the elimination of time. Furthermore, relational time consists in temporal relations of before, after, and simultaneous with, which hold either between the parts of an intrinsically temporally extended entity, or between two or more temporally located entities. Thus, the existence of just a single instantaneous (i.e., temporally unextended) event cannot give rise to relational time, and it is necessary that if there is such an event, then time is absolute. In conclusion, a Humean counterexample to the sufficiency of a naive independence criterion of substance is unsuccessful: there could not be an instantaneous event and nothing else.

Based on the foregoing argument, we can now make this observation: the assertion that, possibly, there is just one instantaneous event and absolute time is less objectionable than the assertion that, possibly, there is just one instantaneous event and nothing else. We will construct our analysis of substance so that it is compatible with the former possibility. In doing so, that analysis will turn out to be compatible with the latter possibility as well.

tential entailments. Recall that these existential entailments create problems for an independence criterion of substance because they suggest that independence is not a logically necessary condition of being a substance. Because the category of Substance (if instantiable) is at level C, and because the instantiation of this category does not have the aforementioned troublesome existential entailments, these problems can be solved by stating an independence criterion of substance in terms of a category variable that ranges only over ontological categories at level C of generality. Moreover, being a substance subsumes more specific properties like being a husband and being a torus (thereby ensuring that the latter properties are not level C categories). This is the strategy which we shall pursue in formulating our analysis of substance in terms of independence. Our way of avoiding the problems created by lower-level kinds of substantial entities shows that it is not *qua* substance that there being a husband or a torus entails that there are certain other entities, but *qua* husband or torus.

In this and following sections, we will develop and defend a pair of analyses of the ordinary concept of being a substance. The first analysis does not seem to require that it is possible for there to be a substance which has no other substance as a part. For example, it does not seem to require that either souls or point-particles or indivisible material atoms are possible. This complicates both the statement and defense of our first analysis. Later, we offer a simplified, second analysis which *does* require the possibility of either souls, point-particles, indivisible material atoms, or some other sort of substance which has no substantial parts.

We are now prepared to state our first analysis of substance, which we do in two steps.

(4D1) A level C category $C1$ is *capable-of-having-an-independent-instance* =df. (i) $\Diamond$ [there is a temporal interval t and an x such that x instantiates $C1$ throughout t & $(\forall y)$ ((in t y instantiates $C1$ and in t y is not a part of x) $\rightarrow y = x$)], & (ii) $\Diamond$ $(\exists z)$ [(z instantiates $C1$) & $\sim (\exists x)$ (x instantiates a level C category $C2$ which satisfies (i) and which is not equivalent to $C1$)], & (iii) $\sim \Diamond$ $(\exists x)$ $(\exists y)$ [(x instantiates $C1$) & (y is a part of x) & (y instantiates a level C category (other than a category either equivalent to being a concrete proper part or equivalent to being an abstract proper part) that is not equivalent to $C1$)].

(4D2) x is a substance =df. x instantiates a level C category which is capable-of-having-an-independent-instance.

It might be thought that since Substance is a level C category, and since (4D2) analyzes being a substance in terms of the notion of a level C category, (4D2) is viciously circular. However, while Substance is a level C category, our account of what it is for a category to be at level C does *not* make use of the concept of being a substance at any point. List *L,* our core list of level *C* categories does not include Substance; nor is the concept of substance employed elsewhere in the analysis. We account for the category of Substance being at level *C* in terms of its standing in certain logical relations to the categories on *L.* Hence, (4D2) is not conceptually circular.

(4D1) makes use of the generic concept of parthood, a concept we take as a primitive. Species of generic parthood include spatial parthood, temporal parthood, and logical parthood. Entities of different kinds may have different kinds of parts, for example, spatial parts, temporal parts, or logical parts. But in the generic sense of 'part' that we employ throughout this book, entities of different kinds have parts in the very same sense.

Note that if *both* concrete and abstract proper parts are possible, then a putative *ontological category* of being a proper part would seem to be both below level *B* and not subsumed either by being concrete or by being abstract, something which is impossible. Thus, being a proper part is a *category* only if either just concrete proper parts are possible or just abstract proper parts are possible. But neither of these disjuncts is evidently the case. It is for this reason that in clause (iii) of (4D1) we speak instead of the categories of being a concrete proper part and being an abstract proper part. (The categorial status of *being a concrete proper part* is discussed in note 48.) Nevertheless, for brevity's sake, we will henceforth express the disjunctive expression which occurs within the parentheses in clause (iii) of (4D1) by simply saying 'other than a category equivalent to being a proper part'.

In (4D1) and (4D2), we understand the independence of an entity as something derived from that entity's instantiating a level *C* category. Intuitively, and without reference to category instantiation, there are at least two senses in which it can be said that an entity is independent of certain other entities. The first sense is that the existence of an entity does not entail the existence of those other entities. Accordingly, if an entity could not exist in the absence of certain other entities, then there is a sense in which that entity depends upon those other entities. The second sense is that it is possible for an entity not to have certain other entities as parts. Correspondingly, there is a sense in which certain complex entities depend upon their parts, namely, when it is impossible for such a complex to exist without those parts.[8] Related senses of independence explicable in terms

8 We assume only that, possibly, there exists a complex entity that has its parts essentially. A stronger doctrine of mereological essentialism has been maintained, viz., that, necessarily, any complex entity has its parts essentially. Such a doctrine is controversial, but nevertheless merits serious consideration.

of level C category instantiation include the following three, that correspond to the three clauses of (4D1), respectively.

First, an entity, x, that instantiates a level C category, $C1$, is independent of other entities of category $C1$ (other than parts of x) if the instantiation of $C1$ by x does not entail that there is an instance of $C1$ other than x or a part of x. An entity of such a category will be said to be *independent-within-its-kind*. In virtue of clause (i) of (4D1), (4D2) implies that an entity which instantiates the category of Substance is independent-within-its-kind.

Second, an entity, x, that instantiates a level C category, $C1$, is independent of any other entity that is independent-within-its-kind if the instantiation of $C1$ by x does not entail the instantiation of a nonequivalent level C category by another entity that is independent-within-*its*-kind. In virtue of clause (ii) of (4D1), (4D2) entails that an entity which instantiates the category of Substance is independent of any other entity of a different level C category that is independent-within-its-kind.

Finally, if it is impossible that a level C category, $C1$, be instantiated by an entity having as parts entities instantiating another level C category, $C2$, then this is a sense in which an entity of category $C1$ is independent of any such entities of category $C2$. In virtue of clause (iii) of (4D1), (4D2) implies that an entity which instantiates the category of Substance is in this sense independent of entities of other level C categories.

Notice that in virtue of clause (i) of (4D1), (4D2) allows that if a substance must have parts, then it must in a sense be dependent upon them. However, this general dependence of any complex or extended entity upon its parts is *not* the sort of dependence which distinguishes a substance from entities of other sorts. On the other hand, as we shall see, Substance is distinguished from some other level C categories by not possibly having an instance which depends on parts that do not belong to the same level C category as itself. This is the point of clause (iii) of (4D1).

We shall argue that individual substances possess a type of independence which no other type of entity possesses, namely, the conjunction of the three forms of independence explained earlier. Unlike some previous accounts, our account does not claim that other kinds of entities depend on substance, but not vice versa. Thus, our account does not assert that substances possess a *dyadic* asymmetric independence of all other sorts of entities. Rather, our account asserts the more complex asymmetric independence of substance explicated previously.

In what follows, we confirm the adequacy of (4D2) by arguing that even if it is granted that there could exist abstract and concrete entities of a variety of categories at level C, it is impossible for any entity which is not a substance to instantiate a level C category that is capable-of-having-an-independent-instance.

III. THE FIRST TEST CASE: PROPERTIES

> Now as for shapes and colours and sizes and weights and all the other things predicated . . . as permanent properties . . . we should not think that these are independent natural substances: that is not conceivable.
>
> Epicurus *Letter to Herodotus*

Let us begin with a type of abstract entity, namely, properties. In what follows, we argue that since it is impossible for a property to instantiate a level C category that satisfies clause (i) of (4D1), (4D2) implies that a property could not be a substance. In the first place, the level C category of being a property satisfies clause (i) of (4D1) only if it is possible that there exists a property and no other properties except for that property's parts. However, it is controversial whether a property could have parts. If a property could not have parts, then all that needs to be shown in order to demonstrate that the category of being a property does not satisfy clause (i) of (4D1) is that there could not be one and only one property. That there could not be one and only one property can be shown as follows.[9]

To begin with, if there is a property, then there must be a *first-order property,* a property (such as being blue) that could only be exemplified by a concrete individual. Hence, it is impossible that every property is self-instantiating. Furthermore, there could not be a first-order property unless there were another property, namely, a *second-order property,* a property of a first-order property that could only be exemplified by a first-order property. For example, being blue exemplifies the second-order property of being a first-order property. The notions of a *third-order property,* a

9 There are two important views about the existence conditions of properties and other *abstracta.* According to the first, there are infinite totalities of properties and other *abstracta* which are isomorphic to the infinite totalities of numbers and sets posited by mathematics and set-theory, respectively. According to the second, for example, as held by D. M. Armstrong in his *Nominalism and Realism,* 2 vols. (Cambridge: Cambridge University Press, 1980), the existence condition of a genuine property is that it is exemplified and needed for the purpose of causal explanation. The second view entails a much more parsimonious ontology of properties than the first, more platonistic view. In defending our *first analysis* of substance, we assume what we take to be the more plausible ontology of *abstracta,* viz., the more platonistic view. For an extended argument in favor of a form of property-realism which entails such an ontology, see Gary Rosenkrantz, *Haecceity: An Ontological Essay* (Dordrecht: Kluwer, 1993). Later, in defending our *second analysis* of substance, we require no commitment to one of these views as opposed to the other.

fourth-order property, and so on, *ad infinitum,* can each be defined in a fashion parallel to the way in which a second-order property was defined. For instance, a third-order property, for example, being a second-order property, is a property of a second-order property that could only be exemplified by a second-order property.

As the foregoing discussion shows, there could not be one and only one property. It follows that if it is impossible for a property to have parts, then the category of being a property does not satisfy clause (i) of (4D1). On the other hand, suppose it is possible for a property to have parts. Only if a logically complex property has other properties as *logical* parts, do we need to consider the idea that properties have parts. The idea here would be that a conjunctive property has each of its conjuncts as a logical part, a disjunctive property has each of its disjuncts as a logical part, and so forth. If it is possible for a property to have parts of this kind, then we need to determine whether there could be a logically complex property, for instance, a "huge" disjunctive property, that has every other property as a logical part. If there *could* be such a huge property, then there could be a property which except for its parts is the only property, and our analysis of substance would falsely imply that properties are substances. We argue that there could *not* be a logically complex property of this kind.

In the first place, since it is a necessary truth that an entity is not a proper part of itself, there could not be a logically complex property which had as a logical proper part every property, including itself. Furthermore, we will argue that for any property, $P1$, there must be another property, $P2$, such that $P2$ is not a logical part of $P1$, and $P1$ is not a logical part of $P2$. To begin with, if there is a first-order property, say, being blue, then this entails that blueness has the property of being a first-order property, and that being a first-order property has the property of being a second-order property, and that being a second-order property has the property of being a third-order property, and so on, *ad infinitum.* Each property in such an infinite hierarchy is *not* a logical part of either any of its predecessors or any of its successors in the hierarchy, since it is not possible for a property of a given order to have as a logical part a property of a different order. For instance, being blue (a first-order property) is not a logical part of being a first-order property (a second-order property), and vice versa. Clearly, a parallel argument applies to any pair of properties belonging to an infinite hierarchy of the kind under discussion. It follows that there could not be a property which except for its logical parts is the only property, *unless* there is a logically complex property which has *all* of the properties in such an infinite hierarchy as logical parts. An example of such a logically complex property would be the "infinite" disjunctive property (call it $P^\star$) of being either blue, or a first-order property, or a second-order property, or a third-order property, or . . . If $P^\star$ exists, then this entails that $P^\star$ has the property, $P^{\star\star}$, of being a disjunctive property having an infinite number of disjuncts, the first of which is a first-order property, the second of which is a second-order property, the third of which is a third-order property, and so on, *ad infinitum*. Inasmuch as $P^{\star\star}$ is of a higher order than $P^\star$, $P^\star$ is *not* a logical part of $P^{\star\star}$, and vice versa.

An argument of the foregoing kind applies to every infinite hierarchy of properties and to every logically complex property having infinitely many logical parts. It follows that it is impossible for there to be a property which except for its logical parts is the only property. Consequently, the category of being a property fails to satisfy clause (i) of (4D1). Parallel arguments apply to other categories of abstract entity such as relation and proposition: either an entity of such a kind does not have parts and there cannot be an entity of that kind which is the only entity of that kind, or else there cannot be an entity of such a kind which, except for its parts, is the only entity of that kind. Inasmuch as none of these various general categories of *abstracta* at level C of generality satisfies (4D1), none of these categories of *abstracta* is capable-of-having-an-independent-instance. Moreover, as far as we can tell, there is no other level C category which is capable-of-having-an-independent-instance and which could be instantiated by an abstract entity of any of these kinds. Thus, (4D2) has the desirable implication that neither a property, nor a relation, nor a proposition could be a substance.

IV. TROPES

They cannot be considered as independent of one another.
J. Priestly *Institutes of Natural and Revealed Religion* I. 276 ([1772] 1782)

Turning to *concreta,* let us consider the category of tropes, that is, concrete features or "properties" such as the particular wisdom of Socrates or *that* particular redness.[10] If a trope has parts, then it has either spatial, or

---

10 There are two views about the existence conditions for tropes which parallel the two views about the existence conditions of properties described in n. 9 in Section III of this chapter. As before, in defending our first analysis of substance, we assume what we take to be the more plausible ontology of tropes, viz., the more generous one of an infinite totality of tropes which is isomorphic to the infinite totalities of numbers and sets posited by mathematics and set theory, respectively. Later, in defending our second analysis of substance, we require no commitment to the more generous view as opposed to the other, more stingy, view that, necessarily, a trope exists if and only if it is needed for the

temporal, or logical parts. However, if there is a trope, $P1$, then this entails that there are other tropes of a higher order than $P1$ such that $P1$ is not a part of them and none of them is a part of $P1$.[11] For example, if there is the first-order trope, *that* particular redness, then there must be the second-order trope, *that* particular being a trope, and so forth. Surely, the former is not a spatial or temporal part of the latter, and vice versa. And for reasons parallel to those advanced with respect to abstract properties, the former is not a logical part of the latter, and vice versa. Since an argument of this kind implies that if there is a trope, $P1$, then there must be another trope which is not a part of $P1$, the level C category of being a trope does not satisfy clause (i) of (4D1).[12] And it would seem that there is no other level C category which is capable-of-having-an-independent-instance and which could be instantiated by a trope. Consequently, (4D2) has the welcome consequence that a trope could not be a substance.

V. PLACES, TIMES, AND LIMITS

Yet is space no thingish entity, no tangible object.
                              Open Court [U.S.] 5, June, 2316/2 (1890)

Although time is numbered among continuous quantities yet through its being invisible and without substance it does not altogether fall under the category of geometrical terms, which are divided in figures and bodies of infinite variety, as may constantly be seen to be the case with things visible and things of substance; but it harmonizes with these only as regards its first principles, namely, as to the point and the line.
        E. MacCurdy Leonardo da Vinci's *Notebooks* 76 (1941 trans.)

The external limits of the magnitude of a body are lines and surfaces.
        H. Kater and D. Lardner *A Treatise on Mechanics* i. 4 (1830)

---

purpose of causal explanation. The latter view of the existence conditions of tropes has been advocated by William Mann in "Epistemology Supernaturalized," *Faith and Philosophy* 2 (1985), pp. 436–456. For a criticism of Mann's view, see Gary Rosenkrantz, "Necessity, Contingency, and Mann," *Faith and Philosophy* 2 (1985), pp. 457–463. Mann replies to the latter paper in his "Keeping Epistemology Supernaturalized: A Reply To Rosenkrantz," *Faith and Philosophy* 2 (1985), pp. 464–468.

11 The notion of a first-order trope can be understood as follows. A first-order trope is one that could only be possessed by or belong to a concrete individual other than a trope. A second-order trope is one that could only be possessed by or belong to a first-order trope. Higher-order tropes can then be defined in a fashion parallel to the way in which a second-order trope was defined.

12 If species–genus or determinate–determinable relationships are part–whole or whole–part relationships, our conclusions about properties and tropes stand, since neither of the first two relationships can hold between properties or tropes of different orders.

Other categories of *concreta* include being a place, being a time, and being a limit. In what follows, we will show that these categories also fail to satisfy clause (i) of (4D1). We argue that if there is an entity of one of these three kinds, then this entails that there is a dense continuum of entities of that kind containing both minimum or zero-dimensional entities of that kind, that is, point-positions, instants, and point-limits, respectively, and extended entities of that kind, and that such minimum entities cannot be *parts* of extended places, temporal intervals, or nonzero-dimensional limits.

The first step in reaching this conclusion is to prove that it is impossible for there to be just one place or just one time. Our proof is as follows:[13]

(1i) Necessarily, if a place or a time exists, then it is either an extended place (a place that is not a point, for example, a spatial interval) or a point-position, or an extended time (a time that is not an instant, for instance, a temporal interval) or an instant, respectively.

(1ii) Necessarily, if there is an extended place or an extended time, then there are other, smaller subplaces or subtimes, for example, the extended right and left halves of that extended place, or the extended times which are the first half and the second half of the extended time in question.[13]

(1iii) Necessarily, if there is a point-position or an instant, then there exists an extended place or an extended time of which that point-position or instant is a *limit,* respectively.

(1iv) Necessarily, if there is a limit, then it is not identical with that of which it is a limit.

Therefore,

(1v) Necessarily, if there is a place or a time, then there are other places or times.

It might conceivably be objected to (1iii) that it is possible for space or time to consist of just one point-position, or just a single instant, respectively. In this case, the point-position or instant in question is not a limit of an extended place or an extended time. Our reply is as follows. With respect to the temporal case, we simply find ourselves unable to attach any sense whatever to the notion of unextended time (consisting of just a single

---

13 We find the notion of a minimal, extended place or minimal extended time to be unintelligible. Some philosophers who accept the possibility of discontinuous space and time presuppose the intelligibility of this notion. Below, we argue against the possibility of discontinuous space and time (in a strong sense of 'discontinuous' to be explained later), and in particular, against the coherence of a minimal, extended place or time. However, we shall also argue in Section X of this chapter that a simplified version of our first analysis of substance gives the correct verdict on places and times, viz., that they are nonsubstantial beings, even if both a discontinuous space and time, and a minimal extended place and a minimal extended time, are possible.

instant).[14] The idea of an unextended space (consisting of just a single point-position) is no more intelligible to us.[15] However, it is perhaps understandable how someone might think that there could be space consisting of a single point-position: this could be the result of a confusion between a *point-position* (a place) and a *point-particle*. There could, it seems,

14 It might be objected that the Boethian doctrine that God perceives everything in an eternal "now" implies the possibility of unextended time. We have our doubts about the intelligibility of this doctrine, but for the sake of argument let us waive these doubts. Nevertheless, what this Boethian doctrine says (even according to its proponents) is that God is an *atemporal* being. Thus, if this doctrine is coherent, then it seems not to imply the possibility of unextended time, but rather the possibility of some nontemporal mode of being.

   That a so-called eternal now is not a time can be argued as follows. If there could be an eternal "now," then possibly, just one eternal "now" exists and there does not exist a time which is not identical with that eternal "now." Furthermore, we shall argue in Section X of this chapter, that it is not possible for there to be just a single time, as time must have a structure which is compatible with the occurrence of change. Thus, an eternal "now" is not a time.

15 According to an objection based upon the "Big Bang" theory, this modern cosmological theory conceives of the physical universe as having originated in an initial zero-dimensional "singularity," and the existence of such a singularity entails the existence of unextended space.

   One reply to this objection is simply that it misinterprets the claims of modern cosmology: the "Big Bang" theory implies that the original singularity is outside of space and time, and that space and time begin with the "Big Bang." If this interpretation is accurate, then, of course, the "Big Bang" theory does not entail the existence of unextended space.

   Moreover, we shall argue in Section X of this chapter that there could not be just a single unextended space, as space must have a structure which is compatible with the occurrence of motion. Hence, if the "Big Bang" theory entails the existence of a single unextended place, then that theory is necessarily false. Because the original "singularity" is either an unextended place or a point-particle, and because, as we argued in Chapter 1, Section III, if only a single point-particle exists, then it must reside in an absolute space, it follows that the notion of an original physical "singularity" which is outside of space and time is incoherent. Therefore, the "Big Bang" theory stands in need of an interpretation which does not employ the latter notion. In particular, if the "Big Bang" theory is to be coherent, then the original "singularity" must be thought of as an infinitely dense point-particle which resides in an *extended* absolute space.

   In sum, whether the original "singularity" is regarded as an unextended space or as an unextended particle, the "Big Bang" theory cannot be coherently employed in defense of the idea that the existence of unextended space is possible.

   It is worth noting that even if the "Big Bang" theory is both coherent and entails the existence of unextended space, contrary to our argument, this entailment is not a reason for thinking that an unextended space satisfies our definition of substance. Our reason for saying this is as follows. First of all, on the foregoing hypothesis, the "Big Bang" theory entails that the "Big Bang" is the beginning of both time and extended space. Hence, on the hypothesis in question, the "Big Bang" theory entails that the original zero-dimensional singularity does not exist throughout an interval of time. Thus, even if the existence of an original singularity as envisioned by the "Big Bang" theory entails that

be a single point-particle in an extended space, but such a point-particle is, of course, a substance, not a place.

Having shown that there cannot be just one place or just one time, we next argue that *strongly discontinuous* space and time are impossible.[16] We find it overwhelmingly plausible that necessarily, if space and time exist, then there is a *dense continuum* of places and times.[17] Nevertheless, some

there exists one and only one place, U, it does not entail the possibility of U's existing throughout an interval of time. Therefore, the possibility of U is not a reason to think that the level C category, $C1$, instantiated by U, i.e., Place, satisfies clause (i) of (4D1), inasmuch as this clause requires that, possibly, there is an instance of $C1$ which exists throughout an interval of time. Consequently, U's being possible is not a reason for thinking that U satisfies our account of substance in (4D2). A single unextended place threatens to be a counterexample to (4D2) only if it can persist.

16 Is there any support for atomic space and time to be found in the sciences? Not according to Adolf Grunbaum: "Newtonian physics, relativity theory, and standard quantum mechanics all assume that spatial and temporal betweenness are each dense as opposed to discrete." See his *Modern Science and Zeno's Paradoxes* (Middletown, Conn.: Wesleyan University Press, 1967), p. 37. He also states that: "It is well to bear in mind that there is both a weak sense and a strong sense in which a discrete space and time might be contemplated: (1) The weak sense is to imagine a world of which it would be appropriate to say that it has a granular space and time, and (2) the strong sense is to specify those further empirical conditions which would justify that we *reinterpret* our present information about the physical space and time of our actual world so as to attribute genuine atomicity to them. It is difficult enough to carry out the weaker kind of envisionment. And it is all the more unclear how future developments in quantum theory might implement the stronger program of quantization of space and time." See "Modern Science and Zeno's Paradoxes," in *Zeno's Paradoxes*, ed. Wesley Salmon (Indianapolis: Bobbs-Merrill, 1970), p. 247.

In the passages just cited, Grunbaum does not deny that recent science postulates atomic *motion*, as opposed to atomic space or time. One could define an atomic motion as one with respect to which there is no time at which the transition from one place to the next is only part way through. Thus, atomic motion occurs in instantaneous "leaps" or "jumps" (see Chapter 5, Section IX). If there were atomic spaces, then any object moving into such a space would at one time not occupy any part of the space, and then at a later time would occupy all of the space, and there would be no time at which the object would occupy only part of the space. Thus, the existence of atomized space implies the atomic motion of any object which moves into or out of such a space, but the existence of atomic motion does not imply the existence of atomized space.

17 To say that space or time is *dense* is to say that there are discrete places or times, and that between any two discrete places or times, there is another place or time; and to say that a subregion R of space or time is dense is to say that there are point-positions or instants which bound R, and that between any two discrete places or times which belong to R, there is another place or time. Notice that although, necessarily, every *continuum* is dense, not every densely ordered series is a continuum. E.g., the series of rationals is dense in the sense that between any two rational numbers there is a third, but this series is not a continuum, since the rationals cannot be put into one-to-one correspondence with the real numbers. Nevertheless, it is presumably a necessary truth that if *space* and *time* are dense, then space and time are continua in the sense that places and times can each be put into one-to-one correspondence with the real numbers.

103

philosophers have denied the existence of such a dense continuum, and have postulated minimum or atomic places and times.[18]

We shall distinguish between a weak and a strong sense in which space and time might be said to be continuous. Whenever we say that necessarily, if space and time exist, then space and time are *continuous*, the sense of continuity which we have in mind should be distinguished from another, stronger sense of continuity. Space or time being continuous in the stronger sense entails that between *any* two discrete places or times there is another. Space or time being continuous in this sense implies that there is not a gap in space or time. To say that space or time is continuous in our weaker sense is to say that any place or time belongs to some *region* which is a dense continuum of places or times. The existence of a weakly continuous space or time is compatible with there being a gap in space or time. In our arguments, when we commit ourselves to continuous space and time, we commit ourselves only to the proposition that necessarily, if space and time exist, then space and time are continuous in the weaker sense, given the ordinary or intuitive conceptions of space and time. Accordingly, in arguing against the possibility of discontinuous space and time, we are only arguing against the possibility of *strongly* discontinuous space and time. To say that space and time are discontinuous in this sense is to say not only that there are minimal places and times which have no place and time between them, but also that for every minimal place or time, m, there is a spatial or temporal direction, d, such that there is another minimal place or time, m', which is *next* to m in direction d.

Given that space and time are (strongly) discontinuous, there are two possibilities with respect to the nature of these minimal places and times. The first is that they are spatially or temporally extended, not mere points or instants, but nevertheless such that a smaller place or time does not exist. The second possibility is that minimal places are points and minimal times are instants.

18 For example, both Richard Sorabji, *Time, Creation, and the Continuum* (Ithaca, N.Y.: Cornell University Press, 1983), pp. 19, 345–346, and Nicholas Denyer, "The Atomism of Diodorus Cronus," *Prudentia* 13 (1981), pp. 33–45, ascribe to Diodorus Cronus the view that there are atomic times and places which have size. More, recently, G. J. Whitrow, *The Natural Philosophy of Time* (London: Thomas Nelson, 1961), p. 153, takes the possibility of sized atomic places and times seriously: "since the rise of the quantum theory, it has become commonplace to regard energy as being ultimately atomic. Whether physical length should also be pictured in the same way is still a moot point, although it would seem to be in general accord with the trend of modern ideas to postulate a lower limit to spatial extension in nature. Closely linked with this concept is the hypothesis of minimal natural processes and changes, according to which no process can occur in less than some atomic unit of time, the *chronon*."

Let us further consider the first possibility, that of a discontinuous space and time in which the atomic places and times are extended. We find this view paradoxical. Suppose there is a minimal place, p, with spatial extension, e. p will have a right half and a left half, each of which has a spatial extension of $e/2$. It would seem that each of the halves in question is itself a place, yet on the view in question, either p does not have a right half and a left half, or else it does but they are not places. We find both of these alternatives absurd.[19] A similar argument will apply to the claim that there are times which have a minimal temporal extension.

The second possibility is that of a discontinuous space and time whose atomic places and times are points and instants, that is, unextended places and times. In the case of a discontinuous space, each atomic place is next to another atomic place, and in the case of a discontinuous time, each atomic time is next to another atomic time. If the atomic places and times belonging to a discontinuous space and time are point-positions and instants, then a discontinuous space and time somehow arise out of these unextended point-positions and instants. There are three decisive arguments against this second possibility.

The first argument is that point-positions and instants are not *capable* of independent existence: point-positions and instants are *limits* of extended places and times,[20] and could not exist unless extended places and times exist. Thus, it is incoherent to suppose that there could be a point-position or an instant which was not the beginning or end of an extended place or time.[21] It is therefore a mistake to think of space or time as somehow arising out of unextended point-positions or instants. The dependence relation runs the other way around: point-positions and instants owe their existence to the existence of extended space and time.

19 An anonymous referee for Cambridge University Press suggests the following objection to our claim that the right half of p is a place with extension $e/2$. "If a place were defined as a possible position of an object (wholly occupying it), and if no object could have an extension less than e, then no object could occupy the right half of p, whence that would not qualify as a *place* by the definition." As the objection is stated, its claim that "no object could occupy the right half of p" presupposes that by an *object* is meant a *substance*. However, a *part* of a substance is an object in the sense of "object" relevant to occupying a place, i.e., it is an entity which has spatial extension. Thus, the claim just quoted is false, because the right half of an atomic object which occupies p occupies the right half of p.

20 We remind the reader that when we speak of an extended time we are referring to a time that is not an instant, e.g., a temporal interval; and when we speak of an extended place we are referring to a place that is not a point, e.g., a spatial interval.

21 As Richard Sorabji aptly describes Aristotle's view of the nature of an instant: "An instant is not a very short period, but rather the beginning or end (the boundary) of a period." See *Time, Creation, and the Continuum*, p. 8. As Sorabji correctly observes, on this view points and instants are *limits*.

The second argument against the possibility of a discontinuous space and time whose atomic places and times are point-positions and instants is stated here.

(2i) Necessarily, if there is a point or an instant, then it is a zero-dimensional limit of a one-dimensional place or time.

(2ii) Necessarily, if there is a discontinuous space and time whose atomic places and times are points and instants, then these points and instants are not limits of a one-dimensional place or time: there are points and instants without any places or times between them, and these points and instants do not bound any one-dimensional places or times.

Hence,

(2iii) It is impossible for there to be a discontinuous space and time whose atomic places and times are points and instants.

The third argument against the possibility of a discontinuous space and time whose atomic places and times are point-positions and instants is as follows.

(3i) Necessarily, if space and time are discontinuous and atomic places and times are point-positions and instants, then there are extended places and times which arise solely from entities which are zero-dimensional and (hence) sizeless.

(3ii) Necessarily, extended places and times do not arise solely from zero-dimensional entities which are sizeless.

On the one hand, if time and space are discontinuous and absolute, and there are unextended minimal times and places, then the extendedness of time and space would have to arise solely from those minimal times and places. Since the latter lack extension, extended space and time cannot arise from them.[22]

On the other hand, if time and space are relational, then the extendedness of time and space must arise solely from entities which occupy space and time, for example, bodies and events. If all such entities are themselves unextended, then extended space and time cannot arise from them, since there is no way to define the spatial and temporal dyadic relations, x's being n units of distance from y, and x's being n units of time before or after y. In order to define such relations, there must be occupants of space and time, and the distance or time between x and y is definable in terms of the number of times some spatial or temporal occupant needs to be laid end to

22 We refer those readers who think that Dedekind and Cantor have undermined this intuitive claim to Appendix 2, where we dispute their point-set analysis of continuous space and time.

end in order to cover the distance or time in question. If, as assumed, all spatial and temporal entities are sizeless, then, obviously, such relations are not definable. And unless these relations *are* definable, relational space and time do not arise. Therefore,

(3iii) It is impossible that space and time are discontinuous and atomic places and times are point-positions and instants.

Since both versions of the view that space and time are discontinuous seem to be unintelligible, we are skeptical about the possibility of discontinuous space and time.

We have now shown that (4i) there cannot be just one place or one time; and (4ii) there cannot be discontinuous space or time. Together, (4i) and (4ii) imply that if there is a place or a time, then this entails that there is a dense continuum of places or times containing both minimum or zero-dimensional entities of that kind, that is, point-positions and instants, respectively, and extended places and temporal intervals. We shall next argue that such minimum entities cannot be *parts* of extended places or temporal intervals.

It seems that sizeless point-positions and instants in an extended continuum are not *parts* of that continuum, though there may be infinitely many of them, since extension can never arise by the addition of sizeless entities of these kinds. And in general, it appears to be necessarily true that none of the parts of an extended entity are sizeless.[23]

Aristotle agreed, for he asserts that "it is absurd that a magnitude should consist of things which are not magnitudes."[24] Two principles have been cited by M. J. White as principles to which Aristotle may have implicitly appealed in support of this assertion. According to the first, the principle of "complete additivity, ultra additivity, or super-additivity, if a magnitude is partitioned into a class of parts, then the 'size' or measure of the whole original magnitude must equal the sum of the measures ('sizes') of the parts."[25] The second principle, which White calls the "principle of non-supervenience of positive measure," says that "each partition of a continuous magnitude having positive measure or size into proper parts yields

23 An anonymous referee for Cambridge University Press poses the following question: if *points* exist and lines *contain* them, then what else could they contain them as except as *parts*? As our previous remarks indicate, our answer to this question is that points are "contained" by lines in the sense that they are *limits* of their parts.

24 *Complete Works of Aristotle*, 1:516.

25 M. J. White, *The Continuous and the Discrete* (Oxford: Oxford University Press, 1992), p. 8.

parts the sums of whose measures are all non-nil."[26] To cite Aristotle once again: "Moreover, it is plain that everything continuous is divisible into divisibles that are always divisible."[27] More generally, it seems that necessarily, an entity of $n + 1$ dimensionality does not have any part which is of dimensionality n.

It might be objected that a collection of point-particles is of greater dimensionality than each of the particles which are the parts of the collection. The particles are zero-dimensional, but, the argument goes, the collection is either one-dimensional (if, for example, n particles [where $n \geq 3$] lie in a straight line), or two-dimensional (if the same number, n, of particles do not lie in a straight line, but lie in the same plane), or three-dimensional (if this number, n, of particles do not lie in the same plane). Our reply to this objection is that it misconstrues the location and size of the collection in question. In each of the cases of n point-particles described, the collection of them is located where the particles are located: that is, it is in each case a scattered entity which is located at several points in space. Since the size of a collection is the sum of the sizes of its parts, the size of any collection of point-particles is *zero*. Thus, all three of our collections of n point-particles have zero size. We defend this proposition in the case of a collection of point-particles as follows:

(5i) Necessarily, if there is a collection of just two point-particles, then the only parts of that collection are the point-particles in question.
(5ii) Necessarily, if such a collection is spatially extended, then it has two extended parts, $H1$ and $H2$, which are halves of it.
(5iii) Necessarily, if the only parts of such an extended collection are two point-particles, and if that collection has parts $H1$ and $H2$, which are halves of it, then the extended half $H1$ is identical with one point-particle, and the extended half $H2$ is identical with the other point-particle.
(5iv) Necessarily, a point-particle is not identical with any extended entity.

Therefore,

(5v) Necessarily, a collection of just two point-particles is not extended.

It should be obvious that if a collection of two point-particles is not extended, then, since a larger collection is the sum of some number of pairs of point-particles, none of which has extension, a collection of more than two point-particles will also be unextended. Hence, the size of any collection of point-particles is zero.[28]

26 Ibid., p. 13.
27 *Complete Works of Aristotle*, 1:391.
28 We have claimed that the size of an entity is the sum of the sizes of its discrete proper parts.

Our account of the ontological status of point-positions and instants vis-à-vis space and time closely resembles that of Aristotle. In Appendix 2, we shall defend this Aristotelean account against objections based upon the different accounts of some contemporary mathematicians and argue that in any case, our first analysis of substance is compatible with the accounts of continuous space and time given by the mathematicians.

Let us apply this principle to two possible instances of Substance. Suppose that there is a substantial table, and that it is composed of microscopic portions of matter which are separated from other such parts by relatively huge spaces. What would be the size of this entity? Recall that among the intuitive data for an analysis of the ordinary conception of substance is the proposition that, necessarily, a part of a material object is a piece or portion of matter. Since it is also necessary that a place is not a piece or portion of matter, it follows that, necessarily, a material object does not have a place as a part. Hence, our table, which we are assuming to be a material substance, would not have a place as a part. The parts of this table would be the microscopic portions of matter, the molecules or atoms or more fundamental particles, which compose it. But the sum of the sizes of these particles would be smaller by many orders of magnitude than what would be the apparent size of the table, which is the size that common sense would attribute to our table. The latter, however, includes the sizes of the places between the fundamental particles composing the table. Thus, common sense would be mistaken about the size of the table, if common sense were conceiving of the table as a substance. Of course, at least one reason for this mistake is that such an object would appear to the senses to be continuous matter.

It might be objected that the gaps or interstices between the atoms constituting a table are *parts* of a table, and that therefore one can uphold the ordinary belief that the size of the table is greater than the combined sizes of its constituent atoms, as it includes also the sizes of the gaps between them. After all, it might be argued, a physical object such as a statue can have a hole as part, e.g., a hole in a statue by Henry Moore can be an integral part of it. We answer this objection as follows.

First, in the strict sense of 'part', the parts of a physical object are other physical objects or portions of physical stuff, and not privations. In the sentence about Moore's statue, 'part' is being used in a metaphorical sense. The meaning of that sentence is captured in the following translation: there being a hole in a statue by Henry Moore can be an important aspect of its design. Of course, this translation does not imply that a statue by Henry Moore can have a hole as a part in the strict sense. Second, since holes are ontologically suspect, and a statue by Moore is not, it is doubtful that a statue by Moore can have a hole as a part. (Or at least, if a statue is ontologically suspect, then it could not be ontologically suspect *because* it has a hole in it, from which it follows, inasmuch as holes are ontologically suspect, that it is dubious that a statue can have a hole as a part.) Finally, it seems to be necessarily true that for any physical object, *x*, and any proper part, *y*, of *x*, the existence of *y* does not entail that there is a nonbasic physical object of which *y* is a proper part. Yet, if a hole in a statue by Moore is a proper part of that statue, then the existence of this hole entails that there is a nonbasic physical object of which that hole is a proper part. Thus, a hole in a statue by Moore seems not to be a part of that statue.

Another mistake about the size of physical objects is illustrated by the possible case of an inflated balloon, assumed to be a material substance. It would not be unusual for someone to describe such a balloon as having a certain cubic volume corresponding to a solid sphere. Were this the judgment of common sense, then it, too, would merit deflation. Recall that the intuitive data for an analysis of the ordinary notion of substance implies that necessarily, each part of a complex material substance is joined or physically bonded to another part of that substance in such a way that all of these parts together form

We further defend our contention that point-positions and instants are not parts of the continua in question, with the following two arguments:

(6i) Necessarily, if space and time exist, then space and time are dense continua.

Therefore,

(6ii) Necessarily, no two point-positions or instants are adjacent.

Furthermore,

(6iii) Necessarily, if extended space or time has minimal parts, then these parts are point-positions or instants.

Moreover,

(6iv) Necessarily, if an entity is composed of some number of minimal parts, then in the final analysis it completely resolves into those parts.

Additionally,

(6v) Necessarily, if an entity completely resolves into a number of minimal parts none of which is adjacent to another, then no part of that entity is adjacent to any other part of that entity.

Also,

(6vi) Necessarily, if no part of an entity is adjacent to any other part of that entity, then the entity in question is not continuous.[29]

a unified whole. In the case at hand, it may be assumed that none of the gas particles inside or outside the balloon's rubber skin are joined or physically bonded with that skin in the way required for the skin and those gas particles to be parts of a single substance. Thus, we may assume that the balloon does not have any of the gas particles inside or outside the rubber skin as a part. In that case, our principle that the size of an entity is the sum of the sizes of its discrete proper parts implies that the size (volume) which the inflated sphere actually would have is the sum of the sizes of the discrete parts of the rubber which is stretched by the air inside the balloon into a spherical shape. Certainly, the sum of the sizes of these parts would be minuscule compared with the size (volume) of the corresponding solid sphere. Once again, a commonsense judgment would turn out to be mistaken.

29 A definition of 'x is composed of y and z' which Roderick Chisholm has formulated (following Whitehead) implies that if a continuum has points as parts, then that continuum is composed of (completely resolves into) those points. The definition is as follows: "(a) y is a part of x, (b) z is a part of x, (c) y is discrete from z, and (d) no part of x is discrete from both y and z." See Chisholm, "Scattered Objects," in On Metaphysics (Minneapolis: University of Minnesota Press, 1989), p. 91.

Given (6v) and (6vi), it is clear that those who hold the view that there are minimal spaces and times which are parts of spaces and times should (and in some cases do) hold the view that space and time are discontinuous. Richard Sorabji provides an illuminating discussion of several ancient philosophers who espoused this view. See his Time, Creation, and the Continuum. We cited one of these figures in n. 18. And in Appendix 2, we discuss at greater length issues concerning the metaphysical status of spatial and temporal continua and their constituents in the light of recent mathematical accounts.

Hence,

(6vii) Point-positions are not minimal parts of extended spaces, and instants are not minimal parts of temporal intervals.

In addition,

(6viii) Necessarily, if point-positions or instants are parts of spaces or times, respectively, then they are minimal parts of them.

Consequently,

(6ix) Point-positions are not parts of extended spaces and instants are not parts of temporal intervals.[30]

Our second argument, for this same conclusion, is as follows:

(7i) Necessarily, a limit belonging to an entity is not a part of that entity.

For example, an edge, corner, or surface of a table is not a part of a table, unlike a table top or the legs of a table.[31]

---

30 Since the parts of continua are not sizeless, it follows that their parts are extended. The extended parts of a continuum *are* adjacent to other such parts. Cf. Aristotle: "The *continuous* is a species of the contiguous; two things are called continuous when the limits of each, with which they touch and are kept together, become one and the same, so that plainly the continuous is found in the things out of which a unity naturally arises in virtue of their contact." *Complete Works of Aristotle,* 2:1688.

E.g., if there is a line of finite length, then the right half and the left half of the line are adjacent to one another, each of the quarters of the line is adjacent to another, each of the eighths to another, and so forth, *ad infinitum.* Thus, what makes a continuum continuous is the fact that each of its parts *is* adjacent to another. It is also a fact about a continuum that between any two points on the continuum, there is another. But this latter fact is necessarily equivalent to the former fact and, we believe, it is the fact that each of the parts of a continuum is adjacent to another which *explains* the fact that between any two points on a continuum there is another.

31 It might be alleged that intuition would allow that the boundary of a tennis court is *part* of it. E.g., if it is asked "What part of the court is that player on?" it may be answered "He's on the boundary." We respond that in the strict sense, the parts of a physical object are other physical objects or portions of physical stuff, and not limits. In the foregoing question and answer, 'part' is being used in a figurative sense. In particular, what the question really means is "Where on the court is that player?" – a question which does not presuppose that every location on the court is a part of it in the strict sense of 'part'. Note that when it is said that he is on the boundary, this does not imply that the player is *only* on the boundary of the court, since the court's boundary is one-dimensional and the player is of higher dimensionality. Furthermore, it appears to be necessarily the case that for any proper part, *y*, of a nonbasic physical object, *y*'s existence does not entail that there exists a nonbasic physical object which has *y* as a proper part. But if the boundary of the tennis court is a proper part of it, then the boundary's existence entails that there exists a nonbasic physical object of which that boundary is a proper part. Therefore, the boundary of the tennis court appears not to be a part of it.

(7ii) Point-positions and instants are limits, of extended places and durations, respectively.[32]

Therefore,

(7iii) Point-positions and instants cannot be parts of extended places and temporal intervals, respectively.[33]

Given the conclusion of the foregoing arguments, there cannot be an extended place or temporal interval unless there are also point-positions or instants. Since point-positions are places which are not parts of other, extended places, and since instants are times which are not parts of other, temporal intervals, there cannot be an extended place and no other place, or a temporal interval and no other time, except for its parts.

A third argument deals with limits in general. Here the argument is that while there could be just one limit *of a certain kind,* except for its parts, there could not be just *one limit,* except for its parts. For example, there could be just one *surface* except for its parts, say, if the universe were to consist of a single spherical fundamental particle. But in this case there would not be just one *limit* except for its parts. In our example, there would be not only the surface of the fundamental particle, but infinitely many point-limits, boundaries between the parts of the particle (e.g., between the right and left halves of the particle), and so forth. These point-limits, boundaries, and so forth, are not themselves parts of the original limit, that is, the surface of the spherical particle, which surface has no limits. If in the case of the single spherical particle there could not be just one limit except for its parts, then there could not in general be just one limit except for its parts. Hence, there could not be just one limit except for its parts.[34]

32 Notice that premise (7ii) implies that the level *C* categories, Time and Place, intersect (are coinstantiable) with the level *C* category, Limit. Thus, an instant is both a time and a limit, and a point-position is both a place and a limit. However, because there could be times and places which are not limits, e.g., temporal intervals and three-dimensional places in a three-dimensional space, and limits which are not times or places, e.g., surfaces and edges, the categories, Time and Place, are not equivalent to that of Limit.

33 It might be thought that our reason for saying that the limit of *x* is not a part of *x* is that the limit in question is not detachable from *x*. If that were the reason, then there would be a refutation of our argument for the conclusion that the limit of *x* is not a part of *x*, viz., that there could be nondetachable parts. For example, there could be a Democritean atom or places or times which have such parts. But the reason subject to this criticism is not ours. We simply find it intuitively plausible *a priori* that the limit of a thing is not a part of that thing.

34 The case of the surface of the single spherical particle provides another reason for our ascent to level *C* categories in our definition of substance. While there could be just one *surface* except for its parts, there could not be just one *limit* except for its parts. Thus, while surfaces *qua* surfaces are independent within their kind, surfaces *qua* limits are not independent within their kind.

Consequently, the level C categories of being a place, being a time, and being a limit do not satisfy clause (i) of (4D1). In addition, as far as we can see, there is no other level C category which is capable-of-having-an independent-instance and which could be instantiated by a place, a time, or a limit. Thus, (4D2) has the happy consequence that neither a place, nor a time, nor a limit could be a substance.[35]

VI. EVENTS

But of these incidents and occurrents here-after more.
J. Foxe *Actes and Monuments of these Latter and Perillous Dayes* III.
861 ([1563–1587] 1684)

An argument parallel to the one applied to places and times in the preceding section applies to (concrete) events provided that there could be events which are temporally extended. This is true because of the following two arguments. First, an event is what happens or occurs at a time. Given the density of time, if there is a temporally extended event, E, occurring at a temporal interval, T, then there must also be instantaneous events occurring in T, namely, instantaneous "slices" of E, which are beginnings or endings of either E or some event which is a temporally extended segment of E. Moreover, since time must be a dense continuum, any temporally extended event must be temporally continuous.[36] Therefore, for reasons

35 Notice that our argument in this section implies that there are at least four varieties of zero-dimensional entities. A *point-position*, or geometrical point, is a zero-dimensional place. Such a *concretum* is a limit of a one-dimensional place, i.e., a geometrical line. On the other hand, a *material-point* is a zero-dimensional limit of a piece or portion of material stuff, and may be either *articulated*, e.g., a corner of a material cube, or *unarticulated*, e.g., the centerpoint of a material sphere. Limits of these kinds are neither places nor substances. In contrast, a *point-particle* is neither a place nor a limit, but is a spatially located, zero-dimensional, substance which has causal powers. There are parallel distinctions for cases of *n*-dimensional entities, where *n* is any number of possible spatial dimensions. E.g., in the one-dimensional case there is a distinction between a geometrical line, an articulated edge of an object, an unarticulated boundary of a piece or portion of a material object with another piece or portion of that material object, and a one-dimensional string.

36 There are several possible objections to our claim that if time is a dense continuum, then any temporally extended event must be temporally continuous. First, consider the case where candle c burns for one minute, is extinguished for one second of time, and then resumes burning for an hour. It might be thought that there is a single event of the candle's burning which stretches over sixty-one minutes and one second. We reply that this is simply mistaken: there are two separate events of the candle's burning. There is a first such event, lasting for one minute, then one second during which there is no candle burning, and then there is a second event of the candle's burning. We hold the following

113

parallel to those provided with respect to point-positions and instants in our argument for (6ix) based upon (6i)–(6viii), the instantaneous events which fall within a temporally extended event cannot be parts of that event.

There is a second argument for this conclusion, which goes as follows. Necessarily, if an instantaneous event, *e,* is the beginning or end of a

principle, *EP:* necessarily, for any time, *t,* if there is an event of a candle's burning at *t,* then at *t* there is a candle which is burning at *t.* Since there is no candle which is burning during the second of time in question, it follows that there is no event of the candle burning at that time.

Next, suppose that there is a gap in time, i.e., time "stands still." (Recall that we understand the continuity of time to be "weak" continuity, which is compatible with such gaps. See Section V in this chapter.) Suppose further that a given candle is burning both before and after the gap. In other words, the supposition is that there is an interval when a candle is burning, followed by an interval when the same candle is burning, but there is no time between these intervals at which that candle is burning. In that case, is there an event of the candle's burning which spans the gap? We maintain that there is not. The principle, *EP,* cited earlier, implies that there is no event of the candle's burning which occurs both before and after the temporal gap. Hence, there is no event in the case described which is temporally discontinuous.

It might be objected that in the first example we discussed, there *is* one discontinuous event which occurs at the sixty-one minute and one second interval, namely, an event of the candle's burning intermittently. We are willing to allow that there is an event of the candle's burning intermittently which occurs over this interval of time. But we reject the claim that this event is discontinuous. Rather, we claim, it is a *continuous* event which occurs throughout the interval in question.

However, a referee for Cambridge University Press has suggested that the following kind of example may pose a problem for our claim that a temporally extended event must be continuous. "Suppose the marriage of Tom and Mary has to be interrupted for an hour owing to a fire-alert, and is then resumed. Surely there is just *one* marriage (an event) which takes place over an extended period, but surely, too, the marriage is *not* going on during the interval of the alert (or else it wouldn't be right to speak, as we do, of the marriage ceremony being *resumed*)." Our position with respect to such an example is that the putative event in question, i.e., the marriage ceremony, is not a genuine event at all, but rather a complex of events constructed according to certain arbitrary conventions. There are no hard and fast rules which in general govern such a conventional imposition of unity upon temporally separated episodes of a similar kind. Ontological parsimony favors the view that genuine events which occur other than at a single moment are temporally continuous. Our stance with respect to events parallels our earlier position (see Chapter 1, Sections II and III) in opposition to the existence of material substances whose parts have no principle of unity other than a conventionally imposed one.

In conclusion, given that time is a dense continuum, there are no good objections to our claim that any temporally extended event must be temporally continuous.

In any case, our analysis of substance can be defended independently of our claim that a temporally extended event must be temporally continuous. This is because even if there are temporally discontinuous events, there being an event, *e,* which exists throughout an interval of time entails that there is another (instantaneous) event which exists within that interval of time and which is not a part of *e.*

temporally extended event, e', then e is a limit of e'. Thus, for reasons parallel to those we gave in the preceding section with respect to places and times, namely, the argument we gave for (7iii) based upon (7i) and (7ii), an instantaneous event cannot be part of a temporally extended event.

Hence, there could not be a temporally extended event, E, occurring throughout an interval, T, unless there were other events in T that are not parts of E. Therefore, the category of being an event does not satisfy clause (i) of (4D1). And as in the case of places, times, and limits, an event fails to satisfy (4D2) because it is impossible for there to be an event that instantiates a level C category which satisfies clause (i) of (4D1).

On the other hand, if there could *only* be instantaneous events, then an event does not satisfy (4D2). This is because it would then not be possible for an event to instantiate a level C category, $C1$, which satisfies clause (i) of (4D1)'s requirement that it be possible for $C1$ to be instantiated by an entity *throughout an interval of time*.[37] Thus, (4D2) has the desirable consequence that such instantaneous events would not be substances.

It is plausible that either there could only be instantaneous events, or there could be both such events and ones that are temporally extended. In either case, the foregoing argument implies that (4D2) has the desired consequence that an event is not a substance.

VII. PRIVATIONS

To gyue substance to privation, (that is) beinge to noo beinge.
R. Eden *The Decades of the Newe Worlde or West India* 87 (1555 trans.)

> *Poor Shadow*
> Everything has a shadow –
> A mountain, a bird or a ball –
> Only a poor, poor shadow
> Hasn't a shadow at all!
> Ilo Orleans *I Watch the World Go By* (1961)

Much Adoe About Nothing.
Shakespeare (1599)

---

37 It should be noted that our analysis of substance is not stated in terms of a notion of bare independence, but rather in terms of an enriched notion of independence, viz., independence through an interval of time. (By an *interval* or *period* of time we mean a nonminimal time.) Because of this feature, our analysis has the desirable consequence that an insubstantial entity of an instantaneous sort, e.g., an instantaneous event, is not a substance, even if there being such an entity does not entail that there is any other entity.

Turning to the category of being a privation, we begin by arguing that this category satisfies clause (i) of (4D1). To show this, that is, to show that a privation is independent-within-its-kind, consider the possibility of there being but a single substance which is a torus, or doughnut-shaped material object, whose matter is continuous. This torus, we may suppose, is a true atom whose parts are undetachable. Since there is a torus, there is a privation, namely, a hole (which we call h). Clause (i) of (4D1) requires that it be possible for an instance of a category to be the only instance of that category (over an interval of time) except for its parts. In our imagined situation, h is the only privation except (possibly) for its parts. We conclude that it is possible for there to be a privation without there being any other privation except for its parts, and that the category of being a privation satisfies clause (i) of (4D1).

Clause (ii) of (4D1) requires of a category that its instantiation not entail the instantiation of a nonequivalent level C category by another entity that is independent-within-*its*-kind. For the sake of argument, assume that a substance is independent-within-its-kind: that the category of Substance satisfies clause (i) of (4D1). Does the existence of a privation entail the existence of a substance? If so, then the category of being a privation will not satisfy clause (ii) of (4D1). If there could be events (or tropes) without substances, as event (or trope) ontologists believe, then, there could be a privation without a substance. For example, there could be a silence which exists between two temporally separated noises. On the other hand, if there could not be an event or trope without a substance, then it seems that there could not be a privation without a substance. Thus, whether privations satisfy clause (ii) of (4D1) turns on further metaphysical questions of these kinds. We remain neutral about the answers to these questions.

In what follows, we shall argue that the level C category of being a privation does *not* satisfy clause (iii) of (4D1). To begin with, recall that clause (iii) of (4D1) requires that it be impossible for an entity of a level C category to have as a part an item which instantiates a nonequivalent level C category (other than a category equivalent to being a proper part). But it is possible for there to be a privation which has as a part an item that instantiates a nonequivalent category of this kind. To show this, we begin by analyzing the category of being a privation as follows:

(4D3) p is a privation =df. (i) p is concrete; (ii) p is an absence of a concrete entity or entities; (iii) either p is entirely extended between parts of a bounding concrete entity or p is entirely extended between bounding concrete entities.

For example, the hole in a doughnut is an absence of the sort of cake of which the doughnut is made. This hole is entirely extended between *parts* of the doughnut. Another example is the gap between Lauren Hutton's two front teeth. This gap is entirely extended between Lauren Hutton's two front teeth, for the gap does not extend below the bottom of her two front teeth.[38]

Consider a privation such as a hole in a bagel, or a silence between two temporally separated noises. It would seem that if a hole exists, then it has as a part each one of the extended places inside that hole. For instance, the hole has a certain volume of space as its right half, and another volume of space as its left half.

To this it might be objected that a hole does not have *places* as parts, but other privations. For example, it might be argued that the hole, *abcda*, depicted in Figure 4.1, has as parts the concavities, *abc* and *adc*. This may be

---

38 It might be thought that an example of a privation is the nonexistence of unicorns. We can only make sense of this entity if we understand it to be an *abstract* entity, i.e., a negative proposition or state of affairs, *that there are no unicorns*. Such an entity, being abstract, is, of course, not concrete, and hence fails to satisfy clause (i) of (4D3). Therefore, it is not a privation.

   In addition, as we have defined a privation, clause (iii) of (4D3) implies that an *unbounded* absence is not a privation. For example, a "silence," *s*, which is an absence of noise over the interval of time, *i*, and which is not bounded at either end of the interval by noises, is not, on our definition, a privation. We don't deny that one could define a category of concrete entity, say, Privation⋆, of which *s* is an instance, and which includes all unbounded concrete absences. Privation⋆ differs from Privation in at least this further way: Privation satisfies clause (i) of (4D1), while Privation⋆ does not. As previously, we assume that time and space are (weakly) dense. Now take our example of *s*. Since *s* is an unbounded temporally extended silence over the interval of time, *i*, at every instant within *i* there is an unbounded silence. Such a point-silence within *s* is not a part of *s*. (That a point-silence is not a part of *s* can be established by an argument which parallels our earlier argument that instantaneous events are not parts of extended events.) This point-silence is also a privation⋆. (Note, however, that if there is a bounded silence, a point-silence within it is *not* a bounded silence. This makes it possible for there to be just one silence, and hence, one privation.) As in the case of *s*, each instance of Privation⋆ cannot be the only privation⋆ except for its parts. There must always be either a temporal point-absence or a spatial point-absence in addition to the temporally or spatially extended (or in addition to the temporally or spatially unextended) privation⋆ with which one starts.

   Of course, Privation⋆, not satisfying clause (i) of (4D1), is not capable of having an independent instance, and hence its instances are not substances according to (4D2). This is a welcome consequence. In defining Privation by means of (4D3), we endeavored to capture the more intuitive notion of a privation. There are further notions of what a privation is, logically related in certain ways to the two notions we have already discussed. Some of the level *C* categories corresponding to these notions, like Privation⋆, fail to satisfy clause (i) of (4D1). And an argument like the one we give subsequently seems to imply that all of these categories fail to satisfy clause (iii) of (4D1).

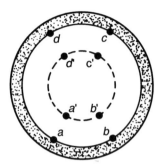

Figure 4.1

correct. But consider the place, $a'b'c'd'a'$, shown in Figure 4.1. This place is a part of *abcda*, but there is no entity which is coincident with $a'b'c'd'a'$ and which is a privation on our definition, since there is no bounded absence which is coincident with $a'b'c'd'a'$. Thus, while some of the parts of *abcda* may be privations, at least some of the other parts of *abcda* must be places and not privations.[39]

Similarly, it seems that if a silence exists between two temporally separated noises, then that silence has as a part each one of the temporal intervals between the noises, that is, the periods of time through which that silence endures. Since every such subinterval of the silence is not bounded by noises, and since (4D3) requires that a silence (or any other privation) be bounded by noises (or by something of a relevant sort), there is no silence, which is coincident with any such interval, and we may assume, no other privation which is coincident with some such subinterval. Hence, every silence has parts which are not privations.

These two examples illustrate the fact that it is possible for some privations to have places or times as parts. But the categories of being a place

---

39 Notice that our view that a hole in a bagel has places as parts implies that: first, when the bagel moves, the hole moves, but, second, when the hole moves, it must lose some or all of these places as parts. To this it may be objected that when a thing moves all of its parts can move with it. Our reply is twofold. First of all, it is true that if by a "thing" is meant a *substance*, then when a thing moves all of its parts can move with it. But, of course, a hole is *not* a thing in this sense, but rather a privation, an insubstantial entity. Second, although we are willing to concede the existence of holes for the purposes of our analysis, it must be admitted that holes are odd entities which are ontologically suspect. In our view, the fact that holes must change some of their parts whenever they move is one aspect of their strangeness.

and being a time are at level C and neither one of these categories is either equivalent to being a proper part or equivalent to being a privation. It follows that the level C category of being a privation does not satisfy clause (iii) of (4D1). Additionally, as far as we can tell, there is no other level C category which is capable-of-having-an-independent-instance and which could be instantiated by a privation. Hence, (4D2) has the desired consequence that a privation could not be a substance.

VIII. COLLECTIONS

> When many ideas of the same kind are joined together, and united in one name, or under one view, it is called a collective idea, so an army, or a parliament, is a collection of men.
> I. Watts *Logick: Or the Right Use of Reason in the Enquiry After Truth* I. iii.
> § 2 (1725)

> The great collective idea of all bodies whatsoever, signified by the name *world.*
> J. Locke *An Essay Concerning Human Understanding* II. xxiv (1690)

Next, let us consider the category of being a (concrete) collection. We begin by arguing that this category satisfies clause (i) of (4D1). It is possible for there to be a collection, *c,* and no other collection which is not a part of *c.* For example, given that there are two or more *concreta,* such a collection would be one which contained or had as a part every *concretum* which is not itself a collection. Such a "universal" collection would also have as a proper part every *concretum* except for itself.[40]

Does the category of being a collection satisfy clause (ii) of (4D1)? It seems that it does. To see why, consider a collection of events. First, such a collection would not have as a part any entity which was an instance of a category not equivalent to being a collection and which satisfies clause (i)

---

40 Unlike sets, which may have a single element, no collection can have but one proper part. E.g., if there is a single point-particle, there is not also a collection which has as its only proper part that point-particle. But for any two *concreta, x* and *y,* there is a third thing, *z,* which is the collection of *x* and *y,* and which has no proper parts which are not parts of either *x* or *y* (or both). Moreover, no collection can fail to have a noncollection as a part, and some formal collection or mereological theories designate the objects of this sort which have no proper parts, "atoms." Examples of the latter might be souls, point-particles, point-positions, or instants. Finally, of collections, as we conceive of them, it is true that no collection can have as proper parts two collections which have a common part which is itself a collection. Thus, a collection which has a finite number of atomic parts must have a finite number of parts overall. For an authoritative discussion of the principles of formal mereological systems, see Peter Simons, *Parts: A Study in Ontology* (Oxford: Oxford University Press, 1987).

of (4D1). Second, for the sake of ontological neutrality we have allowed that there could be events without substances. Third, there could be events without privations.[41] Fourth, as we have seen, none of the other categories on L satisfy clause (i) of (4D1). Hence, it seems that the existence of a collection of events does not entail the existence of an instance of a none-quivalent category which satisfies clause (i) of (4D1), and being a collection seems to satisfy clause (ii) of (4D2).

We will now argue that this level C category fails to satisfy clause (iii) of (4D1). This clause of (4D1) requires that it be impossible for an entity of a level C category to have as a part an item which instantiates a none-quivalent level C category (other than being a proper part). However, a member of a collection is a part of that collection, and it is possible for some collections to have as members items which instantiate a level C category that is equivalent neither to being a proper part nor to the category of being a collection, for example, items such as substances, events, times, and places. Hence, the level C category of being a collection does not satisfy clause (iii) of (4D1). Moreover, as far as we can tell, there is no other level C category which is capable-of-having-an-independent-instance and which could be instantiated by a collection. Therefore, (4D2) has the intuitively plausible consequence that a collection could not be a substance.

IX. SUBSTANCE

substantive, . . . that stands of or by itself; independent, self-existent, self-sufficient.

Oxford English Dictionary (1971)

substance, a being that subsists by itself, a separate or distinct thing.

Oxford English Dictionary (1971)

We are now prepared to discuss the category of being a substance. This level C category appears to satisfy clause (i) of (4D1) because it seems possible that there be a substance, x, which exists throughout some interval of time, t, without any other substance existing in t – except for any parts that x has in t. For example, there could exist throughout t a material object, x, when no substance other than x exists except for any parts that x

---

41 E.g., our collection could be a collection of events which constitute a single, continuous process over a certain period of time, and those events could be the only events that ever occur.

has in t.[42] Also, there could exist throughout t a soul, when no other substance exists.[43]

Moreover, the following line of reasoning shows that the category of Substance also satisfies clause (ii) of (4D1). First of all, it may be supposed that if there is a substance, then this entails that there are in addition entities of one or more of the following other kinds: properties, or times, or concrete occurrences, or propositions, or places, or limits.[44] However, as

42 We would argue that, possibly, during an interval of time, t, there exists a divisible material substance, x, and no other substance except for x's parts. In addition, we have the intuition that, possibly, during an interval of time, t, there exists, in space (as opposed to space-time), an indivisible physical substance and no other substance, e.g., just one point-particle, or just one spatially extended material atom. An atom of the latter sort lacks substantial proper parts and cannot undergo mereological change. However, it might be objected that, necessarily, if such an atom, a, exists throughout t, then during t a con-stitutes another physical substance, o, which is spatially coincident with a at t and which can undergo mereological change. In reply, we will argue that atom a could not constitute a "supervenient" physical substance of this kind, such as a pebble, a snowball, or the like. First of all, there could be such a physical object o only if, possibly, o is constituted by a at t (implying that during t o lacks substantial proper parts) and at a time t' later than t, o is constituted by a material substance which has a and another physical thing as proper parts (implying that at t' o has substantial proper parts). However, since lacking substantial proper parts is the sort of characteristic which is a fundamental intrinsic feature of whatever has it (where an intrinsic feature is fundamental if a thing's having that feature cannot be explained in terms of the thing's parts), it is intuitively plausible that lacking substantial proper parts must be an essential feature of whatever has it. Other such characteristics which must be essential to whatever has them include simplicity and complexity. (Notice that a dualism of supervenient physical substances and constituting material things also implies the possibility of entities which have nontrivial essential characteristics, e.g., a pebble that is essentially small, and a snowball that is essentially roundish.) Accordingly, we take the following principle to be a necessary truth. If there is a substance, x, which lacks substantial proper parts, then x is necessarily such that it lacks substantial proper parts. Yet, as we have seen, if atom a could constitute a supervenient substance o, then, possibly, o lacks substantial proper parts at one time, but *not* at another time. Hence, a could not constitute an object such as o.

43 Spinoza defines a substance as "that which is in itself, and is conceived through itself: in other words, that of which a conception can be formed independently of any other conception" (*Ethics,* part 1, definition 3). Spinoza understands this definition of sub-stance, together with his other definitions and axioms, to imply that necessarily, there is one and only one substance. Thus, our analysis of substance is compatible with Spinoza's ontology of substance, but our analysis, unlike his theory of substance, is compatible with a plurality of substances. This difference illustrates one aspect of the ontological neutrality of our approach.

Another aspect of this ontological neutrality is that our claim that the category of Substance satisfies clause (i) of (4D1) is compatible with the view that every human being is necessarily such that he originated from certain other *temporally prior* substances, i.e., a certain sperm and egg.

44 However, there being a substance does *not* entail that there is a privation. But, there being a torus *does* entail this. This contrast is indicative of how (4D1) provides the solution we promised to the problem of existential entailments, in this case in terms of the distinction

we have argued, the level C categories that these other entities instantiate do not satisfy clause (i) of (4D1). We contend that any level C category the instantiation of which is entailed by the instantiation of the category of being a substance is either not a level C category that satisfies clause (i) of (4D1), or else is equivalent to the level C category of being a substance. It follows that the category of being a substance satisfies clause (ii) of (4D1), a clause requiring the possibility of a level C category being instantiated without there existing an entity of a nonequivalent level C category that satisfies clause (i) of (4D1).

Finally, the category of Substance satisfies clause (iii) of (4D1). To see this, consider that this clause requires that it be impossible for an entity which is an instance of a category, $C1$, to have a part that instantiates a level C category (other than a category equivalent to being a proper part) not equivalent to $C1$. So, let $C1$ = being a substance. Is it possible for a substance to have a part that instantiates a level C category (other than a category equivalent to being a proper part) not equivalent to Substance? For example, is it possible for a material thing or a spirit to have as a part either an event, a property, a time, a place, a privation, or a limit, or a proposition? Clearly not, since a part of a material substance could only be a material substance or a portion of matter, and a spirit is a simple.[45] And in

between x *qua* substance and x *qua* torus. Note that if a putative analysis, (4D1#), of the concept of a category which is capable-of-having-an-independent-instance#, was stated in terms of all kinds of beings rather than just in terms of level C categories, then the analysis would fail. E.g., being a torus is a kind of substance, yet because the instantiation of being a torus entails the instantiation of being a hole (a level D category which is subsumed by the level C category of being a privation), being a torus would not satisfy clause (ii) of (4D1#), where clause (ii) of (4D1#) is identical with clause (ii) of (4D1), except for the difference indicated in the range of the category variable. I.e., clause (ii) of (4D1#) would require that the instantiation of a certain kind does not entail the instantiation of a nonequivalent kind by another entity which is independent-within-its-kind (in the relevant sense). Since the category of being a hole could have just one instance (the universe could contain nothing but a single torus composed of continuous matter), the category of being a hole is in the relevant sense independent-within-its-kind. Hence, being a torus would not count as a category which is capable-of-having-an-independent-instance#, even though a torus is a substance. And for that reason, (4D2#), the parallel to (4D2) which would pair with (4D1#) and provide the analysis of the concept of substance as that which is an instance of a category which is capable-of-having-an-independent-instance#, would falsely imply that a torus is not a substance.

45 A substance can have an entity of another (level C) kind as a part only if a substance is reducible to or identifiable with an entity of that kind or a collection of such. Since we have shown that a substance is *not* reducible to or identifiable with an entity of another kind or ontological category, we conclude that a substance cannot have as a part an entity of another (level C) kind. Arguments supporting the proposition that a substance is not reducible to or identifiable with an entity of another kind or ontological category may be

general, a part of a physical substance could only be a physical substance or a portion of physical stuff. Hence, it appears to be impossible for a substance to have a part that instantiates a level C category (other than a category equivalent to being a proper part) not equivalent to Substance. Thus, the category of Substance seems to satisfy clause (iii) of (4D1).

Since the category of Substance satisfies (4D1), this category is capable-of-having-an-independent-instance. Thus, an instance of this category, namely, a particular individual substance, must satisfy (4D2), our analysis of substance.

As we have seen, the category of Substance satisfies clause (i) of (4D1). However, clause (ii) of (4D1) requires that a category at level C could be instantiated even if there did not exist an entity of a nonequivalent category at level C that satisfies clause (i) of (4D1). Therefore, if the instantiation, by an entity, x, of a level C category, $C1$, not equivalent to Substance, entails the instantiation of the category of Substance, then $C1$ fails to meet clause (ii) of (4D1). Thus, $C1$ is not capable-of-having-an-independent-instance. And if there is no other level C category which is capable-of-having-an-independent-instance and which x instantiates, (4D2) implies that x is not a substance. An Aristotelean would argue that the instantiation of *any* level C category not equivalent to Substance entails the instantiation of the category of Substance. For example, an Aristotelean would argue that necessarily, there is a place only if there are substances which stand in spatial relations to one another; necessarily, there is a time or an event only if there is a substance which undergoes change; necessarily, there is a property or a trope only if there is a substance which exemplifies or possesses a first-order property or trope; necessarily, there is a privation only if there is a *concretum* of a certain kind which bounds that privation, and there being a *concretum* of that kind entails the existence of a substance; necessarily, there is a collection or limit only if there is a *concretum* of a certain kind which is collected or limited, and there being a *concretum* of that kind entails the existence of a substance; and so forth. Such an Aristotelean argument implies that every level C category instantiated by a nonsubstance fails to satisfy clause (ii) of (4D1), and hence that any nonsubstance fails to satisfy (4D2). Although an argument of this kind lends further support to our analysis of substance, and has some

found in Chapter 1, Section I, where we argue that a substance cannot be identified with either a property, an event, a privation, a limit, a place, or a time; in Chapter 1, Section III, where we present certain intuitive data for an analysis of the intuitive notion of an individual substance which prove to be incompatible with a collectionist analysis of this intuitive notion; and in Chapter 3, where we demonstrate this incompatibility.

123

attractions, we do not need or want to appeal to it. Still, it is arguable that at least *some* categories of concrete entities other than Substance could not be instantiated unless the category of Substance were instantiated, for example, being an event, being a trope, and being a privation. Thus, it is arguable that entities of these categories are not substances because of the failure of these categories to satisfy clause (ii) of (4D1).[46] We turn next to our simplified, second analysis of substance.

X. A SECOND SOLUTION AND ITS DEFENSE

Substance is the oldest topic of philosophical inquiry and it is also one of the most entangled.

Anthony Quinton *The Nature of Things* 3 (1973)

The analysis of substance which we have already defended did not seem to assume that it was possible for there to be a substance having no other substance as a part, a substance such as a soul, point-particle, or Democritean atom. We avoided requiring this assumption in order to be as uncommitted as we could, consistent with our basic understanding of the nature of substance. Our not insisting upon this possibility led us to argue that, necessarily, space and time are dense continua. Given that space and time are dense continua, the defense of our analysis required us to argue that the unextended "constituents" of extended entities are not parts of those extended entities. Thus, we argued that point-positions, instants, and instantaneous events are not parts of extended places, times, and events, respectively. Moreover, we were led to argue that there cannot be a single property or trope, except for its logical parts. This argument asserted that if there is a property or trope, then there must be an infinite hierarchy of properties or tropes of higher orders, and that properties or tropes of a

46 We hesitate to insist that events, tropes, and privations depend upon substances for the following reasons. First, some philosophers have held event or trope ontologies, according to which there are events but no substances (e.g., Alfred North Whitehead, *Process and Reality* [Toronto: Collier-Macmillan, 1969]) or tropes without substances. Other philosophers, such as Aristotle, have argued that one cannot conceive of a change without a subject of change. However, we hold that our conceptions of ontological categories are suggested to us by our experiences. Since some of our experiences of events (e.g., seeing a flash of lightning) are not experiences of a substance or any other subject undergoing change, the existence of such events seems to be conceivable. For this second reason we do not insist on ruling out the possibility of events without substances. Of course, one might hold that a flash of lightning does in fact involve substances undergoing change, viz., charged particles in motion. However, it is the *possibility* of there being events without substances which is at issue here. Finally, if there could be events without substances, then there could be privations without substances, as we have already argued.

lower order cannot be logical parts of properties or tropes of a higher order.

Although we remain confident that all of these arguments are sound, some of their premises are controversial, and some are highly controversial. For that reason, all other things being equal, an analysis of substance which does not rely on such arguments is preferable. On the assumption that we declined to require earlier, that there could be a substance which has no other substance as a part, a simpler analysis of substance *can* be formulated and defended which does not need for its defense all of the arguments just listed. Moreover, the assumption in question is, in our view, a highly plausible one, which a great many philosophers would be prepared to concede.

Once we have our second, simplified analysis in hand, we will reexamine the various categories at level C in the context of the revised analysis. As will become clear, our defense of the revised analysis does not require our commitment to at least two of the controversial propositions to which we subscribed in defending (4D1) and (4D2): that the unextended constituents of extended entities are not parts of those extended entities, and that if there are properties (or tropes), then there is an infinite totality of them which is isomorphic to the infinite totality of numbers or sets posited by mathematics or set theory. Furthermore, our argument for saying that places, times, limits, and events are nonsubstantial entities according to the revised analysis, will *not* imply that necessarily, space and time are dense continua, unlike our earlier argument for saying that places, times, limits, and events are nonsubstantial entities according to (4D1) and (4D2).

Thus, we begin by making the simplifying assumption that it is possible that there is a substance that has no other substance as a part, for instance, either a spirit, or a voluminous material atom, or a Boscovichian point-particle. Given this assumption, (4D1) can be simplified by deleting the phrase, 'in t, y is not a part of x', from clause (i) of (4D1). It is obvious why a soul or point-particle has no other substance as a part: since they are *concreta* which lack spatial extension, they have no parts at all. On the other hand, atoms are voluminous and (hence) spatially extended. Thus, their not having a substance as a part calls for some explanation. First, by an *atom* we mean a material substance which has volume and which is necessarily indivisible. Second, because an atom is voluminous, it has parts. Thus, what we maintain is that the parts of an atom are not substances. Unlike typical complex material objects, which depend upon their parts, but whose parts do not depend upon them, an atom is such that it depends upon its parts and its parts depend upon it. That is, neither can exist without the other. This fact about atoms is a consequence of their metaphysical indivisibility, which entails the impossibility of the parts of an atom existing apart from the atom. Thus, assuming that there could be a contingently existing atom, a, and p is a proper part of a, p could not exist independently of all other contingent substances which are neither proper parts of p nor temporally prior substances that played a role in the production of p: for p cannot exist independently of a, and a is a contingent substance which is neither a proper part of p nor a temporally prior substance that played a role in the production of p. Intuitively, if an entity, e, cannot exist independently of all contingent substances which are other than e and e's proper parts, and other than temporally prior substances which played a role in e's production, then e is not a substance.[47] Hence, it is plausible that the parts of an atom are not substances.[48] It is for this reason that we think that the possibility of there being a single atom and no other substance which is not a part of that atom is, in fact, the possibility of there being a single substance.

The simplified version of (4D1), which we call (4D1$\star$), would consist of the following first clause:

$\Diamond$ [there is a temporal interval t and an x such that x instantiates C1 throughout t and $(\forall y)$ (in t y instantiates C1 $\rightarrow$ $y = x$)],

---

47 Thus, we allow for the following two possibilities: first, that an extended nonatomic substance is dependent upon other substances which are its parts; and, second, that a substance, for instance, a human being, is dependent upon certain other temporally prior substances which played a role in its production, e.g., a certain sperm and egg.

48 If the proper parts of an atom are not substances, then what are they? They are not times, places, events, privations, abstract entities, or tropes. Indeed, they are not instances of any level C category so far admitted. It would seem that these entities are in fact instances of a level C category of *being a concrete proper part*. This category seems to intersect all other level C categories of *concreta* so far mentioned, but is not equivalent to any of them. In fact, this category is not equivalent to any conjunction of the intersections of Concrete Proper Part with the other aforementioned level C categories: for, as we have seen, the proper parts of atoms are not instances of any of those other categories. A further question is this: does the category of being a concrete proper part satisfy clause (i) of (4D1)? It does not. Clearly, there cannot be just one concrete proper part except for its parts: by definition, the existence of a concrete proper part of something implies the existence of at least one other concrete proper part which is not a part of it. Since the category of being a concrete proper part does not satisfy (4D1), it fails to satisfy (4D2), and (4D2) implies, correctly, that a concrete proper part, *qua* concrete proper part, is not a substance. This is compatible, as we have indicated, with there being *some* concrete proper parts which are substances, viz., the detachable parts of substances. Readers can see for themselves, by the same reasoning, that the category of being a concrete proper part does not satisfy the simplified analysis of being capable of having an independent instance which we will now provide in the text.

and a second and third clause which would be identical in wording with clauses (ii) and (iii) of (4D1). Thus, the entire definition (4D1*), and its companion (4D2*) corresponding to (4D2), will read as follows.

(4D1*) A level C category C1 is *capable-of-having-an-independent-instance** =df. (i) $\Diamond$ [there is a temporal interval t and an x such that x instantiates C1 throughout t & ($\forall y$) (in t y instantiates C1 $\rightarrow$ $y = x$)], & (ii) $\Diamond$ ($\exists z$) [(z instantiates C1) & ~ ($\exists x$) (x instantiates a level C category, C2, which satisfies (i) and which is not equivalent to C1)], & (iii) ~ $\Diamond$ ($\exists x$) ($\exists y$) ((x instantiates C1) & (y is a part of x) & (y instantiates a level C category (other than a category equivalent to being a proper part) that is not equivalent to C1)).

(4D2*) x is a substance =df. x instantiates a level C category which is capable-of-having-an-independent-instance*.

(4D1*) has certain advantages. In particular, clause (i) of (4D1*) expresses a simplified sense of an entity's being *independent-within-its-kind*. And as a result, fewer assumptions are needed in the case of (4D1*) than in the case of (4D1) to show that properties, relations, propositions, tropes, times, places, limits, and events do not satisfy clause (i).

Note that according to (4D2*), an entity, x (regardless of whether x is simple or complex), is a substance in virtue of x's instantiating a level C category which is capable-of-having-an-independent-instance*. In this section we try to show that Substance is the only such level C category.

Our earlier argument that the category of being a property does not satisfy clause (i) of (4D1) was complicated by the possibility of infinitely large, logically complex properties. This argument aimed to show that no such property could include all other properties as parts. This earlier argument is no longer needed in order to show that the category of being a property does not satisfy the simplified clause (i) of (4D1*). In order to establish the latter conclusion, all that we need to show is that there could not be just one property. Recall the distinction we made in our defense of (4D2) between the more platonistic theory of the existence conditions of properties and the causal theory of the existence conditions of properties. In defending (4D2), we assumed the former theory, but in defending (4D2*), we shall argue that on either theory properties do not satisfy (4D2*).

On the more platonistic theory, because of the many logical entailments of any property, it is easy to show that there could not be just one property. For example, necessarily, if there is the property of being a human, then there are other properties, for instance, the property of being a primate, the property of being a mammal, and so forth. Moreover, necessarily, if there is

127

the property of being a human, then there is another (higher-order) property, for example, the property of being a property, and so on. An argument of the same kind applies to any property whatsoever and implies that there could not be just one property. Parallel arguments apply to other categories of *abstracta*, such as Relation, Proposition, and Set, and lead to the conclusion that there cannot be an entity of such a sort which is the only entity of that sort. In particular, if there is a relation, R_1, then there must be another relation, R_2, such that R_1's instantiation necessitates R_2's instantiation; if there is a proposition, P_1, then there must be another proposition, P_2, such that either P_1 necessitates P_2 or P_1 necessitates the negation of P_2; and if there is a set, then there must be at least two sets, namely, the null set and the null set's singleton. Inasmuch as none of these various general categories of *abstracta* at level C of generality satisfies (4D1$\star$), none of these categories of *abstracta* is capable-of-having-an-independent-instance$\star$. Moreover, as far as we can tell, there is no other level C category which is capable-of-having-an-independent-instance$\star$ and which could be instantiated by an *abstractum* of any of these kinds. Thus, (4D2$\star$) implies, as it ought to, that neither a property, nor a relation, nor a proposition, nor a set could be a substance.

On the causal theory of the existence conditions of properties, the existence of any property, P, entails that an instance of P, i, figures in some causal relationship, so that i figures in a causal relatum r. Supposing that P figures in some causal relationship, there must be another property, $P\star$, an instance of which, $i\star$, figures in a causal relatum, s, which is either a cause of r or an effect of r. Evidently, every causal relationship must involve a cause and an effect which differ in their attributes. Hence, on the causal theory of properties, there could not be just one property.

Turning our attention to *concreta*, our earlier argument that the category of being a trope does not satisfy clause (i) of (4D1) was also complicated by the possibility of indefinitely large, complex tropes. This argument about tropes, like the argument about properties, aimed to show that no such trope could include all other tropes as parts. Once again, this earlier argument is no longer needed in order to show that the category of being a trope does not satisfy the simplified clause (i) of (4D1$\star$). In order to establish the latter conclusion, all that we need to show is that there could not be just one trope.

Once again, we distinguish between the more and less generous theories of the existence conditions of tropes. When we defended (4D2), we assumed that there must be infinitely many tropes, as many as there are numbers, but in defending (4D2$\star$), we will argue that on either the more generous assumption that there must be an infinite number of tropes, or the less generous one that the existence conditions for tropes are causal in nature, tropes do not satisfy (4D2*).

On the more generous theory, because of the many necessary connections between tropes, it is easy to demonstrate that there could not be just one trope. For example, necessarily, if there is a particular humanity (say, the particular humanity of Socrates), then there are other tropes, for instance, a particular primateness, a particular mammality, and so forth. Moreover, necessarily, if there is a particular humanity (of Socrates), then there is another (higher-order) trope, for example, a particular tropehood (of the particular humanity of Socrates), and so on.

On the causal theory of the existence of tropes, an argument parallel to the one just given with respect to properties on a causal theory of the existence conditions of properties implies that there could not be just one trope.

Since if there is a trope, T1, then there must be another trope, T2, the level C category of being a trope does not satisfy clause (i) of (4D1*). Furthermore, it would seem that there is no other level C category which is capable-of-having-an-independent-instance* and which could be instantiated by a trope. Thus, (4D2*) has the welcome consequence that a trope could not be a substance.

An overall assessment of the status of our second account of substance vis-à-vis properties and tropes is now in order. We have distinguished causal views of properties (tropes) from more platonistic or generous views of properties (tropes). On the former views, empirical science alone provides a rationale for the existence of properties or tropes; whereas on the latter views, *a priori* sciences such as logic and mathematics provide such a rationale. Observe that it is highly plausible that if there are properties (tropes), then either the causal view of properties (tropes) or the more generous view of properties (tropes) is correct, the latter view of properties being itself neutral on the question of whether there are unexemplified properties. Since our second account of substance, (4D1*) and (4D2*), gives the correct verdict on the status of properties and tropes on either the causal or the more generous view of properties or tropes, namely, that properties and tropes are not substances, it is highly plausible that our second account of substance gives the correct verdict on the status of properties and tropes.

Our earlier discussion of certain other categories of *concreta,* namely, Place and Time, occurred in the context of (4D1). There we aimed to show that such categories did not satisfy clause (i) of (4D1), and our argument rested upon an assumption, that, necessarily, if space and time exist, then they are dense continua which contain minimum or zero-dimensional points or instants, and on a lemma, whose conclusion is that, necessarily, such minimum entities are not parts of extended places or times. This assumption and this lemma are no longer needed in order to show that the categories of being a place and being a time do not satisfy the simplified clause (i) of (4D1*), a clause which requires that a level C category could have but a single instance throughout a temporal interval (a nonminimal time). The categories of Place and Time fail to satisfy clause (i) of (4D1*) if there could not be just one place or time.

On the assumption that, necessarily, if space and time exist, then they are dense continua, it is obvious that there could not be just one place or just one time. Nevertheless, even granting the possibility of discontinuous space and time, (4D1*) and (4D2*) are adequate to their task. There are two arguments in favor of this conclusion.

To set up the first argument, let us ask the following question. If it is possible that space and time are not continuous, then could there be but *one* minimum place or time?[49] Necessarily, if space exists, then it is either relational or absolute; and likewise for time.[50] If space and time are relational, which seems to be the majority view these days, then given one minimum place or time, there must be other places or times. This is true for the following reasons. First of all, necessarily, there is relational space only if there are at least two (noncoincident) spatial entities which are spatially related to one another; and necessarily, there is relational time only if there are at least two (nonsimultaneous) occurrences which are

---

49 Obviously, if a place or time is not atomic, then it will have parts which are places or times, and there will not be just one place or time.

50 It was shown earlier that relational space and time cannot arise from zero-dimensional entities which are sizeless. Therefore, in order for there to be relational space or time, either there must be at least one spatial entity which has *intrinsic spatial extension* and which occupies some place, or there must be at least one event which has *intrinsic temporal extension* and which lasts for some time, respectively. On the other hand, it seems that given a relational conception of space or time, the existence of even one such spatially extended entity which occupies some place, or the existence of even one such temporally extended entity which lasts for some time, is logically sufficient for there being relational space or time. In that case, it appears that the spatially or temporally extended entity in question has indefinitely many proper parts which have intrinsic spatial or temporal extension, and space or time arises out of spatial or temporal relations between these spatially or temporally extended parts. Thus, it seems that on relational theories of space and time, space would not exist without such spatially extended entities, and time would not exist without such temporally extended entities. In contrast, an absolute theory of space and time implies that space and time would exist even if there were not spatially or temporally extended entities, e.g., no material objects and no events.

temporally related to one another. However, there being at least two such spatial entities entails that there are at least two places, and there being at least two such occurrences entails that there are at least two times. It follows that it is impossible for there to be a relational space or time which consists of just a single minimum place or time. And more generally, we conclude that there cannot be a relational space or time consisting of only one place or time.

On the other hand, suppose that space and time are absolute. In this case, could there be just one minimal place or time? An absolute minimal place or time, existing without any other place or time existing, strikes us as a most peculiar entity. Thus, we don't give much credence to the possibility of there being just one absolute minimal place or time.[51] Moreover, if there could be *just one* minimal place or time, *m,* of an *absolute* nature, then *m* would be a space or time whose existence is *independent* of the existence of any substance and *independent* of the existence of any other place or time. But given the unique independence intuitively possessed only by a substance, we are inclined to think that the independent entities which are alleged to be minimal absolute *places* or *times* have enough of the characteristics of *substances* to make it more plausible that they are substances of some very peculiar sort than that they are places or times. For these reasons, we find it reasonable to deny the possibility of an absolute space or time consisting of only one minimal place or time.

However, our argument that the entities described as independent minimal absolute places and times in the preceding paragraph are more plausibly categorized as very peculiar substances than as places or times might be rejected on the ground that it is question-begging. It might be said that this argument attempts to support our conclusion that there cannot be an absolute space or time consisting of only one minimal place or time by appealing to the idea that there is a unique independence intuitively possessed only by a substance. But our critic could maintain that this idea is mistaken if there can be such an absolute space or time. Whatever the verdict on this dispute, we have a second, more decisive, argument which demonstrates that there cannot be just one place, or just one time, and

---

51 We remind the reader that our goal in this chapter was to "provide an analysis of substance which is ontologically neutral in the sense that it is compatible with the existence of entities belonging to any intelligible categories, given some *plausible* [new emphasis] view about the natures, existence conditions, and interrelationships of entities belonging to those categories." We claim that the view that there could be discontinuous space and time is not a plausible view about the natures, existence conditions, and interrelationships of spaces or times. Even less plausible in these respects is the claim that there could be a single minimal extended absolute place or time.

which is compatible with space and time being discontinuous. It goes as follows.

The notions of time and change are logically interrelated, as are the notions of space and motion. Specifically, each of the following four propositions is a conceptual or a necessary truth: (8i) for any e, if e is a change, then e occurs in time; (8ii) for any x, if x moves, then x's motion occurs in space; (8iii) if time exists, then time allows for the occurrence of change within it (in other words, if time exists, then time has an intrinsic structure which is compatible with the occurrence of change); and (8iv) if space exists, then space allows something to move within it (i.e., if space exists, then space has an intrinsic structure which is compatible with the occurrence of motion). However, necessarily, time allows for the occurrence of change within it only if there are at least *two* times. This is because, necessarily, change occurs only if there are two times t_1 and t_2 such that either something exists at t_1 which does not exist at t_2, or something exists at t_2 which does not exist at t_1, or something has a certain feature at t_1, but lacks that feature at t_2, or something lacks a certain feature at t_1, but has that feature at t_2. Furthermore, necessarily, space allows something to move within it only if there are at least *two* places. This is because necessarily, an entity, x, moves only if there is a temporal interval, t, and two places, p_1 and p_2, such that: x (or a proper part of x) occupies p_1 at the start of t, and x (or a proper part of x) occupies p_2 at the end of t.[52] Hence, it is impossible for there to be just one time, and it is impossible for there to be just one place.

If we turn to the category of being a limit, the following line of reasoning establishes that the existence of a limit is incompatible with the discontinuity of space and time. A limit, for instance, a surface, a point-limit, or a beginning, is a boundary of an extended entity which has at least one more

52 Notice that necessarily, if an object, x, moves in a linear fashion, then x moves from one place to another. On the other hand, it is possible for an object, x, to move without x moving from one place to another. E.g., this would occur if x is a sphere which rotates on its own axis. However, in any such case, there must be a *proper part* of x which moves from one place to another, e.g., one hemisphere of x. Thus, necessarily, if an object, x, moves and x does not have a proper part, i.e., x is a moving point-particle, then x moves from one place to another.

On a proper understanding of what is meant by an atomic or minimal place, the following principle should be affirmed: necessarily, no minimal place is only *partly* occupied by an entity. (See n. 16.) Thus, there cannot be rotational motion in a single, minimum extended place. For if there were such a motion, then, as noted already, a proper part of the rotating object would first occupy only part of the place in question, and then only another part of the place. To put this point another way, the existence of minimal places implies that motions have a minimal size equal to the size of a minimal place. Rotational motion within a single minimal extended place involves angular motions whose sizes are smaller than the size of that minimal place.

dimension than the limit in question. But, necessarily, if space and time are discontinuous, then there are no such boundaries: there are minimal spatial and temporal entities without any spatial or temporal entities between them, and these minimal spatial and temporal entities do not bound any spatial or temporal entities.

If the minimal temporal or spatial entities are unextended, then, obviously, these entities do not have boundaries. And even if they are extended, it follows (paradoxically) that they do not have boundaries. Suppose the extended minimal entities in question are spaces or times. Paradoxically, such extended places or times are not bounded, since if they were bounded, there would be places or times, namely, the boundaries in question, which are smaller than the extended places and times with which we began.[53] Alternatively, suppose the minimal entities in question are extended substances or events. In that case, given the assumption that space and time are discontinuous, there are minimal places or times which the minimal substances or events occupy. Now suppose that a minimal substance or event has a spatial or temporal boundary, respectively. It follows on this assumption that there is a minimal space or time. This minimal place or time corresponds to the boundary of the minimal extended substance or event, and this minimal place or time is the boundary of the extended minimal place or time which is occupied by the substance or event in question. This contradicts the conclusion of our earlier argument that minimal extended places and times cannot have boundaries. Consequently, there being a limit is incompatible with space and time being discontinuous.

We are now positioned to argue that there cannot be just one limit. The foregoing argument implies that if there is a place or a time which is a limit, then space and time are continuous. It follows that if there is a place or time which is a limit, then there are infinitely many other such limits. For example, if there is an instant (a time which is a limit), then there must be infinitely many other instants; and if there is a point-position (a place which is a limit), then there must be infinitely many other point-positions.

But there could be a limit which is not a time or place, for example, a surface, edge, corner, beginning of a process, or ending of a process. We shall now argue that there cannot be just one limit which is not a time or place. This argument will apply not only to limits which are not places or times, but also to those which are. Thus, this second line of reasoning will

---

53 The paradoxical nature of the conclusion that extended minimal places and times do not have boundaries is not unexpected: we argued earlier that such entities are impossible.

imply, independently of the preceding argument, that there could not be just one limit.

Our first premise is that necessarily, if L is a limit of dimension, n, then there is an extended entity, e, of dimension $n + 1$, such that L is a limit of e. For example, if there is a zero-dimensional corner, there must be a one-dimensional edge whose end point it is; if there is a one-dimensional edge, there must be a two-dimensional surface whose edge it is; and if there is a two-dimensional surface, then there must be a three-dimensional object whose surface it is.[54] Our second premise is that necessarily, whatever is extended has extended proper parts. Therefore, necessarily, if there is a limit, L, then there is an extended entity, e, of which L is a limit, and e has infinitely many extended proper parts, for instance, halves, quarters, eighths, and so on, which have boundaries with adjacent extended proper parts of e. Since these boundaries are limits, the existence of L entails that there are infinitely many limits. Hence, there cannot be just one limit.

The foregoing simplified arguments show that Place, Time, and Limit are all such that they cannot have just one instance. Therefore, the level C categories of Place, Time, and Limit do not satisfy clause (i) of (4D1★). In addition, as far as we can tell, there is no other level C category which is capable-of-having-an-independent-instance★ and could be instantiated by a place, a time, or a limit. Thus (4D2★) has the happy consequence that neither a place, nor a time, nor a limit could be a substance.

Finally, we consider the level C category of (concrete) Event in the light of (4D1★) and (4D2★). Here we assume that either there could only be events that are of some minimal temporal length, for example, instantaneous events, or there could be both such events and ones that occur at a temporal interval (i.e., a nonminimal time). If events could only be of some minimal temporal length, then any level C category which could be instantiated by an event does not satisfy clause (i) of (4D1★) because of that clause's requirement that a level C category be capable of having an instance which exists throughout an interval of time. Thus, (4D2★) has the desirable consequence that such events of a minimal temporal length would not be substances.

54 It is necessarily true that a corner, edge, or surface is a limit of some entity, and necessarily true that if L is a limit of some entity, x, then L has fewer dimensions than x. Consequently, a two-dimensional physical substance would not have a surface (a two-dimensional limit). In other words, such a substance would not have an outside. Nor would it have an inside.

Also note that it is not necessarily true that a place is a limit. For instance, there could be a three-dimensional Euclidean space which is not a limit of a four-dimensional entity.

On the other hand, suppose that there could be events which occur at a temporal interval as well as events of some minimal temporal length. Whether time is continuous or discontinuous, if there is a temporally extended event, e, occurring at a temporal interval, t, then there must also be a temporally extended event other than e occurring at a time, $t^\star$, which is a part of t. Such an event will be a temporal part of e. Thus, whether time is continuous or discontinuous, there could not be an event, e, occurring throughout an interval, t, unless there were other events in t. Since it is necessarily true that time is either continuous or discontinuous, whether there could only be events of some minimal temporal length or both such events and events which occur at a temporal interval, the category of Event does not satisfy clause (i) of (4D1$\star$). As in the case of places, times, and limits, an event fails to satisfy (4D2$\star$) because it is impossible for there to be an event that instantiates a level C category which satisfies clause (i) of (4D1$\star$), and (4D2$\star$) has the welcome consequence that an event is not a substance.[55]

The following observations show that there are contrasts between the categories of Event and Substance vis-à-vis the first clauses of (4D1) and (4D1$\star$) which are indicative of a fundamental difference between these categories of *concreta*. As we have seen, the occurrence of a temporally extended event, E, at an interval of time, T, entails both that E has as a temporal part another temporally extended event which occurs at an interval of time, t, such that t is a proper part of T, and that there is a momentary event other than E which is *not* a temporal part of E and which occurs at an instant falling within T. Recall that because of the first entailment, the category of Event does not satisfy clause (i) of (4D1$\star$), and because of the second entailment, the category of Event does not satisfy clause (i) of (4D1). On this basis, we concluded that the category of Event is not capable of having an independent instance in either one of our two

---

55 A possible counterexample to the logical sufficiency of our first analysis, (4D1) and (4D2), was suggested by Peter Simons. Simons makes at least two suppositions: that the entire history of the universe constitutes one event, e, and that the instantaneous events which are slices of e are *parts* of e. The claim is that this would enable the category of Event to satisfy (4D1), and thereby imply that events are substances. In defense of (4D1) and (4D2), we reject Simons's second assumption: we do not understand how any number of temporally unextended events can add up to a temporally extended event. Thus, we think the claim that instantaneous events are parts of temporally extended events is incoherent. Note, however, that we do not need to reject Simons's second assumption in order to defend (4D1$\star$) and (4D2$\star$), our second, simplified analysis, against Simons's counterexample. Since e has other, temporally extended events as parts, e cannot be the only event which occurs. For that reason, e is not a counterexample to our simplified analysis.

related senses, and that an instance of this category fails to satisfy either our first analysis of substance in (4D2) or our second analysis of substance in (4D2⋆).

The contrast between the existential entailments of the occurrence of a temporally extended event and of the existence of a persisting substance vis-à-vis clause (i) of (4D1⋆) can now be brought out as follows. That a substance, $S1$, persists over an interval of time, T, does *not* entail that either $S1$ has a temporal part which persists through an interval of time, t, which is a proper part of T, or $S1$ has a temporal part which exists at an instant, i, which falls within T. In particular, $S1$'s persisting through T does not entail that there is another, shorter-lived, nonmomentary, substance, $S2$, which is a temporal part of $S1$ and which persists through t. For example, possibly, $S1$ is an atom, and T is a period of an hour through which $S1$ persists, but there is no other atom which is a temporal part of $S1$ and which only lasts for the first half of T. Notice that our second analysis of substance requires that $S1$'s persisting through T does not entail that there is such a shorter-lived substance, $S2$, since according to our second analysis, in virtue of clause (i) of (4D1⋆), a substance is an instance of a level C category such that possibly, this category has a single instance over an interval of time.

The contrast between the existential entailments of the occurrence of a temporally extended event and of the existence of a persisting substance vis-à-vis clause (i) of (4D1), is brought into sharper focus by the following considerations. As we have argued, it is a necessary truth that what has no size is not a part of what has size. Hence, it is impossible that a persisting substance, $S1$, has an instantaneous substance as a temporal part. Moreover, $S1$'s persistence through T does *not* entail that there is another, momentary, substance which is not a temporal part of $S1$ and which exists at an instant falling within T. For instance, possibly, $S1$ is a table, and T is a period of an hour through which $S1$ persists, but there is no other table which exists at (and only as long as) the beginning of T (and which therefore is not a temporal part of $S1$).[56] Observe that our first analysis of substance *requires* that $S1$'s persistence through T does *not* entail that there is a momentary substance of this kind, since according to our first analysis, in virtue of clause (i) of (4D1), a substance is an instance of a level C category such that,

---

56 The preceding remarks do not imply, and are not intended to suggest, that most adherents of the doctrine that substances have temporal parts would say that a (proper) temporal part of an atom or a table is itself an atom or a table. In fact, many adherents of this doctrine would not say this.

possibly, this category has a single instance over an interval of time, exclusive of any proper part of this instance during that interval.[57]

With respect to the categories of Privation and Collection, the arguments to show that instances of these categories are not substances according to (4D1★) and (4D2★) are identical with our earlier arguments which proved that they are not substances according to (4D1) and (4D2). The arguments are unchanged in the case of privations because they appeal to the fact that the category of Privation fails to satisfy clause (ii) or (iii) of (4D1), or clause (ii) or (iii) of (4D1★), which are identical clauses in (4D1) or (4D1★). And these arguments are unchanged in the case of collections because they appeal to the fact that the category of Collection fails to satisfy clause (iii) of (4D1) and clause (iii) of (4D1★), which are identical clauses.[58]

We have provided two analyses of substance, which differ only in the first clauses of (4D1) and (4D1★). Thus far, the two analyses have given the same results, though (4D1★) is simpler than (4D1), and justifying (4D1★)

57 We emphasize that our commitment is *either,* via (4D1★), to the possibility of a persisting substance which does not have substantial temporal parts, *or,* via (4D1), to the possibility of a persisting substance which does not have a substantial instantaneous temporal part.

Thus, (4D1★) is incompatible with its being *necessary* for a persisting substance to have substantial temporal parts. Some philosophers who prefer an ontology of space-time to one of space and time seem to think that material substances do in fact have such temporal parts. (See, e.g., Mark Heller, *The Ontology of Physical Objects: Four Dimensional Hunks of Matter* [Cambridge: Cambridge University Press, 1990]. Other four-dimensionalists include McTaggart, Russell, Carnap, Quine, and Smart.) We can allow for this possibility, just so long as the claim is not that four-dimensionality is necessary for the existence of a persisting substance.

On the other hand, (4D1) is compatible even with its being necessary for a persisting substance to have substantial temporal parts, just so long as it is not also claimed that such a substance has an *instantaneous* substantial part.

Of course, both (4D1★) and (4D1) are compatible with its not being possible for there to be a persisting substance which is in space-time. Some philosophers are skeptical about this possibility (e.g., Chisholm, Broad, Prior, Geach, and Simons). Simons, for instance, wonders whether the notion of a persisting physical object in space-time is capable of a coherent formulation on the grounds that all attempts thus far to explicate this notion implicitly appeal to an ontology of three-dimensional continuants, while space-time is supposed to preclude the existence of such continuants (Simons, *Parts,* pp. 121–127). We take no side in this controversy in this work.

58 There appears, however, to be an additional argument which implies that the category of Collection does not satisfy clause (i) of (4D1★). Clause (i) of (4D1★) requires that a category capable-of-having-an-independent-instance★ be capable of having just one instance over an interval of time. Could there be just one collection over an interval of time? It seems not. Since clause (i) of (4D1★) posits an interval of time, there must be indefinitely many times within that interval, and there must be indefinitely many collections which have various times as parts.

requires fewer assumptions than justifying (4D1). There are, however, certain respects in which they yield slightly different results.

To see why, observe first that both of our analyses of substance, that is, the one based on (4D1) and the one based on (4D1*), seem to be compatible with the possibilities of there being one necessary soul, for example, God, and with there being one necessary material object. Since many traditional philosophical theologians have claimed that by definition God is outside of time, we shall consider both the possibility that the one necessary soul or the one necessary material object is atemporal.[59] First, consider the case in which the one necessary substance is in time. In that case, it appears that if there is just one necessary substance, then there could be just one substance which persists through an interval of time, namely, the necessary substance in question. Second, consider the case in which the one necessary substance is atemporal. In that instance, it seems that there could be just one contingent substance which *is* in time and which is the only substance which persists through an interval of time. For example, a necessary, atemporal God could bring it about that a single contingent, created substance persists through some interval of time.[60]

A further observation is that neither analysis of substance is compatible with there being two or more necessary souls which are in time. In that instance, there could not be an interval of time during which just one substance exists, or during which just one substance exists except for its parts.[61]

Consider, however, the possibility of there being two or more necessary material objects which are in time. Our analysis of substance based on (4D1) and (4D2) is compatible with this possibility, because, presumably, all of these objects could combine into a single compound material object which then persists over an interval of time. This compound object would have each of the formerly discrete objects as parts. We would argue that, possibly, this compound object exists over an interval of time, t, without any other substance existing in t – except for this compound object's parts

---

59 The intelligibility of the view that God is atemporal has recently been defended by Norman Kretzmann and Eleonore Stump, "Eternity," *Journal of Philosophy* 78 (1981), pp. 429–458. We are skeptical that their arguments succeed, and question the intelligibility of there both being something which is in time and some substance which is outside of time. Nevertheless, we allow for this possibility.

60 By the same reasoning, the existence of two or more necessary atemporal substances appears to be compatible with both analyses of substance.

61 Unlike material substances, souls cannot be joined to form a single, compound substance which has the things compounded as parts. Souls can, of course, be collected, but such a collection is, as we have argued, not a substance.

in t. This possibility satisfies the requirement of (4D1) and (4D2) which is specified in clause (i) of (4D1). On the other hand, because of clause (i) of (4D1*), (4D1*) and (4D2*) require that, possibly, there is a substance which exists over an interval of time, t, without any other substance existing in t. This possibility is ruled out by the existence of two or more necessary material objects which are in time. Hence, if it is possible for there to be two or more such objects, then (4D2*) does not provide a logically necessary condition for being a substance. In other words, if there are two or more material objects of this kind, then the category of being a substance is not capable-of-having-an-independent-instance*, there could not be a substance that is an instance of a level C category which is capable-of-having-an-independent-instance*, and (4D2*) does not provide a logically necessary condition of substancehood.

To sum up, our first analysis, based on (4D1) and (4D2), is compatible with more ontological possibilities than our second analysis. These additional ontological possibilities are remote. The price for this marginal gain is its commitment to background assumptions to which our second analysis is not committed and its slight additional complexity. These assumptions include the claim that, necessarily, space and time are continuous, the lemma which concludes that sizeless entities cannot be parts of entities with size, and the claim that if there are properties (or tropes), then there is infinite totality of properties (or tropes) which is isomorphic to the totality of numbers or sets postulated by mathematics or set theory. On the other hand, our second analysis is committed to a background assumption to which our first analysis seems not to be committed, namely, that it is possible for there to be a substance having no other substance as a part. Moreover, we are quite confident of all of the background assumptions referred to earlier. Nevertheless, since the greater complexity of the first analysis is slight indeed, and since we judge that being able to accommodate the additional ontological possibilities is slightly more valuable than its costs, we have somewhat of a preference for our first analysis, but we leave the reader to form his or her own preference.

XI. OTHER CATEGORIES

There are more things in heaven and earth, Horatio,
Than are dreamt of in your philosophy.
Shakespeare *The Tragedie of Hamlet, Prince of Denmarke* act 1
scene 5 166 (1602)

Notice that our account in an earlier chapter[62] of a level C category in terms of the list, L, of core categories at level C,[63] and (1D5), our definition of a category being at level C, generates a "list" of categories of being that is *open-ended*. In other words, (1D5) is logically compatible with two things. First, that there are one or more level C categories which are *not* on L. Second, that one or more of the categories on L are *not* at level C (because they are not instantiable). Hence, (1D5) differs from Aristotle's list of the categories of being, which has a *fixed membership*.[64]

Of course, it is extremely plausible that some categories on L are at level C. In addition, it is tempting to argue (*à la* Aristotle) that there is no category at level C that is not on L except for a category equivalent to Substance. Nevertheless, since (1D5) is open-ended, we can allow that there are level C categories not on L other than ones equivalent to being a substance. Some representative candidates for examples of such categories are being a sense-datum, being a nation, and being a sentence-type. However, it seems that each of *these* candidates is a species of a category at level C. For example, it can be argued plausibly that Nation is a species of Collection, that Sense-Datum is a species of Event, and that Sentence-Type is a species of Property. If so, then (1D5) implies that the categories of Nation, Sense-Datum, and Sentence-Type are *not* at level C, and that these categories are too specific to be values of the category variable in (4D1) or (4D1*).

On the other hand, assume for the sake of argument that these categories *are* at level C. We contend that on this assumption these categories fail to satisfy (4D1) or (4D1*). For example, if there is a nation, then it is

---

62 See Chapter 1, Section II.

63 We remind the reader that we are using ordinary or intuitive concepts of the categories on L, and that we assume, plausibly, we believe, that given such intuitive concepts, some actual or possible instance of one of these categories cannot be identified with an instance of another level C category. (The reader should recall that this sort of *irreducibility* of a category on L is compatible with the *eliminability* of an entity of such a category in favor of an entity of another level C category.) While a detailed defense of this presupposition falls outside the scope of the current inquiry, such a defense would in a general way parallel the one provided in Chapters 1 and 3 of the proposition that a substance is not reducible to or identifiable with an instance of another ontological category. For instance, the arguments we marshaled against the reduction of substance to collections or sets of tropes or properties, in particular, the unity problem, can readily be adapted to counter the claim that, say, events or places are identical with collections or sets of features. (Bertrand Russell is an example of a philosopher who has asserted that events and places can be reduced to "complexes" of properties. See his *Human Knowledge: Its Scope and Limits* [New York: Simon and Schuster, 1948], part 1, chap. 3, and part 4, chaps. 4–8.)

64 *Complete Works of Aristotle, Categories,* chap. 4.

possible for a nation to have a city as a part. Moreover, if being a nation is at level C, then being a city is also at level C. Finally, being a nation and being a city are nonequivalent, and being a city is not equivalent to being a proper part. Consequently, being a nation does not satisfy clause (iii) of (4D1) and of (4D1★).

Furthermore, as we stated earlier, we presuppose that an individual substance is not reducible to or identifiable with an entity of another ontological category. Given this presupposition, and assuming that the categories of Nation and Sense-Datum are at level C, it is extremely plausible to suppose that the instantiation of either one of these two categories entails that the category of Substance is instantiated, namely, that there is a piece of territory or a person, or that there is a sensing organism or creature, respectively. For reasons explained earlier, this entailment, together with the fact that neither the category of Nation nor the category of Sense-Datum is equivalent to the category of being a substance, implies the conclusion that the categories of being a nation and being a sense-datum fail to satisfy clause (ii) of (4D1) and of (4D1★). Hence, we infer the truth of this conclusion.

On the other hand, being a sentence-type fails to satisfy clause (i) of (4D1) and clause (i) of (4D1★). This is because if there is a sentence-type, then there must be another sentence-type that is not a part of the former one.

Thus, if the categories of Nation, Sense-Datum, and Sentence-Type are at level C, then none of these categories is capable-of-having-an-independent-instance.[65] In addition, it appears that if the categories of Nation, Sense-Datum, or Sentence-Type are at level C, then there is no other level C category which is capable-of-having-an-independent-instance and which could be coinstantiated with one of the former categories. Therefore, (4D2) and (4D2★) have the welcome implication that neither a nation, nor a sense-datum, nor a sentence-type could be a substance.

Another possible candidate for a category at level C is the category of being a space-time. The concept of space-time does not, of course, belong to the ordinary conceptual scheme, but arises from philosophicoscientific theorizing. Since our system of categories is open to proposals from such sources, our analyses of substance should be adequate to them as well. This

---

65 For stylistic convenience, we ignore the distinction between being capable-of-having-an-independent-instance and being capable-of-having-an-independent-instance★ throughout the remainder of this section. The claims we make apply to both of these properties.

141

category is distinct from the categories of Place and Time, since places have only spatial dimensions, times have only temporal dimensions, but space-times have both spatial and temporal dimensions. On the other hand, intuitively, space-time is like space and time in being both concrete and insubstantial. The insubstantiality of space-time can be argued for as follows:

(9i) Necessarily, if a space-time is a substance, then it is a physical substance.

(9ii) Necessarily, if there is a physical substance, then it possibly moves.[66]

(9iii) Necessarily, if there is a space-time, then it does not possibly move.

Therefore,

(9iv) Necessarily, a space-time is not a substance.[67]

The level C category of Space-Time fails to satisfy clause (i) of (4D1) and clause (i) of (4D1★). Arguments parallel to those which show that the categories of Place and Time fail to satisfy these clauses show that the category of Space-Time can neither have just one instance over an interval of time except for the parts of that one instance, nor just one instance over an interval of time. Accordingly, arguments parallel to those which show that (4D2) and (4D2★) imply that a place or a time is not a substance, show that (4D2) and (4D2★) imply that a space-time is not a substance. This is a desirable outcome.

Arguments parallel to the foregoing ones seem to apply to any other candidate for being a level C category, for example, to categories of *concreta* such as being a rainbow, being a reflection, or being a storm, and to

---

66 Note that in Chapter 1, Section III, we implied that (9ii) is an intuitive datum for the ordinary notion of a physical substance. In other words, we implied that the characteristic of possibly moving, predicated by intuitive datum (9_m), necessarily applies both to all material substances and to all nonmaterial physical substances.

67 Alternatively, this conclusion can be supported by means of the following related argument. (10i) Necessarily, if a space-time is a substance, then it is a physical substance. (10ii) Necessarily, if there is a physical substance, then it *occupies* (or is *in*) either a place or a space-time. (10iii) Necessarily, if there is a space-time, then it does not *occupy* (or is not *in*) either a place or a space-time. Therefore, (10iv) necessarily, a space-time is not a substance. In defense of (10iii), notice that although it can be said that every space-time is either a proper or improper *part* of some space-time, and that every space-time stands in spatiotemporal relations to other space-times, e.g., spatiotemporal distance relations, this is *not* to say that a space-time *occupies* or is *in* a space-time. Similarly, although it can be said that a space-time is *identical with* a space-time, this is *not* to say that a space-time *occupies* or is *in* a space-time. It is an entity such as a physical object, event, or trope, and not a space-time, that could occupy a space-time. In Chapter 5, Section III, we shall defend a proposition which is parallel to (10iii), namely, the proposition that, necessarily, a place cannot occupy (or be *in*) a place: it is an entity such as a physical object, event, or trope that could occupy a place.

142

categories of *abstracta* like being a set, being a number, or being a fact. In other words, either such a category is a species of a category at level C (e.g., Set and Number are species of Property, Fact is a species of Proposition, and Rainbow, Reflection, and Storm are species of Event), or else such a category is at level C but there is no level C category which could be coinstantiated with it and which is capable-of-having-an-independent-instance (e.g., the categories of Set, Number, and Fact do not satisfy clause (i) of (4D1) and clause (i) of (4D1*), and if the categories of Rainbow, Reflection, and Storm are at level C, then these categories do not satisfy clause (ii) of (4D1) and clause (ii) of (4D1*)). Thus, it seems that there is no counterexample to the sufficiency of (4D2) or of (4D2*) in which a nonsubstance instantiates a level C category not on L.

5

Souls and bodies

The Egyptians were the first to advance the idea that the soul is immortal
and that when the body dies it enters into another animal which is then
being born; when it has gone round all the creatures of the land, the sea, and
the air, it enters into the body of a man which is then being born; and this
cycle takes it three thousand years. Some of the Greeks – some earlier, some
later – put forward this idea as though it were their own: I know their names
but I do not transcribe them.

Herodotus Histories II. 193

That, however, which is neither itself a body, nor a force within a body, is
not existent according to man's first notions, and is above all excluded from
the range of imagination.

Maimonides The Guide for the Perplexed I. xlvi

I. THE NATURE OF A SOUL

The ideas we have belonging, and peculiar to Spirit, are Thinking, and Will.
    John Locke *An Essay Concerning Human Understanding* II. xxiii (1695)

The spirit-monad – the monad that has consciousness of itself.
    E. Caird *A Critical Account of the Philosophy of Kant* Introd. V. 79 (1877)

In previous chapters, we have explored the intuitive notion of an individual substance, culminating in our analyses of this notion in Chapter 4. In
this chapter we turn to the *possible extension* of the category of Substance,
and we shall defend the proposition that this possible extension includes
not only material objects and other physical substances, but also immaterial
or Cartesian souls. In other words, we shall argue that immaterial souls
could exist, whether or not they actually do exist. This claim is a conceptual
one and, therefore, can be defended by purely philosophical, *a priori* arguments. Here we remain neutral on the issue of whether souls, or even
material objects, actually exist. The other important conceptual issue concerning souls and bodies which we address in this chapter is that of the

possibility of *interaction* between them. We will defend this possibility as well.

The positions we take on the possible extension of the category of Substance and on the possibility of interaction between souls and bodies are and have been highly controversial. For example, in the philosophical tradition, idealists have argued that *material* substances are impossible and that interaction between substances is possible only in the case of souls or purely spiritual beings. On the other hand, philosophical materialists have argued that *spiritual* substances are impossible and that interaction between substances is possible only in the case of bodies or physical beings. As do most philosophers nowadays who accept the possibility of substances, we accept the possibility of interacting material substances. But many philosophers who accept the possibility of bodies which interact either argue that souls are impossible or else argue for the weaker claim that interaction between souls and bodies is impossible.

In contrast, most systems of religious belief are committed to the existence of purely spiritual beings and to their interaction with bodies. For example, in asserting the existence of God, traditional Western theism asserts the existence of a purely spiritual being. According to this form of theism, God is a disembodied spirit, or soul, with the power to affect material things. In addition, many theists are committed to the existence of other souls that have this power, for example, angels, devils, or human souls. However, it should be noted that although the proposition that there are souls which causally interact with bodies is frequently accepted within religious systems of belief, this proposition does not seem to entail the existence of a deity of any kind.

A variety of philosophical objections have been raised to the intelligibility of both the notion of a soul and the notion of a soul affecting a material thing. Of course, since traditional Western theism presupposes the intelligibility of these notions, the soundness of any of these objections entails the unintelligibility of this form of theism. However, our principal aim in this chapter is to defend the intelligibility of the concepts of a soul and of dualistic interactionism against philosophical objections.

What is a purely spiritual being or soul? We propose the following initial characterization:

(5D1) *x* is a soul =df. (i) *x* is a substance, and (ii) *x* is unlocated, and (iii) *x* is capable of consciousness.

Let us examine the rationale behind each of the three conditions in (5D1). In the first condition of (5D1), we employ the concept of an individual

145

substance as ordinarily understood, the concept we analyzed in terms of ontological independence in the preceding chapter. Paradigm cases of this ordinary concept seem to be particular material objects and persons. Since a soul is a person or a creature in the ordinary senses of 'person' and 'creature' we rely upon here, and since a person or a creature in these senses is a substance, a soul is a substance.[1] Thus, being a substance is a logically necessary condition of being a soul, and the inclusion of (i) in (5D1) is warranted.

Clauses (i) and (ii) of (5D1), which together say that a soul is an unlocated substance, entail that a soul is *unextended*. Being unextended and being unlocated are not equivalent. For example, Boscovichian point-particles are unextended but located; and places (other than points) are extended but unlocated. Finally, point-positions are neither extended nor located. In other words, to be located is to occupy or be in a place. Although a place is unlocated, a place is not a substance.

It is not possible for a spiritual substance to be spatially extended, and it is a necessary truth that whatever is spatially extended is physical. Thus, a "ghost" that literally possesses spatial extension does not count as a soul. It would be either an exotic type of physical entity, or else a subtle type of physical stuff. (An extended but massless particle in physics is an example of an "exotic" physical entity, whereas a gas or plasma is a case of a "subtle" type of physical stuff.) It is arguable that there could be a substance that is conscious and unextended, but occupies a point of space. It can be further argued that such an entity is a soul or spirit. However, it is not obvious that either of these are genuine possibilities. But, even if there could be an unextended spiritual substance occupying a point of space, it would not be a *purely* spiritual being. That is, it would not be *wholly* outside of the physical world, inasmuch as it would occupy a point of space. When

1 Descartes distinguishes between the human person and the soul, the former being formed from the "substantial union" of the soul and the body. However, in asserting that a soul is a person or a creature in the relevant ordinary senses, one does not imply that a soul is a *human* person or creature. Furthermore, it may seem that Hume and Locke deny that a person in our sense is a substance. But either Hume and Locke *are* issuing such a denial, i.e., are attempting to *analyze* the relevant ordinary concept of personhood in terms of collections or sequences of nonsubstantial items, or else they are not denying that a person in the relevant ordinary sense is a substance, but instead are proposing to *eliminate* persons of this kind in favor of such collections or sequences. We have already criticized collectionist and sequentialist strategies of the first sort in Chapter 3. The main criticisms of those strategies we gave in Chapter 3 are no less applicable in the case of personal substances than in the case of nonpersonal substances. On the other hand, collectionist and sequentialist strategies of the second sort are compatible with our claim that a person in the ordinary sense in question is a substance.

traditional Western theism affirms the existence of God, angels, and so forth, it is affirming the existence of purely spiritual beings, and this is what we mean by the term 'soul' or 'spirit'. For the foregoing reasons, we regard unlocatedness as a logically necessary condition of being a soul, as specified in clause (ii) of (5D1).

Finally, in clause (iii) of (5D1), we require that a soul be capable of consciousness. Descartes seems to hold that a soul is and must be conscious at every moment that it exists. However, perhaps there could be a soul that is unconscious for a time. Clause (iii) of (5D1) is compatible with this possibility. On the other hand, this clause is also logically consistent with what appears to be Descartes's overall position on souls, which, as we have indicated, is that any soul would be essentially conscious.[2] Thus, if Descartes is right, then there being a soul that is *capable* of consciousness entails that this soul *is* conscious. And, of course, if a soul is conscious, then it must be capable of consciousness. Therefore, on Cartesian assumptions, consciousness and the capacity for consciousness are equivalent. It follows that clause (iii) of (5D1) is logically compatible with Descartes's view that a soul is conscious at every moment of its existence.

But could there be a soul that is unconscious, yet capable of consciousness? Apparently, some capacities or dispositions of a physical thing are *basic,* that is, are not explained by any occurrent structural properties of that thing together with nonfundamental laws of nature. Rather, such capacities are grounded in some very general features of that thing, features involved in being the sort of thing that it is, together with some fundamental law or laws. For example, it seems that a material object has a basic capacity to move; it does not have this capacity in virtue of any of its structural characteristics, for instance, its shape, size, or order and arrangement of parts. Rather, it seems to be capable of motion simply in virtue of its being a *spatial* substance. Similarly, perhaps a soul has a basic capacity for consciousness simply in virtue of its being a *nonspatial* substance. On (5D1), a soul has neither a structural nor any other plausible basis for its capacity for consciousness.

However, if there could be an unconscious soul that is capable of consciousness, then there seems to be an interesting difference between material and spiritual substances. This can be brought out in terms of the following comparison. It seems clear that a material object, *m,* that is

2 René Descartes, *Meditations on First Philosophy,* in *The Philosophical Writings of Descartes, Volume 2,* trans. John Cottingham, Robert Stoothoff, and Dugald Murdoch (Cambridge: Cambridge University Press, 1984), meditations 2 and 6.

currently stationary has a number of positive, occurrent, intrinsic qualities that are wholly in the present,[3] and it seems that these qualities of it are neither universal essential properties nor equivalent to ontic categories. For example, *m* has a certain shape and size. In contrast, it is arguable that a currently unconscious soul would lack any such occurrent qualities. We agree with this point, unless the questionable Leibnizean view that a soul always has "unconscious mental states" is acceptable. This having been said, the following somewhat plausible principle seems to create a challenge to the coherence of the notion of an unconscious soul:

(P1) A substance must have some positive, occurrent, intrinsic, wholly present quality that is neither a universal essential property nor equivalent to an ontic category.

We are not sure of the truth or falsity of (P1). For instance, (P1) would appear to rule out the possibility of an ontology of Boscovichian point-particles. This might be thought to cast some doubt on (P1). If, however, (P1) is true, and if unconscious mental states of souls are disallowed, then it would seem that a soul must be conscious at all times.[4] In that case, clause (iii) of (5D1) should be replaced with '*x* is conscious'. Otherwise, clause (iii) of (5D1) would be unnecessarily misleading by suggesting that a soul could be unconscious. Call this revised characterization (5D2).

For the purposes of this book, we do not argue specifically for (5D1) or for (5D2). One of them must be correct, though we do not display any preference.

II. IS A SOUL WHOLLY NEGATIVE IN NATURE?

We can but imperfectly describe the conditions of its actuality by negational terms.

D. W. Thompson *Odds & Ends* iii. 6 (1865)

Not by way of negation, as if nothing were necessary but this; but by way of comparison.

Bp. Hall *The Residue of the Contemplations upon the New Testament* iv. xvii (1634)

---

3 For example, the property of being conscious is wholly present, but the property of having been conscious at some previous time is not.

4 Note that if a human person can exist when unconscious, it is open to one who agrees with Descartes that souls are conscious at all times to respond that while human persons are capable of consciousness whenever they exist, they are material objects. It is formally consistent with this view of human persons that souls are possible. This response is not one Descartes himself would make, for he also holds that material bodies are incapable of consciousness.

It has been argued that the notion of a disembodied spirit or soul is unintelligible, on the ground that this notion can only be understood in *negative* terms. For example, a soul might be defined as a *nonphysical* or *unlocated* thing. An argument of this kind seems to have been defended by Douglas Long.[5] Such an argument presupposes the following principle:[6]

(P2) If a putative ontological category, *C*, stands in need of explication, and if *C* can only be explicated in terms of negative characteristics, then *C* is not an intelligible ontological category.

However, (P2) is ambiguous, and can be read in either of two ways. Let us designate the first such reading (P2A).

(P2A) If a putative ontological category, *C*, stands in need of explication, and if *C* can only be explicated in terms of a set of characteristics *all of which* are negative, then *C* is not an intelligible ontological category.

(P2A) has much intuitive plausibility. For example, in some places Plotinus says that the only way to "explicate" the transcendent "One" is in wholly negative terms, and his critics were rightly skeptical of the coherence of such an explication.[7] In general, to explicate an ontological category in wholly negative terms is, after all, not to distinguish it from other such categories which can also be described in those negative terms.[8] To explicate a category and to distinguish it from a different one, something must be said about the positive nature of that category. Thus, we accept principle (P2A), at least as it applies to the category of souls.

Nevertheless, an argument against the intelligibility of the notion of a soul based upon (P2A) is unsound, for as we have argued in terms of (5D1)

---

5 Douglas Long, "Disembodied Existence, Physicalism, and the Mind-Body Problem," *Philosophical Studies* 31 (1977), pp. 307–316.

6 Long never explicitly states this principle, but his argument against the intelligibility of the notion of a soul depends upon it.

7 Plotinus, *Enneads,* 2nd ed. rev., trans. Stephen Mackenna (London: Faber and Faber, 1969).

8 The only kind of exception may occur in a case such as the explication of an *abstract entity* as a *nonconcrete entity.* This sort of exception may occur because this pair of ontological categories is at a certain very high level of generality, i.e., level *B.* See Appendix 1 for an argument that Abstractness is in fact explicable as Non-Concreteness, and especially n. 6 in that appendix, where it is argued that no intelligible ontological category below level *B* can be explicated in wholly negative terms, but that such considerations do not apply to intelligible ontological categories at level *B.* Of course, the category of being a soul is below level *B,* since it is subsumed by being a substance, a level *C* category. For this reason, the foregoing sort of possible exception to the prohibition on a wholly negative explication of an intelligible ontological category does not apply in the case of the category of being a soul. In other words, the category of being a soul is not at the very high level of generality which permits the wholly negative characterization of an ontological kind.

149

and (5D2), this notion can be explicated in terms of a set of three characteristics, *only one* of which is negative.

One arrives at the second reading of (P2), which we shall call (P2B), simply by replacing '*all of which* are negative' in (P2A) with '*some of which* are negative'. It does appear that the explication of the notion of a soul must include a negative characteristic such as being unlocated.[9] Thus, we need to ask whether an argument against the intelligibility of the notion of a soul based upon (P2B) is successful. We maintain that such an argument is unsound. To begin with, (P2B) suffers in a comparison with (P2A). Unlike (P2A), (P2B) has no intuitive plausibility. There seems to be no objection to the inclusion of negative characteristics in an explication, provided that they are individually meaningful. Furthermore, there seems to be a variety of counterexamples to (P2B). For example, consider the following apparent cases of intelligible ontological categories that stand in need of explication, and which can only be explicated in terms of a set of characteristics that includes a negative feature. First, take photons. It seems that in order to explicate the notion of a photon, there must be reference to the negative characteristic of masslessness. Second, there is the category of Number. To explicate this category, there must be reference to abstract entities whose nature involves a negative component, namely, zero, the empty set, or the like. Third, what are the correct explications of the categories of Instants and (spatial) Points? They seem to be that an instant is an *unextended* time, and that a point is an *unextended* place.

For the foregoing reasons, (P2B) is implausible. Hence, it cannot be shown that the notion of a soul is unintelligible by appealing to either (P2A) or to (P2B). On either reading, (P2) cannot be utilized to show that the notion of a soul is unintelligible.

III. DO SOULS NEED A PRINCIPLE OF INDIVIDUATION?

Zeno's puzzle – "if place exists, in what does it exist?" – is not hard to solve. Further, if [place] is itself an existent, where will it exist? For Zeno's puzzle demands some explanation. For if every existence is in a place, clearly there will have to be a place of a place, and so on, *ad infinitum.*

Aristotle *Physics* 210b23 and 209a23

---

9 On the other hand, an explication of the concept of a soul needs to include a negative characteristic only if there could be a conscious material body. If, as Descartes supposed, it is impossible for a material body to be conscious, then the concept of a soul can be explicated in *wholly positive terms,* either as a substance that is capable of consciousness, or as a substance that is conscious.

A second challenge to the intelligibility of the concept of a soul is based on the premise that for any intelligible ontological category, there must be an adequate criterion of individuation for entities of that category. Leibniz, for example, argued that any two entities must differ qualitatively.[10] Most philosophers now reject "Leibniz's Law," and allow for the possibility of two qualitatively indistinguishable concrete entities. Nevertheless, these philosophers often accept the premise that for such entities there must be a criterion of individuation. If they are correct, then it follows that the criterion of individuation for these entities is not solely in terms of qualitative universals – namely, the criterion involves either nonqualitative properties or relations to other concrete entities.

Let us assume that if there could be souls, then there could be two souls, each of which has the same qualitative properties as the other. Two such souls would exist at the same times and, at any given time of their existence, would be qualitatively indistinguishable in their thoughts, experiences, and so forth. Keith Campbell is representative of those philosophers who argue that since two souls of this kind would lack a criterion of individuation, the concept of a soul is unintelligible. Entities which are intelligible, Campbell assumes, do not lack such a criterion of individuation, for example, bodies, which are individuated by their different locations.

Note that Campbell is referring to synchronic individuation, or individuation at a time. As he says,

> Atoms, and material things generally, are individuated and counted by their positions. Non-spatial spirits cannot, of course, be individuated and counted in this way. But then, in what way can they be individuated and counted? If there really is no difference between one spirit and two spirits of exactly similar history and contents, then spirits are a very suspect sort of thing indeed.[11]

The problem with this argument is that it presupposes that with respect to Campbell's demand for a criterion of individuation, bodies are *better off* than souls. Two bodies, he thinks, can be individuated at a time by their different places, even if they are qualitatively indistinguishable, whereas souls, lacking location, cannot be individuated at a time when they are qualitatively indistinguishable.

---

10 According to "Leibniz's Law," necessarily, for any x and y, $x = y$ if and only if for any property P, x has P iff y has P. 'P' ranges over qualitative properties, including intrinsic and relational ones.

11 Keith Campbell, *Body and Mind* (Garden City, N.Y.: Anchor Books, 1970), pp. 44–45.

Suppose that we have two qualitatively indistinguishable bodies, x and y, and that x occupies place p_1 and y occupies place p_2. Campbell presupposes that x differs from y in that x occupies place p_1 while y does not.

But if two qualitatively indistinguishable bodies must have a criterion of synchronic individuation, then so must two qualitatively indistinguishable places, that is, p_1 and p_2. Thus, let us ask: what is the criterion of individuation for two qualitatively indistinguishable places?[12]

The answer to this question will depend on whether space is relational or absolute. If space is relational, then the existence of places depends on the existence of spatially located entities, and the individuation of places must involve their relations to such entities. Since Campbell assumes a substance ontology, so shall we. Thus, if space is relational, and p_1 and p_2 are different places, then one of these places has a relation to a body that the other lacks, and it is this which individuates that place. This will not do for the purposes of Campbell's argument, since it seems viciously circular to individuate bodies in terms of places, and places in terms of bodies.

The appearance of vicious circularity is more than a mere appearance. The demand for a criterion of individuation is a demand for an *explanation* of the diversity of entities of a certain category, an explanation that is logically necessary and sufficient. In other words, a criterion of individuation provides an *analysis* of the diversity of entities of that category.[13] Thus, the demand for a criterion of individuation seems to rest on something like the following premises:

(A1) There could be two entities, each of which has the same qualitative properties.

(A2) For each of these entities, there would be some fact about it that accounts for or explains its diversity from any other entity.

(A3) In the case of qualitatively indistinguishable entities, this fact can only be that each entity has either a nonqualitative property, or a relation to some other (concrete) entity, that any other entity lacks.

Since the demand for a criterion of individuation is based on the demand for a certain kind of explanation, and since explanations cannot be circular, the individuation of bodies in terms of places, combined with the individuation of places in terms of bodies, is *viciously* circular. The following general principle applies in this context: for diverse ontological categories,

---

12 Campbell and others who give this kind of argument never seem to pose this crucial question.

13 The analysis of the diversity of bodies which is at issue might be stated as follows. At a moment t_1, a body x and a body y are diverse =df. the places that x and y occupy at t_1 are diverse.

F and G, it is viciously circular to individuate Fs in terms of Gs, *and* to individuate Gs in terms of Fs.

The alternative remaining to be considered is that bodies are individuated by their places and that such spaces are absolute. If space is absolute, then places are not individuated by their relations to bodies, since places could exist without bodies. Thus, if space is absolute, and if bodies are individuated by their places, then what individuates places?[14] The only replies to this question that need to be considered are the following three.

First, nothing individuates places. If this is the reply, then the diversity of places has no explanation. But if this is so, then why suppose that the diversity of souls is in need of an explanation? On the other hand, if places stand in need of a criterion of individuation, but do not have one, then places are unintelligible. Hence, if bodies stand in need of a criterion of individuation, but have no such criterion unless it is in terms of their locations, and places are unintelligible, then bodies are unintelligible as well.

Second, places are individuated either by their exemplification of different nonqualitative properties or by their possession of different individual qualitative properties. An example of a nonqualitative property would be *being identical with that* (where *that* = the place in question), and an example of an individual qualitative property (or trope) would be *a particular shape* (of the place in question). In either of these cases, souls could be individuated by the same sorts of properties, for instance, by the nonqualitative property, *being identical with that* (where *that* = the soul under discussion), or by an individual qualitative property, for example, *a particular consciousness* (of the soul in question).

Third, places are individuated by their parts, so that one place differs from another in that the former has different proper parts than the latter. Such parts, of course, would be places themselves. According to this approach the synchronic diversity (diversity at a time) of places can be analyzed in the following manner:

(IP) At time t, a place x is diverse from a place y =df. There exists a place z such that (i) at t z is a proper part of x, and (ii) at t y does not have z as a proper part.

---

14 Note that a place cannot be individuated by its location, i.e., in terms of the place it occupies. Why? Because a place does not *occupy* (or is not *in*) a place, though of course every place is either a proper or improper *part* of some place, and stands in spatial relations to other places, e.g., relations of distance. Similarly, although a place is *identical with* a place, a place's being identical with a place is by no means the same thing as a place's *occupying* (or being *in*) a place.

We will argue that there is a serious problem with any such approach on the ground that it *presupposes* a vicious form of *circular individuation*.

To begin with, let us say that for any ontological category C, an attempted explication, A, of the synchronic diversity of instances of C *presupposes circular individuation* if in every possible case A seeks to explain the synchronic diversity of two instances of C (x and y) by relating x (or y) to *another* entity, z, which is an instance of C in such a way that x and z's (or y and z's) being so related *entails* that $x \neq z$ (or $y \neq z$). For example, a purported analysis, A, of the synchronic diversity of *places* (or *bodies*) presupposes circular individuation if in every possible case A seeks to explain the synchronic diversity of places (or bodies) x and y by relating x or y to *another* place (body) z in such a way that x and z's (or y and z's) being so related *entails* that $x \neq z$ (or $y \neq z$). In what follows, we give a formal statement of conditions under which a proposed analysis of the synchronic diversity of entities of a given ontological category, being a G, presupposes circular individuation, and explain why an adequate analysis of such diversity cannot presuppose circular individuation.

Where being a G is a category, a proposed analysis, A, of a particular G, x, being synchronically diverse from a particular G, y, presupposes circular individuation if A meets the following three conditions:

(CI) (i) It is possible that A's *analysandum* and A's *analysans* are jointly satisfied, and (ii) Where being an F is a category, either A has the structure: (S1) *a G, x, is diverse from a G, y, at t =df. There is an F, z, such that (i) x is related in way R to z at t, and (ii) y is not related in way R to z at t,* or A has the structure: (S2) *a G, x, is diverse from a G, y, at t =df. at t, x is related in way R to y,* and (iii) When A has structure (S1), it is necessarily true that if A's *analysandum* and A's *analysans* are satisfied, then z is a G which is diverse from x (or y) at t; and when A has structure (S2), it is necessarily true that if A's *analysandum* and A's *analysans* are satisfied, then y is a G which is diverse from x at t.

Let us explain why an analysis of the synchronic diversity of entities of a given ontological category, being a G, cannot presuppose circular individuation as specified in (CI). To begin with, the purpose of clause (i) of (CI) is to prevent a proposed analysis of synchronic diversity whose *analysandum* and *analysans* are not jointly satisfiable from trivially satisfying (CI). We are prepared to grant that the *analysandum* and *analysans* could be jointly satisfied in the proposed analyses of synchronic diversity with which we are concerned, for instance, (IP). So, henceforth we ignore clause (i) of (CI). Now, suppose that A is a proposed analysis of the synchronic diversity of Gs which satisfies (CI). In that case, A entails that if x and y are Gs, then x is individuated from y by virtue of x being *related* in a certain way to something, z, (clause (ii) of (CI)), and z is a G *other than* x (clause (iii) of (CI)). If there are Gs, and if A explicates their synchronic diversity, then it follows that one G is individuated from another *by virtue of* a G's being related in a certain way at a time to *another* G. Specifically, when A has structure (S1), a G, x, is individuated from another G, y, *by virtue of x's* being related in a certain way at a time to a third G, z, and when A has structure (S2), a G, x, is individuated from a G, y, *by virtue of x's* being related in a certain way at a time to y. However, *p by virtue of q* entails that *q helps to explain p*. For example, if the car moves down the road *by virtue of* the car's wheels' rotating, then this entails that the car's wheels' rotating helps to explain why the car moves down the road. Therefore, if A is an analysis of the synchronic diversity of Gs, then a G's being related in a certain way at a time to *another* G helps to explain why a G is synchronically diverse from a G. But this consequence is an impossibility. That a G is related in a certain way at a time to *another* G *could not* help to explain the synchronic diversity of Gs, since any such attempt to explain the synchronic diversity of Gs seeks to explain a fact in terms of itself – something which is viciously circular. This means that A's being an analysis of the synchronic diversity of Gs implies an impossibility. Since whatever implies an impossibility is itself impossible, A could not be an analysis of the synchronic diversity of Gs. Hence, an analysis of the synchronic diversity of Gs cannot presuppose circular individuation as specified in (CI).

Lest one think that the prohibition on circular individuation as specified in (CI) rules out *all* attempts to analyze the synchronic diversity of entities belonging to a given ontological category, being a G, it should be observed that this prohibition is consistent with such an attempt if it seeks to analyze the synchronic diversity of Gs by relating Gs to non-Gs. For example, the prohibition in question is compatible with each of the following traditional views: first, *bodies* are synchronically diverse because they occupy different *places,* and, second, *concreta* are synchronically diverse because they exemplify different *properties.*

The following principle is a corollary of (CI):

(P3) For any ontological category, C, if in every possible case one instance of C is individuated from another by the former's bearing to the latter an irreflexive relation (a relation that nothing can bear to itself), then this presupposes circular individuation.

Moreover, we have seen that any attempt to analyze the synchronic diversity of Gs which presupposes circular individuation is inadmissibly circular. Hence, it is inadmissibly circular to attempt to analyze the synchronic diversity of Gs in terms of a G's bearing an irreflexive relation R to a G. Intuitively speaking, the problem with trying to analyze the synchronic diversity of Gs in terms of Gs' bearing an irreflexive relation R to Gs is that, necessarily, R is a *relation* that a G can bear to a G only if the former G is diverse from the latter one. In this sense, the instantiation of R presupposes the diversity of these Gs. Yet, a G's bearing R to a G is supposed to *explain* in what a G's diversity from some other G consists. It is viciously circular to explain the diversity of two Gs in terms of a relation whose instantiation presupposes the diversity of Gs.

In the case at issue, the diversity of two entities, x and y, belonging to the same ontological category, namely, Place, is to be explained [by (IP)'s *analysans*] in terms of a relation, R, that place x bears to another place which is a proper part of x, namely, the proper parthood relation between places. In this case, because no place can be a proper part of itself, the instantiation of R entails the diversity of a place from a place which is a proper part of it. This means that R is an irreflexive relation. Hence, (P3) is satisfied, and the diversity of places cannot be explained in terms of R upon pain of vicious circularity. Our argument implies that this is true in virtue of the fact that (IP) has structure (S1) and (IP) satisfies the conditions in (CI) which pertain to proposed analyses having structure (S1).[15]

In conclusion, whether space is relational or absolute, the attempt to individuate bodies in terms of places does not yield any result that makes bodies any better off than souls with respect to individuation. Therefore, if bodies or places are intelligible, arguments like Campbell's do not establish any unintelligibility in the concept of a soul.

IV. DO SOULS NEED A PRINCIPLE OF SEPARATION?

Though we might at first suppose that there are many souls – Socrates', yours, mine, and so on – Plotinus rejects this commonsense view, and believes there is only one Soul. He argues that the common belief in many souls depends on belief in matter; for we distinguish different souls by the different bodies they belong to, and if we admit the unreality of bodies, we cannot recognize distinct material bodies.

Terence Irwin Classical Thought 189 (1989)

Spatial separation is not the same as spiritual independence.

W. Alger The Solitudes of Nature and of Man III. 23 (1866)

---

15 This argument is based upon principles set forth by Gary Rosenkrantz in *Haecceity: An Ontological Essay* (Dordrecht: Kluwer, 1993), chap. 2, sec. 4.

In a subtle and interesting essay, Ernest Sosa discusses the argument from individuation against the intelligibility of souls. While criticizing this argument, Sosa argues that, nevertheless, there is an important lesson to be learned from it.[16] According to Sosa, if there are two pieces of matter, then the relation of *spatial apartness* must hold between these two material objects. Generalizing from this case, Sosa argues that if *a* is diverse from *b*, then there must be some relation *other than diversity* that holds between them (such as spatial apartness), that nothing can bear to itself.[17] He calls this the Principle that Diversity Cannot Stand Alone (DCSA). Sosa maintains that for souls there is no obviously acceptable relation to stand alongside diversity in the way that spatial apartness stands alongside diversity for pieces of matter. Note that Sosa, in setting out (DCSA), does not state that (DCSA) implies that an entity has a criterion of individuation, which, we have argued, must be explanatory. In this respect, Sosa's argument differs from Campbell's.

Thus, Sosa maintains that in the case of two material objects with all the same qualitative properties, their diversity does not stand alone, because the qualitative relation, _____ is spatially apart from _____, stands alongside their diversity. On the other hand, in the case of two qualitatively indistinguishable souls (Sosa argues), no comparable qualitative relation stands alongside the diversity of the two souls. This, Sosa says, casts doubt on the intelligibility of souls.

A first response to Sosa is to question (DCSA). What reason is there to accept this principle? The only reason Sosa provides is the following:

> Perhaps the lesson is simply that entities *x* and *y* cannot possibly *be related simply by diversity*. Otherwise, you might have not just one right foot but indefinitely many of them, all related only by diversity![18]

All this argument shows, if Sosa is right that no two pieces of matter can exhaustively coincide in space,[19] is that in the case of pieces of matter diversity cannot stand alone. Of course, this fact is explained by the spatial nature of such objects. Sosa generalizes from this case to get (DCSA), but it is not obvious why the generalization is warranted. He has not, for example, pointed out any unintelligibility in the supposition that there are

---

16 Ernest Sosa, "Subjects Among Other Things," in *Philosophical Perspectives, 1, Metaphysics* (Atascadero, Calif.: Ridgeview, 1987), pp. 155–187 (esp. pp. 160–164).

17 Ibid., p. 162.

18 Ibid..

19 Sosa also assumes that a piece of matter cannot be located in two different places at the same time.

indefinitely many souls, all qualitatively indistinguishable. Why can't there be indefinitely many souls of this kind?

However, perhaps this question can be answered by appealing to the following two premises. First, necessarily, for any x and y, if x is qualitatively indistinguishable from y, and x does not bear an irreflexive relation other than diversity to y of the sort Sosa requires, then nothing separates x from y. Second, necessarily, for any x and y, if x is qualitatively indistinguishable from y, and nothing separates x from y, then x and y are numerically one and the same. These two premises together imply that the diversity of qualitatively indistinguishable things cannot stand alone.

If (DCSA) is correct, then the diversity of souls cannot stand alone. In that case, the defender of the intelligibility of souls must provide an irreflexive relation other than diversity which one soul must bear to another, and which does for souls what spatial apartness does for pieces of matter.

We think that such a relation in fact holds between any two souls, namely, the relation: being a soul x which is incapable of directly experiencing a mental state of a soul y. Thus, if we are right, then souls are "epistemically apart" in a way that parallels the spatial apartness of pieces of matter.[20] We assume that necessarily, a soul is capable of directly experiencing some of its own mental states, and that necessarily, no soul is capable of directly experiencing a mental state of another soul. On these assumptions, if there are two souls which are qualitatively indistinguishable, then this irreflexive relation will stand alongside their diversity in the way spatial apartness stands alongside the diversity of two pieces of matter.

Sosa considers and rejects this second reply to (DCSA):

> It might be suggested that no soul x could directly experience the mental states of another soul y and that this provides us with the desired relation to accompany with necessity every case of diversity among souls. But this seems to me to put things backwards. For the (transitive) *experiencing* done by substances like souls is a causal matter which is a form of 'causally registering a state of'. And direct experiencing is then a form of 'causally registering a state of, without reliance on causally intermediary states'. Now either *self*-registering states are allowed or they are not. If they are allowed, then the only states directly experienced would be those which are self-registering. And then it follows that one cannot directly experience states of anyone else. For to *register* a state X is to *have* a state Y with an appropriate causal relation to X. But if the only states directly registered by one are those states of one's own which are *self*-registering (as a limiting causal relation),

20 This point was originally made by Gary Rosenkrantz in "Comments on 'Subjects Among Other Things,'" delivered at the Tenth Annual Symposium in Philosophy at the University of North Carolina at Greensboro, April, 1986.

then it follows trivially that one can only register directly states of one's own, and hence that these are the only states one can experience directly. But this follows only because of the way experiencing is understood as a form of registering and because of the way the *directness* of such registering is conceived.[21]

Sosa goes on to maintain that if self-registering states are *not* allowed, then it is arguable that a soul can directly experience a mental state of another soul. For example, God would directly experience a mental state, *Y*, of a human soul, *x*, if God has a mental state, *Z*, such that *Z* and *Y* are qualitatively alike, and God's having *Z* is *directly* caused by *x*'s having *Y*. Since the epistemic apartness of souls, as we understand it, entails that a soul *x* directly experiences a mental state of a soul *y* only if that state is, in Sosa's terminology, 'self-registering', we shall just consider Sosa's objection to epistemic apartness of this kind. The crucial objection Sosa makes to this idea of epistemic apartness for souls is that it "puts things backwards," because of the "trivial" way that the epistemic apartness of souls follows from the conception of direct experience.

There are two responses we shall make to Sosa's criticism. The first is that his criticism introduces a new requirement that any relation must meet if it is to be a *proper* "accompaniment" to diversity, a requirement which Sosa never mentions until he voices this criticism. As we have indicated, Sosa complains that epistemic apartness is somehow not a proper accompaniment because of its triviality. This seems to be because

(SI) 'direct experience' must be defined in a certain way, and consequently,
(SII) it "trivially follows" (that is, logically follows from the definition) that a soul can only directly experience one of its own mental states.

Thus, it appears that Sosa's further requirement for a proper accompaniment to diversity is that it not be trivial as spelled out by these two conditions. It is not clear why triviality in this sense is unacceptable. It seems that in condition (SI), Sosa implies that it is *analytic* that a soul can only directly experience its own mental states. Hence, Sosa appears to claim that his definition of 'direct experience' provides a *synonym* for it.

Given this reading of Sosa, there are two replies to his use of condition (SI) to criticize our proposed use of the epistemic apartness of souls. First, the rationale for the employment of (SI), though unstated, is plausibly that if condition (SI) is met, then epistemic apartness cannot *explain* the diver-

---

21 Sosa, "Subjects Among Other Things," p. 163.

sity of souls.[22] However, a principle we defended earlier, that is, (P3), implies that the spatial apartness of two bodies cannot explain their diversity either. Since spatial apartness is an irreflexive relation, (P3) implies that such an explanation would be viciously circular. Hence, bodies are no better off than souls in this regard.

Second, there are serious doubts about the claim that Sosa's definition of 'direct experience' is really a synonymy. If, for example, the traditional view that souls can directly experience universals without causally interacting with them is correct, then Sosa's definition of 'direct experience' must be mistaken. Furthermore, if this traditional view, although false, is epistemically possible, then Sosa's definition of 'direct experience' cannot be a synonymy. But in any case, whatever triviality there is in the case of the epistemic apartness of souls appears to obtain as well in the case of the spatial apartness of two pieces of matter, x and y.[23] Consider what their spatial apartness really is, after all. It is not just that x is at some nonzero distance from y. This is true for two reasons: first, x can be at some nonzero distance from x (as, e.g., when x is on the surface of a sphere, and a great circle is drawn from x in any direction around the sphere and back to x);[24] and second, x can be spatially apart from y even though x is at zero distance from y (in a case where x and y are touching). Furthermore, on certain plausible definitions of the concept of distance, a piece of matter is at zero distance from itself.[25] Thus, the notion of spatial apartness is not definable just in terms of the distance relation, and no dyadic spatial relation holding between material things seems to be adequate by itself to define it. What, then, is spatial apartness? We maintain that to define the spatial apartness of x and y one must presuppose the diversity of the places of x and y. That is,

22 Sosa might reply that a proper accompaniment to diversity need not explain diversity so long as it *analyzes* it. In our view, part of the difference between an analysans and a synonym is that the former, but not the latter, is explanatory.

23 We shall assume that x and y are spatially extended.

24 Moreover, apparently, there could be a curved universe, e.g., a three-dimensional spherical universe with a finite radius. In such a spherical universe, a body is at a finite nonzero distance from itself along *every* geodesic intersecting it, each of which is a great circle.

25 If we understand object x being at zero distance from object y in terms of there being a point on the surface of x which is identical with a point on the surface of y, then it follows that an object can be at zero distance from itself. Given that between any two points there is a third point, x being at zero distance from y cannot be understood in terms of there being a point on the surface of x that is *adjacent* to a point on the surface of y.

As our examples have illustrated, an object x is at a *nonzero* distance from an object y only relative to a direction along some line that intersects x and y. Of course, if x is at *zero* distance from y, then this distance is *not* relative to such a direction. Thus, there is no inconsistency in an object's both being at many nonzero distances from itself (relative to different directed lines) and being at a zero distance from itself.

to say that x and y are spatially apart is to say that x and y are in or occupy *different* places, or at least it is to say that x is in a certain place, and that y is not in that place.

Recall our earlier discussion of the individuation of places. We pointed out there that if space is relational, then places are individuated in terms of bodies. Moreover, if space is relational, then the concept of a place is defined in terms of certain relations between pieces or portions of matter. Hence, given that the definition of the spatial apartness of two bodies is in terms of the occupation of a place or places by those bodies, this definition involves a relation to a place or space, and the spatial apartness of two bodies is as trivial an accompaniment to their diversity as one could imagine.[26] If space is absolute, then the diversity of the two places which is presupposed by the relation of spatial apartness, and which accompanies the diversity of two bodies, will not *itself* be accompanied by any irreflexive relation of the required sort. Note that the two places will not be spatially apart, since spatial apartness presupposes that the entities which are apart occupy diverse places, and because places do not occupy places.

For all these reasons, we conclude that Sosa has not shown both that there *is* a relation of the required sort which accompanies the diversity of pieces of matter and that there *is not* such a relation which accompanies the diversity of souls.

V. DOES DUALISTIC INTERACTION VIOLATE THE SUPERVENIENCE OF CAUSAL PROPERTIES UPON NONCAUSAL PROPERTIES?

We can always easily convert an hypothetical syllogism of one form into another, the *modus ponens* into the *modus tollens*.
    W. Hamilton *Lectures on Metaphysics & Logic* I. 344 (1860)

Sosa and others have challenged the intelligibility of causal interaction between souls and bodies.[27] In this argument, we are invited to consider the possibility of a world, W_1, in which there are two qualitatively indistinguishable souls, s_1 and s_2, and two qualitatively indistinguishable bodies, b_1 and b_2, such that: s_1 and b_1 causally interact, s_2 and b_2 causally interact,

---

26 We have employed 'distance' in its usual metrical sense. In the light of our argument, it is interesting to observe that another sense of 'distance', now obsolete, was *diversity*.

27 Sosa, "Subjects Among Other Things," pp. 166–167. John Foster appears to have originated this type of argument against the intelligibility of interaction. See his "Psychophysical Causal Relations," *American Philosophical Quarterly* 5 (1968), pp. 64–70. Note, however, that Foster introduced the argument only to refute it. We will cite his replies to the argument.

but s_1 does not interact with b_2, and s_2 does not interact with b_1. Sosa defends the plausible thesis that an object's causal properties *supervene upon* its noncausal properties. Sosa means by this that no single possible world, such as W_1, could contain two pairs of entities exactly alike noncausally but each differently interrelated causally. Therefore, it could not be the case that s_1 interacts with b_1 but not with b_2, while s_2 interacts with b_2, but not with b_1. In order for s_1, s_2, b_1, and b_2 to interact as described in W_1, there must be some noncausal relation between s_1 and b_1 which does not hold between s_1 and b_2, and so forth. Inasmuch as this relation cannot be a spatial one, and we have no idea what relation it might be, it is, Sosa says, "a great mystery how souls could interact causally with bodies."[28]

This argument has the following key presupposition:

(P4) If souls and bodies could interact, then there is a possible world such as W_1.

But it is not clear why a defender of the intelligibility of dualistic interaction should grant (P4). After all, such a defender might reason as follows. Take a world, W_2, in which there is a pair of qualitatively indistinguishable souls, s_1 and s_2, and a pair of qualitatively indistinguishable bodies, b_1 and b_2, such that: s_1 and b_1 causally interact, and s_2 and b_2 causally interact. Since no single world could contain two pairs of entities exactly alike noncausally but each differently interrelated causally, and inasmuch as we have no hint of any relation holding between s_1 and b_1 which does not also hold between s_1 and b_2, and so forth, it is plausible that in W_2 s_1 must interact causally with *both* b_1 and b_2, and s_2 must interact causally with *both* b_1 and b_2. In other words, the situation in W_2 is one in which the effects of interaction in the respective bodies and souls are causally overdetermined. Admittedly, such a situation is strange, but then so is a symmetrical world containing a pair of qualitatively indistinguishable bodies and a pair of qualitatively indistinguishable souls. Nor does it seem to be *impossible* that a soul causally interacts with two bodies, and a body causally interacts with two souls. The foregoing argument entails the falsity of (P4).

On the other hand, suppose that there is a convincing argument that implies that it is impossible for a soul to interact causally with two bodies or a body to interact causally with two souls. Suppose, too, that no single world could contain two pairs of entities exactly alike noncausally but each differently interrelated causally. Now, if we consider a world, W_3, containing two qualitatively indistinguishable souls, s_1 and s_2, and two qualitatively indistinguishable bodies, b_1 and b_2, then we do not have the slightest

28 Sosa, "Subjects Among Other Things," p. 166.

hint of any relation holding between s_1 and b_1 which does not hold as well between s_1 and b_2, and so forth. In the light of this, and the foregoing two suppositions, it is plausible to conclude that in a world such as W_3, there simply could not be any causal interaction between either s_1 and b_1 or b_2, or s_2 and b_1 or b_2. And once again, we arrive at a conclusion incompatible with (P4).[29]

Since each of the foregoing lines of argument seems no less plausible than Sosa's argument against the intelligibility of dualistic interaction, we conclude that if Sosa's argument is to be convincing, then further substantive support for his key assumption (P4) is needed. At present, we have no idea of how such support might be provided. On the other hand, if no support of this kind is available, our reply to Sosa's argument reveals an interesting and hitherto unnoticed implication of dualistic interactionism, namely, that there are no possible worlds such as W_1, but only ones such as W_2 or W_3.

VI. THE CLASSICAL ATTACK ON DUALISTIC INTERACTION: A REPLY

Heraclitus well compares the soul to a spider and the body to a spider's web. Just as a spider, he says, standing in the middle of its web, is aware as soon as a fly has broken one of its threads and runs there quickly as though grieving over the cutting of the thread, so a man's soul, when some part of his body is hurt, hurries there as if unable to bear the hurt to the body to which it is firmly and proportionately joined.

Hisdosus *On Plato's World-Soul* 17v

But, we ask, how, possibly, can these affections pass from body to soul? Body may communicate qualities or conditions to another body; but − body to soul? Something happens to A; does that make it happen to B?

Plotinus *Enneads* I. 2

The classical attack on the intelligibility of causal interaction between souls and bodies is based on the following argument.

29 Foster also has two replies to this kind of antiinteractionist argument. See Foster, "Psychophysical Causal Relations," and "In *Self*-Defense," in *Perception and Identity,* ed. G. F. MacDonald (London: Macmillan, 1979), pp. 168–170. The two replies are summarized in Foster, "A Defense of Dualism," in *The Case for Dualism,* ed. John Smythies and John Beloff (Charlottesville: University Press of Virginia, 1989), pp. 1–23. Both of Foster's replies, however, involve the rejection of Sosa's premise that all causal relations supervene on purely qualitative noncausal facts. We do not reject this premise in making our two replies to Sosa.

163

(B1) Necessarily, a body, but not a soul, has spatial location.

(B2) Necessarily, a soul and a body interact only if they both have spatial location.

(B3) It is impossible for a soul and a body to interact.

(B1) is unquestionably true. However, it is not clear that (B2) is true. Sosa's argument from the supervenience of causal properties upon non-causal properties is an example of an attempt to defend (B2). We have rejected that argument. However, there is another, more traditional, argument for (B2). In what follows, we try to show that this traditional argument, and certain related ones, are unsuccessful.

According to this traditional argument, the production of motion in a body can only be understood in terms of the transference of motion from one object to another. (Typically, this transference is characterized in terms of the collision of bodies and the transference of motion by impact.) This argument's assumption that the production of motion in a body can only be understood in terms of the transference of motion might be defended by appeal to the following *principle of transference:*

Necessarily, if *a* brings it about that *b* is *F,* then *a* does so in virtue of the transference of *F*-ness from *a* to *b.*

Let *b* be a body, and let *F* be motion. In that case, the transference principle implies that *a* could not bring it about that *b* is in motion unless *a* is in motion and transfers that motion to *b.* However, body–soul interaction is possible only if it is possible for a soul to produce motion in a body. Hence, body–soul interaction is possible only if motion could be transferred from a soul to a body. Since the transference of motion from *a* to *b* requires that both *a* and *b* have spatial location, it follows that necessarily, a soul and a body interact only if they both have spatial location.

The transference principle presupposes the necessity of what Jonathan Barnes has called the *synonymy principle:*

If *a* brings it about that *b* is φ, then *a* is φ.[30]

However, as Barnes points out, the synonymy principle is false.[31] For example, a piece of clay can be caused to be square by an object which is not square, for example, a rolling pin. It follows that the transference

30 Jonathan Barnes, *The Presocratics, Volume I* (Boston: Routledge and Kegan Paul, 1979), p. 119.
31 Ibid.

principle is false as well. Thus, neither the transference principle nor the synonymy principle can be used to provide a plausible defense of the crucial assumption that the production of motion in a body must be understood in terms of transference of motion.[32] It is not obvious that a plausible defense of this assumption can be provided in terms of some alternative principle. Is this assumption acceptable? We shall argue that it is not.

It is extremely plausible that causal interaction can be understood in terms of universally quantified general laws. If causal interaction is understood in terms of such general laws, then there can be functional or correlational causal relationships which do not involve the production of motion by the transference of motion. (This seems to be true whether or not a Humean is correct in denying that these laws express some kind of objective necessary connection.) For instance, consider the law of universal gravitation. According to this law, there is mutual gravitational attraction between any two pieces of matter. As a result, two such pieces of matter accelerate toward each other. It is a law that each acquires a motion, but it is not the case that motion is *transferred* from one to the other. Must there be a deeper explanation of the accelerations in question in terms of transference of motion? Not necessarily. In a domain of causal activity, one could eventually arrive at laws or causal principles which are basic or fundamental, and which therefore describe interactions unexplainable in terms of any more general laws or principles. As far as we know, the law of

32 It should be noted that, unlike the transference principle, the synonymy principle says nothing about the *transference* of properties. The transference principle is based on the intuition that if a brings it about that b is F, then there is a transfer of F-ness from a to b – a transfer in which F-ness is *conserved*. It is logically consistent to reject this intuition, and yet affirm the synonymy principle based on another intuition, viz., that *like can only be produced by like*. Instead of appealing to the transference principle to defend (B2), one can appeal *instead* to the necessity of the synonymy principle. Such a defense of (B2) begins with the following observation. If the synonymy principle is necessarily true, then motion in a body can only be brought about by something that is in motion. But, if something is not located in space, then it cannot be in motion. It follows that motion in a body can only be brought about by something that is located in space. However, body–soul interaction is possible only if it is possible for a soul to produce motion in a body. Hence, (B2) is true.

However, since the synonymy principle is false, the foregoing defense of (B2) is unsound. The defender of (B2) might retreat to the following *restricted* synonymy principle:

If a brings it about that b is ϕ, then there is *some* property that a and b have in common.

Although this restricted principle is necessarily true, it is only *trivially* so. Any two entities must have *some* property in common, e.g., being self-identical. Since a soul and a body have a property in common, e.g., being concrete, being a substance, the restricted synonymy principle cannot be used to support (B2).

gravitation is a basic principle or law, correlating one physical phenomenon with another, a principle or law which is *itself* physically inexplicable.[33]

Therefore, it seems that the aforementioned accelerations are causally related to one another in virtue of some functional law, but this causal interaction is neither a transference of motion, nor explainable in terms of other transferences of motion. Hence, production of motion in a body need not be understood in terms of the transference of motion. Since the argument for (B2) makes the key assumption that the production of motion in a body must be understood in terms of the transference of motion, the argument for (B2) is unsuccessful. It seems that if a soul interacts with a body, then this entails that there is a psychophysical correlation law which cannot be explained in terms of any more general or more basic physical

---

33 Of course, if it should turn out that the law of gravitation *is* explicable in terms of some deeper law, e.g., a law about how bodies affect the geometry of space-time, or a law about the transmission or propagation of gravitons or gravity waves, then this raises the prospect that such a deeper law is inexplicable. Observe that if either the law of gravitation or a deeper law of this kind is a fundamental law, then even the following *restricted* transference principle is false (and hence is not a necessary truth):

(RTP) If *a* brings it about that *b* is ϕ, then *a* does so in virtue of the transference of *some* property from *a* to *b*.

In addition, it appears that (RTP) does not imply (B2). (RTP) implies (B2) only if the following lemma is true:

(*Lemma*) There *could not* be a property, *P*, had by *both* a material substance, *x*, and an unlocated soul, *y*, such that *P* is transferred between *x* and *y*, and it is in virtue of the transference of *P* between *x* and *y* that *x* and *y* interact.

There appear to be two kinds of possible cases which refute (*Lemma*). First, it seems that, *possibly*, a material substance and a soul *both* have the property of consciousness, and interaction between them occurs in virtue of a transfer of consciousness from a soul to a material substance, followed by a transfer of consciousness in the opposite direction. (It could happen that a transfer of consciousness from a soul *to a material substance* is the first link in a causal chain that results in the motion of that material substance, and that a transfer of consciousness *to a soul* from a material substance results in a change in the state of consciousness of that soul.) Thus, for example, a human soul could interact in this manner with certain living parts or cells of a human body, or a nonhuman spirit, e.g., an angel, could interact in this way with another life form that is a material substance, e.g., a human or some other creature. As a result, a soul would produce motion in a body, and a body would produce a change of consciousness in a soul. In the second case, a body and a soul *both* have the property of having energy or the ability to do work, and interaction between them occurs in virtue of transfers of energy. In this context, *the ability to do work* can be taken to mean *either* the ability to produce some physical effect or a more generic ability, viz., *the ability to do something*. There are many things souls have the ability to do, e.g., solve mathematical problems, which a body could enhance by interaction with a soul. Clearly, the same holds for the enhancement of bodily abilities by souls.

law. However, it appears that a correlation law of this kind is unintelligible only if a physically inexplicable *physical*–physical correlation law is unintelligible. But, as we argued, a correlation law of the latter kind is not unintelligible. In particular, it seems both that universal gravitation is such a law, and that universal gravitation is intelligible. Since a physically inexplicable physical–physical correlation law is not unintelligible, there seems to be no reason to reject the intelligibility of a physically inexplicable psychophysical correlation law. (Although there is a sense in which an inexplicable psychophysical correlation is mysterious, an inexplicable physical–physical correlation law is no less mysterious.)

Is there another way to justify (B2) that is more plausible than the traditional argument we have criticized? We cannot think of one.[34] As far as we can tell, there is no good reason to accept (B2). Since the classical attack on the intelligibility of body–soul interaction is based on (B2), we conclude that this attack is ineffective.

VII. DO DUALISTIC INTERACTIONS VIOLATE THE LAWS OF NATURE?

The 'laws of nature', by those who first used the term in this sense, were viewed as commands imposed by the Deity upon matter.
"Laws of Nature" *Oxford English Dictionary* (1971)

Stated in its complete logical form a law is always a universal hypothetical judgement, which states that whenever C is or holds good, E is or holds good.
Lotze's (R. H.) *Metaphysic* 333 (1884 trans.)

In the argument against miracles the first objection is that they are against law.
J. Mozley *Eight Lectures on Miracles* ii. 39 (1865)

The following argument implies that body–soul interaction is unintelligible.

Argument C

(C1) If it is possible that there is body–soul interaction, then it is possible that a physical law is violated.

(C2) It is not possible that a physical law is violated.

(C3) It is impossible that there is body–soul interaction.

34 See nn. 32 and 33 for criticisms of certain related arguments for (B2).

167

It would appear that (C2) is entailed by a plausible account of lawfulness. Necessarily, if L is a law, then L is a true universally quantified conditional. Necessarily, a universally quantified conditional is violated just when there exists a counterinstance to that conditional. For example, the conditional $(\forall x)(Fx \rightarrow Gx)$ is violated if and only if $(\exists x)(Fx \,\&\, \sim Gx)$. Necessarily, there does not exist a counterinstance to a *true* universally quantified conditional. It follows that it is not possible that a law is violated. Therefore, (C2) is true. We shall not question (C2).

It might appear that (C1) is true; nevertheless, we shall argue that it is false. To begin, consider a typical physical law of the form: for any physical object, x, if x is F, then x is G. Unless the defender of Argument C is simply begging the question, he must concede that such a law says implicitly that for any physical object, x, if Fx then Gx, provided that there is no true conjunction of a nonphysical law and initial conditions which implies that x is both F and $\sim G$. Since this law describes only interaction between physical states, it is appropriate to classify it as a *physical* law. An implicit *ceteris paribus* provision of the kind indicated guarantees the inviolability of a physical law of the form in question in the face of interventions by supernatural influences. It accomplishes this by limiting the scope of such a physical law to physical interactions. Parallel remarks apply to physical laws of any kind.

Suppose that a physical state, P_1, is produced by a soul-state, S_1, and that if S_1 were to fail to exist, then there would be a true conjunction of a physical law, L, and physical initial conditions which implies that P_1 fails to exist. Although, as we have argued, L is not *violated* in such a case, it is accurate to say that L is *superseded* or *overruled*. Observe that a law's being superseded in this sense *does not* have the implication that a law is false. On the other hand, a law's being violated *does* have this apparently absurd implication. Hence, a law's being superseded does not imply that a law is violated, and it is a mistake to conflate the supersedence of a law with the violation of a law. If the supersedence of a law is assimilated to the violation of a law, a deceptive appearance is created that certain kinds of supernatural interventions would violate a physical law.

The foregoing considerations imply that (C1) is false. Hence, the argument for the unintelligibility of body–soul interaction based on (C1) is unsound.[35]

35 The argument in this section parallels the one given in Joshua Hoffman's "Comments on 'Miracles and the Laws of Nature' by George Mavrodes," *Faith and Philosophy* 4 (1985),

VIII. DO SOULS NEED A CRITERION OF PERSISTENCE?

> The soul is revealed intuitively as a perduring living agent or entity.
>
> J. Skinner *Dissert. Metaphysics* 109 (1890)
>
> What is this necessary axiom . . . but the perdurability of material substance."
>
> F. Bowen *Modern Philosophy* xv. 269 (1877)

The concept of a soul is the concept of a substance. A substance can endure through time. Thus, a soul can have identity over time. To say that an entity, x, has identity over time is to say that x exists at one time and is identical with something that exists at another time. (An entity's identity over time is the same thing as its persistence, at least in the case where the entity in question is a substance which exists in time, as opposed to space-time.) Yet another challenge to the intelligibility of souls questions the coherence of the idea of a persisting soul. This challenge parallels the earlier one which claimed that the synchronic diversity of souls is unintelligible.

This argument goes as follows:

Argument D

(D1) A criterion for the identity over time of a soul must provide an explanation (and an analysis) of such identity.[36]

(D2) If an entity of a certain category can persist, then there must be a criterion of identity over time for entities of that category.

pp. 347–352. Note that Argument C and the other arguments which we criticize in Chapter 5 are *conceptual* objections to the *intelligibility* of souls or dualistic interaction. We do not consider *empirical* objections to dualistic interaction such as those "based on appeals to a principle of the 'causal closure' of the physical world, or the 'explanatory completeness' of physics, plus the implausibility of systematic causal overdetermination" (anonymous referee for Cambridge University Press).

36 The notion of identity over (one-dimensional) time employed here should be distinguished from the notion of identity over (four-dimensional) space-time. Since it is impossible that a soul has spatial dimensions, it is impossible that there be a soul which exists in space-time. Presumably, it is *possible* that a body persists (in time, as opposed to in space-time), and hence not *necessary* that if a body persists, then it persists through space-time. In what follows, we reply to Argument D by arguing that the effort to analyze the persistence of a body (in time, not in space-time) in terms of a criterion involving spatiotemporal continuity does not yield any result that makes bodies any better off than souls with respect to such an effort. Inasmuch as it is *possible* that a body persists (in time, as opposed to in space-time), such an argument, if successful, suffices as an answer to Argument D.

(D3) A soul does not have a criterion for identity over time.[37]

(D4) If it is possible that a soul exists, then it is possible that a soul persists.

(D5) It is impossible for there to be a soul.

Those who defend an argument of this sort are usually committed to the proposition that pieces of matter or bodies possess a criterion for persistence. This criterion is usually thought to involve spatiotemporal continuity, so we shall confine our attention to those who hold this view.[38] Since souls are not in space, they obviously cannot possess a criterion of persistence involving spatiotemporal continuity.

Given the assumption that if bodies have a criterion of persistence, then that criterion involves spatiotemporal continuity, we will argue that if (D2) is true, then neither bodies nor places are intelligible. Hence, we will show that given this assumption souls are no worse off than bodies and places with respect to possessing a criterion of persistence.

Our argument is based on the following two claims. First, if a body persists in virtue of its momentary stages being spatiotemporally continuous, then this *entails* that places persist. Second, the notion of a body's persisting in virtue of its stages being spatiotemporally continuous *involves* the notion of a persisting place. The argument for these two claims goes as follows.

The notion of the stages of a body, b, being spatiotemporally continuous involves the idea that, necessarily, if a momentary stage of b in a place p_1 at a moment of time t_1 is spatiotemporally continuous with a momentary stage of b in a place p_2 at another moment of time t_2, then either (i) p_1 at $t_1 = p_2$ at t_2, or (ii) there exists a third place p_3 between p_1 and p_2, at a third time, t_3, between t_1 and t_2, and p_3 is occupied by a momentary stage of b. (i) is satisfied if b is stationary from t_1 to t_2. (i) explicitly entails the identity of a place over time. (ii) is satisfied if b is in motion at some time during $[t_1-t_2]$. In the case of (ii), since at time t_3, p_3 is between p_1 and p_2, it logically follows

37 E.g., John Perry, "A Dialogue on Personal Identity and Immortality," in *Reason and Responsibility,* 7th ed., ed. Joel Feinberg (Belmont, Calif.: Wadsworth, 1989), pp. 323–341.

38 E.g., Richard Swinburne, *Space and Time* (New York: St. Martin's Press, 1968), chap. 1; C. D. Broad, *Scientific Thought* (Paterson, N.J.: Littlefield, Adams, 1959), p. 393; Robert Coburn, "Identity and Spatiotemporal Continuity," in *Identity and Individuation,* ed. M. Munitz (New York: New York University Press, 1971), pp. 51–101; Sydney Shoemaker, *Self-Knowledge and Self-Identity* (Ithaca, N.Y.: Cornell University Press, 1967), pp. 4–5; and David Wiggins, *Identity and Spatiotemporal Continuity* (Oxford: Basil Blackwell, 1971). In Section IX, we explicate the notion of spatiotemporal continuity as it applies to bodies and criticize the claim that spatiotemporal continuity is a criterion of persistence for bodies.

that p_1 exists at both t_1 and t_3, and p_2 exists at both t_1 and t_3. Consequently, if a body's stages exhibit spatiotemporal continuity, then this *entails* that places have identity across time.

Furthermore, if one says that an entity, x, exists (or has some property or bears some relation) at *two* times, then this is tantamount to saying that x has identity across time. Let $x = p_1$. Since by hypothesis p_1 exists at t_1, and since (ii) says that at another time t_3, another place p_3 is between p_1 and p_2, it follows that in virtue of (ii) the notion of a body's stages being spatiotemporally continuous involves a notion tantamount to the persistence of a place. In addition, in virtue of (i) the notion of a body's stages being spatiotemporally continuous explicitly involves the idea that a place persists. Therefore, the notion of a body's persisting in virtue of its stages being spatiotemporally continuous involves the notion of a persisting place.[39]

What, then, is the criterion of persistence for places? As in the case of synchronic diversity (or identity) of places, the answer to this question will depend on whether space is relational or absolute. If space is relational, then the existence of places depends on the existence of bodies, and the persistence of places must involve their relations to persisting bodies. Thus, if space is relational, and p_1 at t_1 is the same place as p_2 at t_2, then p_1 and p_2 must bear the same relations at the same times to bodies which persist from t_1 to t_2. Hence, if space is relational, then the criterion of persistence for places involves the persistence of bodies. As we have seen, however, if the criterion of persistence for bodies involves spatiotemporal continuity, then

---

39 The notion of a spatiotemporally continuous sequence of body-stages stands in need of explanation, but it is hard to see how it can be adequately explained without making reference to the places occupied by those stages. E.g., suppose that one claims that there is a primitive relation of (partial or total) "spatial overlap" between successive stages, and then one attempts to define a spatiotemporally continuous sequence of body-stages as a temporally continuous sequence of body-stages, each of the members of which (except for the first) spatially overlaps an earlier member of that sequence. We have two responses to such a ploy. First, no two stages of a body *literally* overlap in space, since they do not coexist. Rather, it is the places which are occupied by the stages in question which overlap. Second, even if we waive the first criticism, an attempted definition of a spatiotemporally continuous sequence of body-stages along the lines just suggested is inadequate, for as our argument in the next section implies, there could be a sequence of body-stages which satisfies such a proposed definition and which is not spatiotemporally continuous. As we shall argue, it is possible that there be a material object which has a temporally continuous sequence of body-stages and which moves in a spatially discontinuous manner. An object of this kind may wholly occupy an extended place and then discontinuously "jump" to another extended place which partly overlaps the former one. This possibility involves a sequence of body-stages which satisfies an attempted definition of a spatiotemporally continuous sequence of body-stages in terms of a primitive relation of spatial overlap between successive stages, but this sequence is not spatiotemporally continuous.

171

this criterion involves the persistence of places. It is circular to give a criterion for the persistence of bodies in terms of the persistence of places, and the persistence of places in terms of the persistence of bodies. As in the case of synchronic diversity, the demand for a criterion of the persistence of bodies is a demand for a certain kind of explanation. Since an explanation cannot be circular, if space is relational, then the circularity of a purported criterion of the persistence of bodies in terms of the persistence of places is vicious. In general, for diverse ontological categories F and G, it is viciously circular to explain the persistence of Fs in terms of a criterion involving the persistence of Gs, and the persistence of Gs in terms of a criterion involving the persistence of Fs.

Even if space is absolute, it is viciously circular to explain the persistence of bodies in terms of a criterion involving the persistence of places, and the persistence of places in terms of a criterion involving the persistence of bodies. So, if space is absolute and the persistence of bodies is explained in terms of a criterion involving the persistence of places, then what explains the persistence of places?[40] The only replies to this question that need to be considered are the following.

First, places persist, but have no criterion of persistence. If this is the reply, then the persistence of a place has no explanation. But if this is so, why suppose that the persistence of a soul is in need of an explanation?[41] Moreover, note that if persisting places have no criterion of persistence, then it is false that for any ontological category of persisting entity, there must be a criterion of persistence for entities of that category. This would mean that (D2) is false.

Second, suppose (D2) is granted. In that case, since places lack a criterion of persistence, places are unintelligible (given that if it is possible for there to be places, then it is possible for places to persist). In addition, given that bodies have no criterion of persistence unless they have one involving

---

40 Notice that a criterion of persistence for a place cannot be in terms of spatiotemporal continuity. The reasons for this are parallel to those which imply that a place cannot be individuated at a time by its location. (See n. 14.)

41 An anonymous referee for Cambridge University Press suggests that souls stand in need of a criterion of persistence, even though places do not, because souls, unlike places, are capable of undergoing intrinsic change. We respond as follows. This objection fails because it implies that, e.g., physical objects which can undergo intrinsic change require a criterion of persistence, whereas physical objects which cannot undergo intrinsic change, e.g., Democritean atoms, do not require such a criterion. However, possibly, at a time t, there is a Democritean atom, a', and at a later time t', a' exists along with another qualitatively indistinguishable atom a''. In the light of this possibility, immutable Democritean atoms stand no less in need of a criterion of persistence than mutable complexes of them.

spatiotemporal continuity, and given that spatiotemporal continuity requires the persistence of places, it follows also that bodies are unintelligible.

Third, the persistence of a place can be explained in terms of a criterion involving either a nonqualitative haecceity or a trope that a place exemplifies or possesses at different times. An example of a nonqualitative haecceity would be the property of *being identical with that* (where *that* = the place in question), and an example of a trope would be *that particular shape* (of the place in question). In this case, the persistence of a soul can be explained in terms of a criterion involving the same kind of property or trope, for example, by the nonqualitative haecceity, *being identical with that* (where *that* = the soul under discussion), or by the trope *that particular consciousness* (of the soul under discussion).

In conclusion, whether space is relational or absolute, the attempt to provide an explanatory criterion or analysis of the persistence of a body in terms of a criterion involving spatiotemporal continuity does not yield any result that makes bodies any better off than souls with respect to such an attempt. Therefore, if bodies or places are intelligible, the argument under discussion does not establish any unintelligibility in the concept of a soul.

IX. IS SPATIOTEMPORAL CONTINUITY A CRITERION OF PERSISTENCE FOR BODIES?

All that shall be, hath a stint and dependance of that which is, by a certeine continuite, which proceedeth from the beginning to the end.
P. Holland, trans., *Plutarch's Philosophie, commonly called, the Morals*
1356 (1603)

As we have observed, since souls are nonspatial, souls lack a criterion of persistence in terms of spatiotemporal continuity. We shall now argue that bodies also lack a criterion of persistence in terms of spatiotemporal continuity, and hence that bodies are no better off than souls in this respect. We begin our argument by providing a formal account of the relevant notion of spatiotemporal continuity. The following series of four definitions culminates in an account of the notion of a spatiotemporally continuous sequence of body-stages.

A *sequence of body-stages* is a sequence of instantaneous temporal slices of a body or bodies, ordered so that each member of the sequence exists at a moment which is later than the moment at which any preceding member of the sequence exists and which is earlier than the moment at which any subsequent member of the sequence exists.

The notion of a *spatiotemporally continuous* sequence of body-stages can be defined in three steps, as follows:

S is a *spatially discontinuous* sequence of body-stages =df. S is a sequence of body-stages such that: (i) S has a subsequence $S^\star$, which has a member, x, which exists at a moment of time t_1 in a place p_1, and a member, y, which exists at a moment of time t_2 in a place p_2, where t_1 is not identical with t_2 and p_1 is not identical with p_2; and (ii) no member of $S^\star$ exists at a time between t_1 and t_2 in a place other than p_1 and other than p_2.

S is a *temporally discontinuous* sequence of body-stages =df. S is a sequence of body-stages such that: (i) S has a subsequence $S^\star$, and a member of $S^\star$ exists at a time t_1 and a member of $S^\star$ exists at a time t_2, where t_1 is not identical with t_2; and (ii) no member of $S^\star$ exists at a time between t_1 and t_2.

S is a *spatiotemporally continuous sequence* of body-stages =df. S is a sequence of body-stages that is neither spatially discontinuous nor temporally discontinuous.[42]

In this context, to say that a body is spatiotemporally continuous is to say that its stages constitute a spatiotemporally continuous sequence. We shall argue that a body lacks an analysis or criterion of persistence involving spatiotemporal continuity among a sequence of body-stages. (The following is a simple analysis of this kind: a body x that exists at a moment t_1 is identical with a body y that exists at another moment t_2 =df. the body-stage of x at t_1 and the body-stage of y at t_2 belong to a spatiotemporally continuous sequence of body-stages.)

To begin with, it might be thought that spatial and temporal discontinuity are not logically independent, and in particular that any spatial discontinuity of necessity involves a temporal discontinuity. If this were so, then by proving the possibility of the former one would prove the possibility of the latter. In fact, the two are logically independent, as the following argument shows. Consider the spatial discontinuity of a temporally continuous sequence of object-stages as illustrated by Figure 5.1. Material object x is in place p_1 from time t_0 until time t_1. In other words, t_1 is the last moment of x's existence in place p_1. Now, because time is a continuum, we can say both that physical object y does not exist at t_1, and that for any time t, such that $t_1 < t < t_2$, y is in place p_2. This implies that there is no first moment of y's being in place p_2, and that there is no time between t_1 and t_2 at which y does not exist. It should be noted that this example does not

---

42 In effect, this account characterizes a spatiotemporally continuous sequence of body-stages as a sequence of body-stages which is densely ordered with respect to space and time. Although, in general, density does not entail continuity, we have argued that *space* and *time's* being dense entails their continuity. See Chapter 4, n. 17. For these reasons, we think that this account of a spatiotemporally continuous sequence of body-stages is correct.

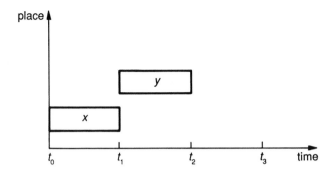

Figure 5.1

involve our saying anything about continuous space or time which we would not have to say anyhow in order to solve certain well-known paradoxes of qualitative and substantial change.[43] For example, we must say of something which comes into existence either that it has a last moment of nonexistence and no first moment of existence, or vice versa. A similar strategy must be adopted to deal with other changes. Since, in our example, the path traced in time by the stages of x and y from t_0 until t_2 is continuous even though the path traced by them in space is not, a sequence's being spatially discontinuous does not entail its being temporally discontinuous.

Since the following case (Case A) seems possible, spatiotemporal continuity among some sequence of body-stages does not appear to be a logically necessary condition of the persistence of a body. Body b occupies place p_1 at time t_1. There is another place p_2 such that at every time between t_1 and a later time t_2, b occupies p_2. In this sort of case, b instantaneously "jumps" in space. That is, b persists, and although b's stages belong to a *temporally continuous* sequence, some of these stages are *spatially discontinuous*. It also seems possible that b persists, and some of its stages are temporally discontinuous. In such a case (Case B) an object "jumps" in time, for example as follows. A body b occupies place p_1 at a moment of time t_1. At every time between t_1 and a later moment of time t_2, b (and each of its parts) fails to exist. At t_2, b occupies p_1. This case presupposes

43 These problems are discussed in a historical context by Norman Kretzmann, "Incipit/Desinit," in *Motion and Time, Space and Matter,* ed. Peter Machamer and Robert Turnbull (Columbus: Ohio State University Press, 1976), pp. 101–136.

that, possibly, a body is totally annihilated and then comes back into existence.[44] The possibility of such a case also implies that the spatiotemporal continuity of some sequence of body-stages is not a logically necessary condition of the persistence of a body.

The possibility of a body making a spatial or temporal "jump" might be attacked as follows. This possibility presupposes that in some possible world someone has conclusive evidence (or at least justification) for believing that such a "jump" occurred. But, there is no such possible world.

Our reply is this. For an observer to reidentify even a spatiotemporally continuous body (other than himself), an *inductive* or *nonconclusive* justification is needed (at least implicitly).[45] Such a justification is ultimately based on nonsimultaneous perceptions of a body which reveal a similarity in a body's sensory properties at diverse times.[46] An inductive justification for such a reidentification may involve inference to the best explanation, causal reasoning, testimony, and so forth.[47]

The need for such inductive justifications of reidentification claims can be brought out by considering the following possible example. Suppose that person, S, has a material object, x, under observation at time, t, in ordinary conditions. It seems to S that from t to a later time, t', he has observed x continuously. On the basis of this evidence, S identifies the object he sees at t' with the object he saw at t. But it may be that while S was watching x, x had zoomed away too fast for S to notice, and that another object, y, indistinguishable from x in its intrinsic qualitative properties, had zoomed in, again too fast for S to notice. It is possible for S to be in a situation like this, and thus, to have the very best evidence he can have for reidentifying a material object. Nevertheless, S may be mistaken in his reidentification of x. True, S may anticipate a possibility such as the one described and endeavor to rule it out, but there are others he cannot

---

44 The denial of this possibility is often attributed to John Locke on the basis of the following quotation: "one thing cannot have two beginnings of existence" (*An Essay Concerning Human Understanding,* ed. John Yolton [London: Everyman, 1974], book 2, chap. 27, "Of Identity and Diversity"). However, we believe that this is a misreading of Locke and that he never meant to deny the possibility of intermittent existence. For an argument to this effect, see Joshua Hoffman, "Locke on Whether a Thing Can Have Two Beginnings of Existence," *Ratio* 22 (1980), pp. 106–111.

45 We leave open the possibility that each of us is a material object and can reidentify himself on wholly deductive grounds. For an argument which implies that each of us can reidentify himself on wholly deductive grounds in virtue of grasping his own nonqualitative haecceity, see Rosenkrantz, *Haecceity.*

46 For arguments in support of this claim, see John Pollock, *Knowledge and Justification* (Princeton: Princeton University Press, 1974), chap. 6.

47 Ibid.

anticipate. Furthermore, there are possibilities which S can anticipate but cannot rule out, because of the inherent limitation of the accuracy of the observations he can make. Finally, there are some possibilities S can rule out only by presupposing other reidentifications which are themselves uncertain. In the light of the fact that the possibilities of such failures to observe are endless, it is clear that none of us can reidentify a material object other than himself without relying (at least implicitly) upon an inductive or nonconclusive justification for the reidentification in question.

An inductive justification for reidentifying a body need not involve the premise that the stages of this body form a spatiotemporally continuous sequence. Hence, given that an inductive justification is possible when an observer seeks to reidentify an external body whose stages form a spatiotemporally continuous sequence, an inductive justification is possible also when an observer seeks to reidentify an external body that "jumps" in space or time. For example, take a possible case of an apparent spatial "jump." Suppose that while you are staring at a ball of distinctive appearance, it disappears from its spot on the left side of your desk, and a ball which is indistinguishable in its sensible qualities instantly appears on the right side.[48] Alternatively, in a possible case of an apparent temporal "jump," the ball vanishes from its spot, and two minutes later a ball that is indistinguishable in its sensible qualities appears in the same spot. In either of these cases, the following circumstances could obtain. First, the most sophisticated and exhaustive empirical tests fail to detect any spatiotemporally continuous sequence of body-stages connecting "prejump" and "postjump" stages of the ball (or any of its parts). Second, the body-stages observed immediately before and after the apparent "jump" appear to be indistinguishable in their intrinsic qualitative properties and velocities when examined with our most accurate instruments, within the limits of experimental error. Third, such an apparent "jump" invariably occurs under replicable conditions of a certain kind. In these circumstances, all other things being equal, one would possess an inductive justification for believing that the ball had made a "jump" in space or time.

Since objects do not ordinarily appear to "jump" in space or time, if there was an isolated case in which one seems to observe that an object

---

48 By two objects being indistinguishable in sensible qualities, we mean in this context their being indistinguishable relative to inspection by means of the unaided senses. By a sensible quality in this context we mean an intrinsic qualitative sensible property, where a qualitative property is one which may be expressed by a term making no reference to any *concretum*.

"jumps" in space or time, then perhaps the most reasonable hypothesis would be that one has experienced an illusion. But since in possible scenarios like those just envisioned objects *do* regularly appear to "jump" in space or time, in such scenarios the hypothesis that one has experienced an illusion would not be a reasonable one. Alternatively, in scenarios of this kind it can be hypothesized that the first object one observes has been totally destroyed and that the perceptually indistinguishable object one observes later is a newly created twin. It can be further supposed that this twinning phenomenon is a sheer coincidence, or that it is the work of some unobservable agent or mechanism. Other, more implausible hypotheses are also available. Clearly, however, the simplest and best explanation, and the one we are therefore justified in accepting in the possible situations under discussion, is the hypothesis of a spatial or temporal "jump."[49]

Finally, it seems that there could be a case (Case C) which involves either the total annihilation of a body, and/or the total creation of another body, and/or one or more bodies that "jump" in space, and implies that the spatiotemporal continuity of a sequence of body-stages is not a logically sufficient condition for the persistence of a body. In this sort of case, a body b occupies a place p_1 at time t_1, and b occupies p_1 at every time after t_1 up to, but not including, t_2. In addition, at t_2, b (and each of its parts) either fails to exist or makes a "jump" to another place. Lastly, at t_2, *another* body $b\star$ (together with each of its parts) either comes into being in p_1 or makes a "jump" into p_1 from another place. This implies both that there is a spatiotemporally continuous sequence of body-stages, and that the bodies to which these stages belong are diverse. Hence, if one observes a spatiotemporally continuous sequence of body-stages, this does not provide logically conclusive grounds for the reidentification of a body, even if in fact all of these stages do belong to the same body.

In what follows, we give a more detailed description of two of the basic sorts of (Case C)-type situations just described: a first sort involving spatial "jumping," and a second sort involving total destruction, total creation, and a temporal "jump."

In Figure 5.2, object x is in place p_1 from time t_0 up to and including time t_1. x "jumps" in space to place p_2, so that x is in place p_2 at every time after t_1 up to and including time t_2. x makes a second "jump" in space from

---

49 The conclusion that it is possible for a material object to "jump" in space receives further support from contemporary quantum physics – at least on some interpretations. From a historical point of view, Leibniz (as well as Hume) allowed for the logical possibility of spatial jumping. See *Gottfried Wilhelm Leibniz: Philosophical Papers and Letters,* ed. Leroy E. Loemker (Dordrecht: Reidel, 1969), pp. 515–516.

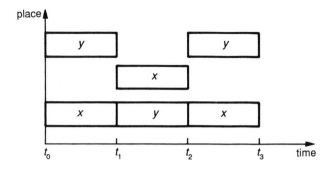

place

y | y

x

x | y | x

t_0 t_1 t_2 t_3 time

Figure 5.2

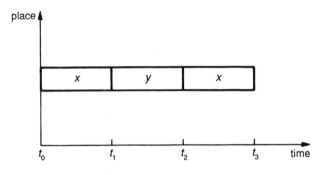

place

x | y | x

t_0 t_1 t_2 t_3 time

Figure 5.3

place p_2 back to place p_1, so that x is in place p_1 again at every time after t_2 up to and including time t_3. Object y is in place p_3 from time t_0 up to and including time t_1. y "jumps" from p_3 to p_1, so that y is in p_1 at every time after t_1 up to and including t_2. y makes a second "jump" from p_1 back to p_3, so that y is in p_3 at every time after t_2 up to and including time t_3.

As Figure 5.2 shows, in this case there is a spatiotemporally continuous sequence of object-stages in place p_1 from t_0 to t_3. Furthermore, certain stages of x are members of the sequence at times t_0 and t_3, even though x "jumps" in space in the interim.

Next, in Figure 5.3, x is a material object which is in place p from t_0 up to and including time t_1. x then undergoes total destruction, and consequently at every moment after t_1 up to and including time t_2, x fails to

179

exist. Material object y is created *ex nihilo* in place p, and is such that it exists in p at every time after t_1 up to and including time t_2. Finally, at every time after t_2 up to and including time t_3, x exists again in place p, x having been created *ex nihilo* and y having undergone total destruction. In this case, a stage of x existing at t_0 and a stage of x existing at t_3 are members of a continuous sequence of object-stages existing in p from t_0 to t_3, even though x fails to exist between t_1 and t_2.

A logical positivist might challenge the intelligibility of the case represented in Figure 5.3 on the ground that there is no empirically discernible difference between such a purported case of temporary-annihiliation-with-replacement and the ordinary persistence of a single object. However, we have already stipulated that in the possible case in question there are good inductive reasons for believing that the case is as we have described it. A logical positivist might reject this empirical evidence, but as we have argued, in doing so, he would be undermining the legitimacy of all reidentifications of external objects. This is an illustration of the well-known fact that logical positivism never succeeded in providing an adequate criterion of either empirical verifiability or cognitive significance.

Enough has now been said to make it plausible that spatiotemporal continuity among some sequence of body-stages is neither a logically necessary nor a logically sufficient condition for the persistence of a body.[50] Hence, although souls lack an analysis or criterion of persistence involving spatiotemporal continuity among a sequence of stages, so do bodies.[51]

---

50 Baruch Brody, in *Identity and Essence* (Princeton: Princeton University Press, 1980), chap. 3, criticizes an analysis of the persistence of physical objects couched in terms of spatiotemporal continuity. Brody's somewhat abbreviated argument is, like some of our arguments, based on the possibility of spatial jumping. He does not, as we do, confront the epistemic argument with which defenders of the continuity analysis would oppose the idea of spatial jumping, but instead invokes the authority of contemporary quantum physics in support of the claim that spatial jumping is possible. The development of the argument we have presented in favor of the possibility of spatial jumping preceded our discovery of a parallel approach in Brody.

51 Our criticisms of criteria of bodily persistence involving spatiotemporal continuity apply to *any* conceivable version of such a criterion, since in each of our examples *both* a body and all of its parts are spatially or temporally discontinuous. Thus, a criterion for the persistence of bodies cannot involve a spatiotemporally continuous sequence of stages of either *entire* bodies or any *proper parts* of bodies.

Alternatively, a causal account of bodily persistence along the following lines might be proposed. (CA) A material object, x, at time $t1$, and a material object, y, at time $t2$, are identical if and only if x has a stage x' at $t1$ and y has a stage y' at $t2$, where those stages are members of a sequence, s, of object-stages such that each of the members of s (except the first) bears a relation of causal dependence to earlier members of s.

As far as such a causal account of the persistence of bodies is concerned, note that

Once again, souls turn out to be no worse off than bodies in this respect.[52]

because temporal stages of souls can be causally related to one another no less than temporal stages of bodies, there is no reason to think that there is a (wholly) causal account of persistence in the case of bodies, but not in the case of souls.

Furthermore, as the example to be described illustrates, there is a serious difficulty which confronts a causal account of bodily persistence such as (CA). Consider the following possible state of affairs. There is a machine which can make a perfect copy of an object, at a place of one's choosing within a given radius, by reading off the object's properties and creating a duplicate. Suppose that there is a sphere sitting on a table and that the duplicating machine is turned on, copies the sphere, and creates a perfect copy. This copy is projected into the place where the sphere is resting at the precise time the original sphere is totally destroyed. The result is that the duplicate sphere has a stage which is a member of a sequence of sphere-stages all of whose members are (let us say) qualitatively indistinguishable. Furthermore, what properties the initial stage of the duplicate sphere instantiates *is* causally dependent upon what properties the last stage of the original sphere instantiated. Thus, (CA) is satisfied, but the series in question consists of stages from histories of different things, and our imagined state of affairs is a counterexample to the logical sufficiency of (CA). Notice that since such a series is spatiotemporally continuous and consists of stages which are qualitatively indistinguishable from one another, our imagined state of affairs is also a counterexample to the logical sufficiency of a proposed analysis of bodily persistence consisting of spatiotemporal continuity supplemented with causal dependence and/or with some requirement of similarity among stages. Also observe that for the same reason our imagined state of affairs is a counterexample to the logical sufficiency of a proposed analysis of bodily persistence consisting of causal dependence supplemented with such a similarity requirement. For an example of a philosopher who suggests that bodily persistence can be analyzed in terms of relations of causal dependence and similarity between body-stages, see Andrew Brennan, *Conditions of Identity* (Cambridge: Cambridge University Press, 1988).

Because "deviant" causal sequences of the sort described earlier are possible, a proposed causal account of bodily persistence, (C*), is adequate only if (C*) replaces the crucial but vague notion of causal dependence used in (CA) with a precisely delineated concept of causal dependence which renders (C*) immune to counterexamples of the foregoing sort and which is satisfactory in all other respects. However, it is far from clear that there is any such concept of causal dependence. Thus, it is doubtful that a causal account of the persistence of material objects can succeed. (Note that if one postulates a condition, A, in order to define a suitable concept of causal dependence, and A employs or presupposes the notion of bodily persistence, e.g., A employs either the idea of the relation of causal dependence that must hold between two body-stages existing at different times just provided that these stages belong to the *same* body, or the idea of a sequence of body-stages such that no two of its members belong to *different* bodies, then A thereby employs or presupposes the very idea which has been targeted for analysis and, therefore, is inadmissibly circular in this context.)

52 This section is based on Joshua Hoffman's "The Persistence of Physical Objects," unpublished manuscript.

181

The concrete–abstract distinction

A concrete name is a name which stands for a thing; an abstract name is a name which stands for an attribute of a thing.

J. S. Mill *A System of Logic* I. ii. § 4 (1846)

Realists and antirealists presuppose an intuitive distinction between *abstracta* and *concreta* in their debates about the problem of universals. Examples of *abstracta* are squareness (a property), betweenness (a relation), *there being horses* (a proposition), the null set, and the number 7. Examples of *concreta* are a stone (a material substance), God (a disembodied spiritual substance), Hurricane Andrew (an event), instants and seconds (times), points and expanses of space (places), the particular wisdom of Socrates (a trope), the sum of Earth and Mars (a collection), the Earth's surface (a limit), and shadows and holes (privations). It is desirable that a philosophical analysis of the concrete–abstract distinction allow for the possibility of entities of any intelligible sorts, given some plausible view about the nature, existence conditions, and interrelationships of entities of those sorts. This *desideratum* seems to require allowing for the possibility of entities of the aforementioned kinds. Six attempts have been made to analyze the concrete–abstract distinction.

(1) Unlike *abstracta, concreta* are spatially located or spatially related to something.

(2) Unlike *abstracta, concreta* are capable of moving or undergoing intrinsic change.

(3) *Concreta* have contingent existence, whereas *abstracta* have necessary existence.

(4) Unlike *concreta, abstracta* are exemplifiable.

(5) Unlike *concreta, abstracta* are (intellectually) graspable.

(6) Unlike *abstracta, concreta* can be causes or effects.

(1) is inadequate because a disembodied spirit is concrete but neither spatially located nor spatially related to something. Alternatively, we might amend (1) to read as follows.

(1') Unlike *abstracta*, *concreta* are spatially or temporally located, or spatially or temporally related to something.

Arguably, it is necessary that a soul is temporally located or enters into temporal relations. Still, (1') is flawed: properties are abstract, but it seems that some properties enter into temporal relations, for example, sobriety is exemplified by Socrates at one time and not at another. Although some philosophers claim that *abstracta* are outside of time, this claim is problematic, for as the example of sobriety and Socrates implies, *abstracta* undergo relational change. An entity's being temporal does not imply that it undergoes nonrelational change, for instance, a sphere which does not undergo nonrelational change and which other spheres orbit is in time.

(2) is inadequate because point-positions and instants are concrete but incapable of either moving or undergoing intrinsic change.

(3) is subject to three complaints or difficulties. First, a being such as the theistic God is concrete yet has necessary existence. Second, according to Aristotelean Realism a property cannot exist unexemplified. Aristotelean Realism implies that some properties are abstract yet have contingent existence. Third, sets of ordinary *concreta* are abstract but seem to have contingent existence.

(4) is objectionable because sets, propositions, and properties such as being a spherical cube are abstract but could not be exemplified.

(5) is unsatisfactory because it would seem that *abstracta* of certain kinds could not be grasped, for instance, sets of *concreta* or haecceities which can be exemplified by necessarily nonconscious material substances.[1]

(6) is unsatisfactory for the following reasons. According to one camp, causes and effects are concrete events.[2] On this view, (6) has the absurd implication that substances are nonconcrete. One reply is that substances (but not *abstracta*) can be *involved* in causal relations. But, if causes and effects are concrete events, then it is hard to fathom the sense of "involvement" intended. For according to an event ontology, an event's occurring does *not* entail that a substance exists, and an event is *not* a substance's

1 For an argument that such haecceities are ungraspable, see Gary Rosenkrantz, *Haecceity: An Ontological Essay* (Dordrecht: Kluwer, 1993), chap. 5, sec. 10.
2 See Donald Davidson, "The Individuation of Events," in *Essays in Honor of C. G. Hempel*, ed. N. Rescher (Dordrecht: D. Reidel, 1971), pp. 216–234; "Causal Relations," *Journal of Philosophy* 64 (1967), pp. 691–703; and "Events as Particulars," *Nous* 4 (1970), pp. 25–32.

exemplifying a property at a time or the like. Moreover, since causal relations hold in virtue of *laws* correlating *properties* of things, in a sense *abstracta* are *involved* in causal relations. Finally, there is evidence that facts or the like can be causes or effects, but facts are *abstracta*.[3]

We will attempt to devise an adequate analysis of the concrete–abstract distinction.[4] The basic idea of this analysis is that an entity is abstract or concrete in virtue of meeting certain conditions *qua* being an instance of the level *C* ontological category to which it belongs.[5]

(A1D1) x is concrete =df. x instantiates a level *C* category which possibly has an instance having spatial or temporal parts.

(A1D2) x is abstract =df. x is nonconcrete.[6]

---

3 These observations provide a reply to the following argument.

  (i) An abstract entity cannot enter into causal relations.
  (ii) We have knowledge about an entity only if that entity enters into causal relations.

  (iii) We cannot have knowledge about an abstract entity.

  In the light of those observations, it would seem that either (i) or (ii) is false. That is, either (i) is false because facts or the like are abstract and can enter into causal relations, or (ii) is false for either of the following two reasons. First, we have knowledge about material substances which cannot enter into causal relations. Second, although *abstracta* cannot enter into causal relations, there is a sense in which *abstracta* are involved in causal relations, and we can have knowledge about an entity if it is involved in causal relations in that sense. Cf. Jaegwon Kim, "The Role of Perception in *A Priori* Knowledge: Some Remarks," *Philosophical Studies* 40 (1981), pp. 339–354.

4 It seems that a consideration of difficulties such as the foregoing ones has led some philosophers to doubt whether there is such a thing as the concrete–abstract distinction at all. E.g., Kim ("*A Priori* Knowledge," p. 348) has written as follows. "The force of saying that something is 'abstract' or 'platonic' has never been made clear. One sense sometimes attached to 'abstract' is that of 'eternal'; an abstract object in this sense neither comes into being nor perishes. Another closely related sense is that of not being in space and time. Abstract entities in this sense are atemporal and nonspatial: they lack location in space-time. A third sense is that of 'necessary'; abstract entities in this sense are said to 'exist necessarily'. It is by no means obvious that these three senses are equivalent: for example, one traditional concept of God makes him abstract in the first and third sense but not in the second." Kim's skepticism about the very existence of the concrete–abstract distinction will prove to be unwarranted if we succeed in providing a philosophical analysis of this distinction, and in arguing that this analysis is adequate to the intuitions philosophers have had about how the distinction applies to particular cases.

5 For an account of our conception of a level *C* ontological category, see Chapter 1, Section II.

6 As (A1D2) illustrates, Abstractness can be explicated in wholly negative terms, since the concrete–abstract distinction is exhaustive and mutually exclusive. Observe that a categorial division of this sort is possible only at level *B*. No intelligible ontological category below level *B* can be explicated in wholly negative terms. Attempting to explicate such a category, *x*, in wholly negative terms is, after all, not to distinguish *x* from other categories which are at the same level of generality as *x* and which can also be described in those negative terms. To explicate such a category and to distinguish it from other catego-

This analysis of the concrete–abstract distinction incorporates the classical notion that the concrete–abstract distinction can be understood in terms of spatiality and temporality. Furthermore, it isn't difficult to see that this analysis adequately handles the problem cases presented earlier.

To begin with, notice that a disembodied spirit instantiates the level C category of Substance. Likewise, for a necessary being such as the theistic God. However, the category of Substance possibly has an instance having spatial parts, that is, a complex material substance. Hence, a disembodied spirit, or the theistic God, satisfies (A1D1): it instantiates a level C category which possibly has an instance having spatial parts. Thus, (A1D1) has the welcome implication that a disembodied spirit, or the theistic God, is a *concretum*. (A1D1) has this welcome implication even if God is a soul who has necessary existence and who is neither spatially located nor spatially related to anything.

A point-position instantiates the level C category of Place, and an instant instantiates the level C category of Time. Yet, the former category possibly has an instance having spatial parts, for example, some expanse of space, and the latter category possibly has an instance having temporal parts, for instance, some period of time. Thus, (A1D1) has the happy consequence that point-positions and instants are *concreta*. (A1D1) has this happy consequence despite the fact that point-positions and instants are incapable of either motion or intrinsic change.

Notice that the level C categories of Property and Trope could not be coinstantiated. Unlike the category of Trope, the category of Property does *not* possibly have an instance which has spatial or temporal parts. A property (e.g., blueness) does not satisfy (A1D1): it does not instantiate a level C category which possibly has an instance having spatial or temporal parts. Therefore, a property is not a concrete entity. Hence, (A1D2) has the desired result that a property is an abstract entity. (A1D2) has this desired result with respect to a property, P, even if P has contingent existence, P is necessarily unexemplified, P is necessarily ungraspable, P is temporally located, or P enters into temporal relations.

Note that the level C categories of Proposition and Event could not be coinstantiated. Unlike the category of Event, the category of Proposition does *not* possibly have an instance which has spatial or temporal parts. A proposition does not satisfy (A1D1): it does not instantiate a level C

ries at the same level of generality, one must sufficiently characterize the positive nature of that category. Of course, these considerations do not apply to an explication of Abstractness, since it is at level B, and Concreteness is the only other category at level B.

185

category which possibly has an instance having spatial or temporal parts. Therefore, a proposition is not a concrete entity. Hence, (A1D2) has the desirable result that a proposition is an abstract entity. (A1D2) has this desirable result despite the fact that a proposition cannot be exemplified.

Finally, the level C category of Set could not be instantiated by something having spatial or temporal parts. This follows from the fact that a set cannot have *parts*. Aside from any elements a set may have, a set has no parts. For example, the empty set has no parts. Although a set can have elements, it is demonstrable that an element of a set is not a part of that set. It is axiomatic that the relation of proper parthood is transitive: necessarily, if x is part of y, and y is part of z, then x is part of z. But the relation of elementhood is not transitive: for example, x is an element of $\{x\}$, $\{x\}$ is an element of $\{\{x\}\}$, but x is *not* an element of $\{\{x\}\}$. Therefore, elementhood cannot be identified with parthood. Since aside from its elements a set has no parts, a set cannot have parts. Hence, unlike the level C category of Collection, the level C category of Set could not be instantiated by something having spatial or temporal parts. A set does not satisfy (A1D1): it does not instantiate a level C category which possibly has an instance having spatial or temporal parts. Therefore, a set is not a concrete entity. Consequently, (A1D2) has the desired result that a set is an abstract entity.[7]

7 In his *Parts of Classes* (Oxford: Basil Blackwell, 1991), David Lewis argues that the singleton subsets of a set, *s*, *are* parts of *s* (though *not* spatial or temporal parts), and *s* is the mereological sum of those singletons. Unlike the elementhood relation, the subset relation *is* transitive. Yet, it is not clear that Lewis employs the standard notion of a set that we employ: he is explicitly skeptical about its intelligibility. If this notion is unintelligible, then *our* category, Set, is noninstantiable. Moreover, Lewis's view of the natures of sums and sets is incompatible with our classificatory system of ontic categories. He permits the mereological addition of any two entities (even if one assumes that there are both *concreta* and *abstracta*), but we cannot, because we uphold the concrete–abstract distinction as exhaustive and exclusive, and because the sum of a *concretum* and an (equally complex) *abstractum*, e.g., the sum of a point and a (simple) property, respectively, has an equal claim *both* to be concrete and to be abstract. Unless Lewis's conceptions of sumhood and sethood fit into an alternative system of ontic classification which is at least as good as the one that we have presented, these Lewisian claims about sums and sets can reasonably be rejected. We would argue that there is no such alternative system.

Penelope Maddy, in her *Realism in Mathematics* (Oxford: Clarendon Press, 1990), in contradistinction to Lewis, denies that sets of *concreta* are *abstracta*. However, Maddy operates with an inadequate understanding of abstractness. She accepts the view that abstractness can be identified with not being in space and time, a view whose inadequacy follows from a criticism presented earlier. In particular, souls would not be in both space and time, but they would not be abstract entities. Moreover, it should be noted that her substantive thesis that a set of *concreta* is *located in space and time* is formally consistent with our claim that a set of *concreta* is an abstract entity which lacks *spatial or temporal parts*, since an entity's being located in space and time does not entail that it has spatial or temporal

(A1D2) has this desired result with respect to a set, S, even if S has contingent existence, and even though S is necessarily unexemplified and necessarily ungraspable.

We shall conclude by answering a possible criticism of (A1D1) and (A1D2). It might be objected that (A1D1) is viciously circular, on the ground that (A1D1) employs the notion of a level C ontological category, while our intuitive characterization of an ontological category's being at level C makes use of the level B distinction between the categories of the concrete and the abstract.[8] However, although this is true of our *intuitive characterization* of what it is for an ontological category to be at level C, our *formal account* of this notion in no way utilizes the level B notions of abstractness or concreteness. Our formal account captures the notion of a level C category solely in terms of certain logical relationships that such a category must bear to our core list L of categories. Hence, (A1D1) is not conceptually circular in the way alleged, and the criticism under discussion is unsound.[9]

---

parts, as illustrated by the possible case of a spatially and temporally located point-particle which lacks both spatial parts and temporal parts.

8 See Chapter 1, Section I.

9 This appendix is based on Gary Rosenkrantz, "Concrete/Abstract," in *Companion to Metaphysics,* ed. Jaegwon Kim and Ernest Sosa (Oxford: Basil Blackwell, forthcoming).

Continuous space and time and their parts: A defense of an Aristotelean account

It is absurd that a magnitude should be constituted from non-magnitudes.
Aristotle *On Generation and Corruption* 1.2

Mathematical continuity, at least in the versions of Dedekind, Cantor, and their successors, is clearly not instantiated in experience. This raises the question of the relation of mathematical continuity to experience.
Stephan Korner "Continuity" *The Encyclopedia of Philosophy* (1967)

We have maintained that point-positions and instants are *not* parts of space and time, respectively. Rather, we have taken the neo-Aristotelean view that such entities are dependent on places and times of higher dimensionality.[1] Thus, we said that a point-position can be a limit of a line, or the place of a corner of a material object, or a place where two spheres touch, and so forth, but a point-position cannot exist apart from a place of higher than zero-dimensionality. Thus, our view has been an antifoundationalist one when it comes to space and time, one aspect of this antifoundationalism being that space and time are not composed of unextended parts.[2]

However, many philosophers, taking their lead from certain mathematicians[3] and, we believe, from the logicist tradition, hold that extended spaces and temporal intervals have a nondenumerable number of zero-dimensional parts. M. J. White has aptly described the contrast between the two views in question:

The tendency of contemporary mathematics, of course, has been to . . . [treat] continuous magnitudes as constituted of indivisible elements (e.g.,

---

1 However, our view of the nature of space and time is not in all respects that of Aristotle. He maintains that a line belonging to space or an interval of time does not actually contain infinitely many line-segments or subintervals. We disagree.
2 The other aspect is that space and time are not composed of extended atomic places and times.
3 By "certain mathematicians" we mean, of course, Cantor, Dedekind, and their followers, and not those who could be described as intuitionists or constructivists.

sets of points) that are in a certain intuitive sense 'discrete'. It then becomes possible to 'reconstitute' the properties of continuous magnitudes using these indivisibles. Such a procedure may suggest an ultimately 'atomistic' ontology of magnitude very much at odds with the Aristotelian dictum that 'every magnitude is divisible into magnitudes . . .'.[4]

He continues:

> Where Aristotle and classical modern conceptions differ is in their *ontology* of the continuous. The classical modern conception, as I understand it here, appeals to a point-set ontology of the continuous. That is, a continuous n-dimensional magnitude is conceived as a set of $(n - 1)$-dimensional entities. In the particular case of a linear or 1-dimensional magnitude (e.g., a lapse of time, a linear spatial interval), the magnitude is conceived as a set of points. Such a set will be a non-denumerably infinite, linearly ordered collection of points satisfying certain other requirements . . . the most important of these are density and Dedekind continuity.[5]

White himself seems to accept this "classical modern conception" of space and time, as do many other commentators on Aristotle's treatment of space and time.[6]

In the remainder of this appendix, we will argue that the idea that space and time are composed of point-positions and instants is wrong. We will also show that even if this idea were correct, neither space nor time would satisfy our two accounts of substance, in (4D1) and (4D2), and (4D1*) and (4D2*), respectively.

Let us begin by formulating more precisely the Dedekind–Cantor continuum theory. According to this theory, ·

> a [linear] continuum is a nondenumerably infinite set, say K, the elements of which constitute a series that, apart from its serial order, also conforms to the following postulates . . . : (1) If K_1 and K_2 are any two nonempty parts of K, such that every element of K belongs either to K_1 or K_2 and every element of K_1 precedes every element of K_2, then there is at least one element X in K such that any element that precedes X belongs to K_1, and

4 M. J. White, *The Continuous and the Discrete* (Oxford: Oxford University Press, 1992), p. 31.
5 Ibid., p. 33.
6 An interesting case is that of David Bostock, in "Aristotle on Continuity in *Physics* VI," in *Aristotle's Physics: A Collection of Essays,* ed. Lindsay Judson (Oxford: Oxford University Press, 1991), pp. 179–212. Bostock seems to defer to the authority of the mathematicians, but expresses residual doubts. Speaking of the view that a line is composed of point-positions, he observes: "But although we have a proof of this fact, must we not still admit that it is absolutely amazing? No point that has been put down touches any of the others, and yet the result is a line with no gaps in it anywhere! No wonder that Aristotle could not see how such a construction of the line could succeed. Indeed, I think I would admit that I cannot exactly 'see' it myself" (p. 186).

every element that follows X belongs to K_2. (2) If a and b are elements of the class K and a precedes b, then there exists at least one element x in K such that a precedes x and x precedes b. ... (3) The class K contains a denumerable subclass R in such a way that between any two elements of the class K there is an element of R.[7]

When this general definition of a continuum is applied to a line belonging to space or to a temporal interval, then, of course, the elements of K are point-positions or instants. In sum, we shall criticize the view that a line or an interval of time (and so, any extended place or time) is composed of point-positions or instants because it is identifiable with *a set whose elements are point-positions or instants* which stand in certain set-theoretical relations to one another.

As we see it, this view involves a pair of category mistakes. The first is involved in the identification of the *elements* of a set with the *parts* of a line or a temporal interval. The view we are considering is that a line or a temporal interval is *composed* of point-positions or instants, where 'is composed of' means, literally, "has as parts." But an element of a set is *not* a part of that set. Nor is it possible for a set to have proper parts. And a part of a line or a temporal interval is not an *element* of that line or temporal interval. We prove that this is so by appealing to an argument already given in Appendix 1, and we repeat the relevant part of that argument, as follows. While the dyadic relation, x being a proper part of y, is a transitive relation, the dyadic relation, x being an element of y, is *not* a transitive relation. For example, if x is an element of $\{x\}$, and if $\{x\}$ is an element of $\{\{x\}\}$, it does not follow that (and is not true that) x is an element of $\{\{x\}\}$. On the other hand, if x is a proper part of y, and y is a proper part of z, then it does follow that x is a proper part of z.

We sum up our first criticism of the identification of lines and temporal intervals with sets by means of the following argument:

(1i) Necessarily, if an extended place or time exists, then it has places or times as proper parts.

(1ii) Necessarily, if a set exists, then it does not have proper parts, though possibly it has elements.

Therefore,

(1iii) Necessarily, if an extended place or time exists, then it is not a set of point-positions or instants.

7 S. Korner, "Continuity," in *The Encyclopedia of Philosophy, Volume 1*, ed. P. Edwards (New York: Macmillan, 1967), p. 206.

Thus, to identify the elements of a set with the parts of a line or temporal interval is to commit a category mistake.

The second category mistake parallels the first. A *set* is an *abstract* entity, in the sense of 'abstract' defined in Appendix 1. On the other hand, a line and an interval of time are *concrete* entities, again in the sense of Appendix 1. Thus, to identify an abstract entity like a set with a concrete entity like a line or an interval of time is once again to commit a category mistake. We state this argument formally as follows:

(2i) Necessarily, if an extended place or time is a set of point-positions or instants, then an extended place or time is an abstract entity.

(2ii) Necessarily, if an extended place or time exists, then it is a concrete entity.

(2iii) Necessarily, for any *x*, *x* is not both abstract and concrete.

Therefore,

(2iv) Necessarily, if an extended place or time exists, then it is not a set of point-positions or instants.

The identification of an extended place or time with a set of point-positions or instants is a particularly egregious category mistake, for the whole idea behind the concrete–abstract distinction is that spatiality and temporality are the determinants of concreteness (as they are in our analysis of the concrete–abstract distinction). Yet, if one identifies places and times with sets, then one is implying that space and time are themselves abstract entities, and the concrete–abstract distinction breaks down completely.

The idea that lines and temporal intervals are sets of positions and instants involves a reduction of lines and temporal intervals to ordered sets of point-positions and instants. For those following the logicist program, natural further steps include the reduction of points and instants to ordered *n*-tuples of numbers, and the reduction of numbers to sets generated from the empty set by iterated nestings. If all three reductions are carried out, then there could hardly be anything more abstract than the sets with which places and times are identified. Thus, there could hardly be anything more incongruous than identifying such quintessentially concrete entities as places and times with sets of this kind. Our arguments block the first and second reductions. The first reduction is blocked by the second of our category mistake arguments stated previously,[8] and the second reduction is blocked by the following parallel category mistake argument:

8 Frequently, those who try to construct an extended line, for instance, out of a set of extensionless elements (in order to support the reduction of the former to the latter) presuppose the existence of extension in carrying out the construction. Of course, such a procedure is inadmissable due to its vicious circularity. E.g., Dedekind says the following

(3i) Necessarily, if a point-position or an instant is an ordered n-tuple of numbers, then a point-position or an instant is an abstract entity.

(3ii) Necessarily, if a point-position or an instant exists, then it is a concrete entity.

(3iii) Necessarily, for any x, x is not both abstract and concrete.

Therefore,

(3iv) Necessarily, if a point-position or an instant exists, then it is not an ordered n-tuple of numbers.

It is true, of course, that point-positions on a line and instants belonging to an interval of time bear certain relations to one another which the elements of a mathematical continuum bear to one another. It is also true that the parts of one's hand bear to one another certain relations that a set of elements equal in number to the parts of one's hand bear to one another. So a set may be a *model* for an entity, such as a line or a hand, which is not a set. It does not follow, of course, that one's hand *is* a set. Nor does it follow that a line or a temporal interval is a set.

Finally, even if places and times are sets of spatial points and instants, places and times do not qualify as substances on either of our two accounts of substance. This is true with respect to our analysis of substance in (4D1) and (4D2) provided that there cannot be just one place except for its parts and that there cannot be just one time except for its parts. But given that necessarily, if space and time exist, then space and time are dense continua,

about such a construction: "I find the essence of continuity . . . in the following principle: 'if all points of the straight line fall into two classes such that every point of the first class *lies to the left* [our emphasis] of every point of the second class, then there exists one and only one point which produces this division of all points into two classes, this severing of the straight line into two portions.'" See *Essays on the Theory of Numbers*, trans. Wooster W. Beman (Chicago: Open Court, 1909), p. 11.

Notice the illegitimate use that Dedekind makes of the spatial notion of something *being to the left of* something else. This notion is not available until the construction of space has already been carried out. Hence, such a notion cannot be employed to construct extension out of points.

Similarly, observe the language employed by David Bostock in describing the same sort of construction: "First set down a denumerable infinity of points that is dense in the line, for example by putting down the two end-points of the desired line, and then by setting down a further point *in the middle* of any stretch *between* two points already set down [our emphases]" ("Aristotle on Continuity in *Physics* VI," p. 186). Bostock speaks illegitimately of locating a point belonging to the reducing set *between* two other points, and *in the middle* of a stretch, when these notions are not available until space has been constructed. It might be replied that he means only that there is some (nonspatial) ordering of the points whereby one point is "between" two others; but then, it does not seem that such an ordering is capable of generating *extension*. It is an equivocation between the nonspatial and the spatial senses of 'between' and related terms that lends the reduction whatever plausibility it has. Similarly for Dedekind's language. Basically, the reductionists are equivocating between two senses of 'point', a spatial sense, and a nonspatial sense.

and given that extended places and times are *sets* of points, it follows that there cannot be just one place or time except for its parts. If, for example, there is an extended place, or a temporal interval, then there are, in addition, infinitely many point-positions, or infinitely many instants which, on the view in question, are not *parts* of the extended place, or the temporal interval, but *elements* of it.

Places and times do not qualify as substances according to our second analysis of substance in (4D1*) and (4D2*) provided that there cannot be just one place (including its parts) and that there cannot be just one time (including its parts). Clearly, if it is a necessary truth that if space and time exist, then space and time are dense continua, and extended places and times are sets of the sort in question, then there cannot be but one place or time.

Thus, if extended places or times are sets of point-positions or instants, then both of our analyses of substance have the desirable consequence that a place or a time is not a substance.[9]

9 For an insightful and historically important account of some of the topics discussed in this appendix, see Franz Brentano's *Philosophical Investigations on Space, Time, and the Continuum,* trans. Barry Smith (London: Croom Helm, 1988).

Index

inherence theory of substance, 52
instants, 101–2, 105–7, 109–12, 150, 185,
    188–93
Irwin, Terence, 156

Johnson, Samuel, 22
Judson, Lindsay, 189n6

Kant, Immanuel, 6, 7, 9, 25n35, 144
Kater, H., 100
Kelvin, Lord William Thomson, 25n35
Kim, Jaegwon, ix, 184n3, n4, 187n9
King, John, ix
Korner, Stephan, 188, 190n7
Kretzmann, Norman, 138n59, 175n43
Kripke, Saul, 57

Lardner, D., 100
laws of nature, 74, 165–8
    supercession of, 168
    violation of, 167–8
Leibniz, Gottfried Wilhelm, 6, 12, 86n45,
    151, 178n49
Lesniewski, Stanislaw, 15n19
Lewis, David, 30n4, 86n45, 186n7
Lewis, Frank, 44–5n23
Limit, category of, 100–12, 132–4
limits, 105, 188
    as distinguished from substances, 100–
    12, 132–4
    not parts of extended entities, 111–12
Locke, John, 6, 25n35, 47–8, 49n33,
    63n14, 119, 144, 146n1, 176n44
Loeb, Louis, 47n26, 55n47
Loemker, Leroy E., 178n49
Long, Douglas, 149
Lotze, R. H., 167
Loux, Michael, 23n31, 51n36, 61n12
Lowe, Jonathan, ix

MacCurdy, E. 100
MacDonald, G. F., 163n29
Machamer, Peter, 175n43
MacKenna, Stephen, 149n7
McTaggart, J. M. E., 137n57
Maddy, Penelope, 186n7
Maimonides, 144
Mann, William, 54n44, 100n10
Martin, C. B., ix
material objects
    metaphysical natures of, 24
    vs. nonmaterial physical objects, 24n34
material points, 113n35

Mavrodes, George, 168n35
Maxwell, James Clerk, 25n35
Mellor, D. H., 32n5, 69n25
mereology, 15–16n19, 63n16, 79, 119n40,
    186
Mill, John Stuart, 182
modalities
    de dicto, 16–17n21, 90
    de re, 16–17n21, 86n45, 90
Moore, Henry, 109n28
motion
    atomic, 103n16
    discontinuous, 103n16
    transference of, 164–5
Mozley, J., 167
Munitz, Milton, 170n38
Murdoch, Dugald, 13, 47n28, 91n3,
    147n2

Neale, E., 62
necessary entity, 20n27, 138–9
nominalism, 15n19, 22n30, 90
nonmaterial physical objects, metaphysical
    features of, 25
Noonan, Harold, 86n45, 87n45
Number, category of, 150

O'Connor, D. J., 47n26
ontological neutrality, 33, 45, 54, 57, 89–
    90, 119, 121n43, 131n51
ontology, analytic, 7
Orleans, Ilo, 115

Paley, W., 93
particulars, 61n11
    bare, 2, 23n31, 46–57
parts
    different kinds of, 60n8, 95
    as individuators, 153
    of lines, 190–1
    of physical object, 109n28
    of times, 190–1
    unity of, in substance, 20–1n28
Pearson, Bp., 89
Perry, John, 170n37
persistence
    through qualitative change, 51
    of substances, 29–30, 48, 51, 83n43,
    137n57
Place, category of, 90, 100–12, 118, 130–
    2, 142, 185
places as distinguished from substances,
    100–12, 130–2